Sleeping with the Devil

ALSO BY ROBERT BAER

*See No Evil: The True Story of a Ground Soldier
in the CIA's War on Terrorism*

Sleeping with the Devil

How Washington Sold Our Soul for Saudi Crude

ROBERT BAER

THREE RIVERS PRESS • NEW YORK

Robert Baer is available for select
readings and lectures. To inquire about a possible appearance,
please contact the Random House Speakers Bureau at
rhspeakers@randomhouse.com.

CIA's Publications Review Board has reviewed the manuscript for this book to assist the author in eliminating classified information and poses no security objection to its publication. This review, however, should not be construed as an official release of information, confirmation of its accuracy, or an endorsement of the author's views.

The author has chosen to indicate parts of the book censored by the CIA by blacking out paragraphs, sentences, and, in some cases, individual words. Although the redactions will not add to the reader's understanding of the subject, they will tell the reader that the author would have been better able to substantiate his arguments if the CIA had not considered the material still classified. The author, as a former CIA employee, is legally obligated to submit in advance certain intelligence-related writing to the CIA to give the CIA the opportunity to remove information it deems classified.

Grateful acknowledgment is made to *Commentary* for permission to reprint an excerpt from "Oil: The Issue of American Intervention" by Robert W. Tucker that appeared in *Commentary* (January 1975). All rights reserved. Reprinted by permission of *Commentary*.

Published by Three Rivers Press, New York, New York.
Member of the Crown Publishing Group, a division of Random House, Inc.
www.crownpublishing.com

THREE RIVERS PRESS and the Tugboat design are registered trademarks of Random House, Inc.

Originally published in hardcover by Crown Publishers, New York, New York, a division of Random House, Inc., in 2003.

Design by Lauren Dong

Library of Congress Cataloging-in-Publication Data is available upon request.

978-1-4000-5268-4

First Paperback Edition

146122990

To DANNY PEARL, in recognition of his courage and relentless search for the truth.

Acknowledgments

I WOULD LIKE TO THANK the Saudi experts, petroleum specialists, and Islamic scholars for keeping me on the right track. Thanks to their true expertise, I hope I managed to get the story right. I would also like to thank the numerous talented journalists—all new-found friends since leaving the CIA—whose interests in the Middle East coincide with mine. Our interminable discussions helped me immeasurably to understand the subject. Unfortunately, there are too many to mention by name. Finally, I would like to thank my many Arab friends who patiently tried to explain Saudi Arabia to me. The book could not have been written without them. I hope I got it right and they do not look at this as an anti-Arab or anti-Saudi book. As harsh as some of my views may appear, my sole intention is to attempt to explain why relations between Saudi Arabia and the United States have reached such a low point—and threaten to get worse. Again, as in *See No Evil*, this book would not have been possible without the research and editorial dictums of Rafe Sagalyn, Howard Means, Kristin Kiser, and Steve Ross, and support from Claudia Gabel, Amy Boorstein, Derek McNally, and Lauren Dong. But, of course, at the end of the day any errors, faulty judgments, and oversights that often pop up in a book like this are all my own.

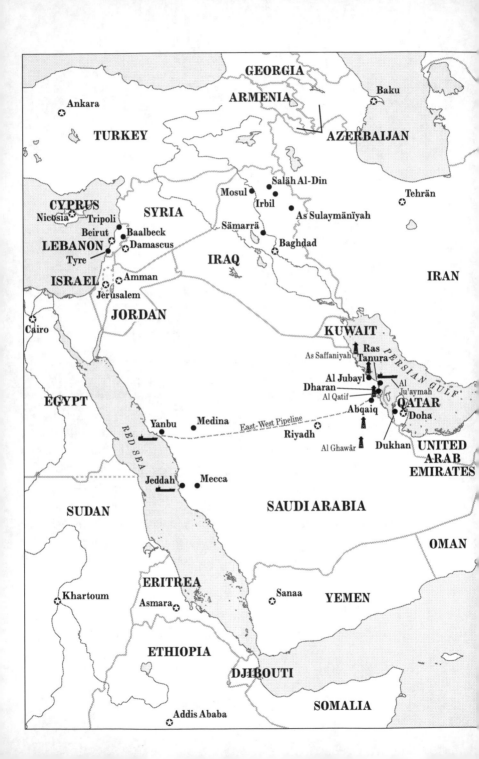

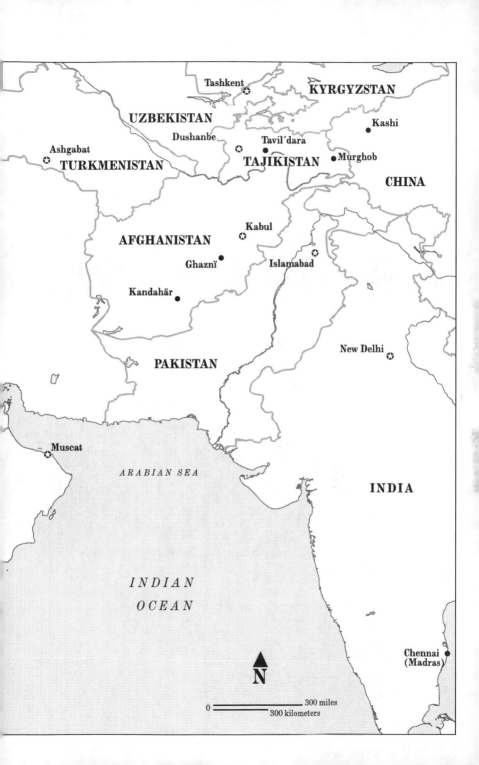

The House of Sa'ud: An Abbreviated Family Tree

KING IBN SA'UD (also known as 'Abd-al-'Aziz) united Saudi Arabia into a single kingdom in 1932 and ruled it until his death in 1953. He had at least forty-three sons, eight of whom died before the age of twenty. Among the most prominent of the survivors:

SA'UD. Succeeded his father as king November 1953. Deposed November 1964.

FAYSAL. Proclaimed king November 1964. Assassinated March 1975.

KHALID. Named crown prince March 1975. Died of natural causes June, 1982.

FAHD. Named crown prince March 1975. Proclaimed king June 1982. Incapacitated by a stroke November 1995. King Fahd has seven sons, including his youngest, 'Abd-al-'Aziz (or "Azouzi"), by his favorite wife, Jawhara Al Ibrahim.

SULTAN. Minister of Defense and Aviation and chairman of
Saudi Arabian Airlines, among other titles. Father of
Prince Bandar, long-time Saudi ambassador to the United
States.

TURKI. Resigned as head of Saudi intelligence just days before
the September 11 terrorist attacks. The closest of the
princes to the Taliban. Attended Georgetown University
with Bill Clinton.

SALMAN. Governor of Riyadh for more than forty years and
de facto head of the Saudi charities some of whose money
found its way into al Qaeda.

'ABDALLAH. Named crown prince June 1982. Commander of
the National Guard since 1963.

NAIF. Current Minister of Interior.

Contents

CONTENTS

Prologue: The Doomsday Scenario

THE WHITE FORD PICKUP rolled quietly to a stop below Tower Number Seven, one of ten large cylindrical structures at Abqaiq that are used to remove sulfur from petroleum, or turn it from "sour" to "sweet," in oil-patch jargon. A dirty tarp covered the cargo bed; extra-heavy shocks kept the bed from sagging onto the axle. To the east, across the Saudi desert, a hint of the morning sun peeked over the horizon. The truck driver, one of thousands of Shi'a Muslims who work the Saudi oil fields, cut the engine, checked his watch one last time, and began reciting verses from the Qur'an, memorized long ago. The lights of the world's largest oil-processing facility twinkled all around him.

Three hours earlier, a fishing boat equipped with twin two-hundred-fifty-horsepower Evinrude engines had set out from Deyyer, on the southern coast of Iran. By dark, the boat had sprinted across the Persian Gulf to the Saudi port at al Jubayl. From there, the Iranian pilot had crept south, hugging the coastline, until he came in sight of the Sea Island oil-loading platform at Ras Tanura, forty-five miles to the northeast of Abqaiq. Now, with the water beginning to glow pink, he pointed the bow at Platform Four and slammed the throttle to full.

PROLOGUE: THE DOOMSDAY SCENARIO

Just inland from Ras Tanura, at Qatif Junction, an Egyptian engineer—a Muslim Brother who had made the grand tour of militant Islam, from Cairo to Tehran—flicked on his flashlight and admired his handiwork. The Semtex was expertly crammed into and around every manifold, every valve, every last pipe junction. It was art, really, lacing it all together in a single charge: a work of beauty, of Allah's great creation.

West of Abqaiq, in the foothills of the al Aramah Mountains at a small Bedouin encampment, a Saudi in his mid-twenties bent over a 120-mm Russian-made mortar for what seemed the hundredth time. A Wahhabi, descended from the religious zealots who brought the House of Sa'ud to power, he had been trained in munitions in Afghanistan by a man who was taught by the Central Intelligence Agency. Below him, at the base of the foothills, sat Pump Station One, the first stop on the oil pipeline that carried nearly a million barrels of extra-light crude daily from Abqaiq across the peninsula to the Red Sea port at Yanbu.

A pager vibrated lightly against his chest and went dead. It was time. The Al Sa'ud were coming down. The oil that fed their whoring and corruption would flow no more. Islam would be purified; the American devils, crippled; and their Israeli protectorate, cut free to die on its own. The world would have to take notice, and for the simplest of reasons: The global economy was fucked.

I'VE DOLLED UP the details and updated them, but I didn't invent them. They come courtesy of people who studied the Saudi oil industry from the ground up. From the mid-1930s until well into the 1960s, Saudi Arabia was a branch office of America's oil giants—a Republican internationalist's fantasy. The United States remained secure in the knowledge that Saudi oil would always be there for us, under the sand, cheap, and as safe as if it were locked up in Fort Knox. We built Saudi Arabia's oil business and, for our efforts, got full and easy access to its crude.

The first OPEC (Organization of the Petroleum Exporting Countries) oil embargo in 1973 took the bloom off that rose, but anxiety
turned into full panic in the early 1980s, during the Iran–Iraq
war, especially when it looked as if Iran might take the war to the
Arab side of the Gulf, including Saudi Arabia. With the nightmare
of an Islamic prairie fire taking down the world's economy, disaster planners in and out of government began to ask uncomfortable
questions. What points of the Saudi oil infrastructure were most
vulnerable to terrorist attack? And by what means? What sorts of
disruptions to the flow of oil, short-term and long-term, could be
expected? And with what economic consequences?

Almost to a person, the disaster planners concluded that the
Abqaiq extralight crude complex was both the most vulnerable
point of the Saudi oil system and its most spectacular target. With
a capacity of seven million barrels, Abqaiq is the Godzilla of
oil-processing facilities. Generally, the study groups posited a
multiprong attack on Abqaiq, with severe damage to storage tanks
and the large spheroids used to reduce pressure on oil during the
refining process, and moderate damage to the stabilizing towers
where petroleum is purged of sulfur.

Restoring the pressure-reducing spheroids would require not
much more than the installation of a series of temporary valves,
to be replaced eventually by permanent ones. The storage tanks
wouldn't be much of a problem, either. A few repairs here and
there, and you would have full-production capacity back in no time
at all.

The stabilizing towers are another story. Sulfur and oil go hand
in hand. The same eons-long processes that make one make the
other. But until the sulfur is removed, petroleum is useless. To get
from one state to the other—from sour to sweet—petroleum goes
through a process known as hydrodesulfurization.

At Abqaiq, hydrodesulfurization takes place in ten tall, cylindrical towers. Inside the towers, hydrogen is introduced into
the oil in sufficient quantities to convert sulfur into hydrogen sulfide gas, which then rises to the top of the structure, where it is

harvested and rendered into harmless, environmentally safe, and usable sulfur.

But hydrogen sulfide is no everyday gas. Familiar to generations of high school chemistry students as the rotten-egg (or "fart") gas, it is highly corrosive and potentially fatal to humans. As long as the gas is confined in the stabilizing towers, everything is fine. Blow the top off a tower, or a wide hole through it, or bring it crashing down by detonating a truck loaded with three thousand pounds of explosives at its base, and all hell breaks loose.

In the atmosphere, hydrogen sulfide reacts with moisture to create the acid sulfur dioxide. Once formed, the acid would rapidly settle on surrounding pipes, valve fittings, flanges, connectors, pump stations, and control boxes, and begin eating its way through everything like some bionic omnivorous termite. But the initial release of hydrogen sulfide would have far more serious effects because of what it does to humans.

The federal Agency for Toxic Substance and Disease Registry (ATSDR), a sister agency of the Centers for Disease Control, classifies hydrogen sulfide as a broad-spectrum poison—that is, it attacks multiple systems in the body. "Breathing very high levels of hydrogen sulfide can cause death within just a few breaths," ATSDR reports. "There could be loss of consciousness after one or more breaths. Exposure to lower concentrations can result in eye irritation, a sore throat and cough, shortness of breath, and fluid in the lungs. These symptoms usually go away in a few weeks. Long-term, low-level exposure may result in fatigue, loss of appetite, headaches, irritability, poor memory, and dizziness."

The Occupational Safety and Health Administration (OSHA) wing of the U.S. Department of Labor has established an acceptable ceiling concentration of twenty parts per million (ppm) of hydrogen sulfide in the workplace, with a maximum level of fifty ppm allowed for ten minutes "if no other measurable exposure occurs." The more conservative—and less politically sensitive—National Institute for Occupational Safety and Health recommends a maximum exposure level of ten ppm.

A moderately successful attack on the Abqaiq facility's stabilizing towers would let loose seventeen hundred ppm of hydrogen sulfide into the atmosphere. That strength would dissipate, but not quickly enough to prevent the death of workers in the immediate vicinity and serious injury to others in the general area—or to stop sulfur dioxide from eating into the metallic heart of the Saudi oil infrastructure. The toxicity also would deter the onset of repairs for months.

At the least, a moderate-to-severe attack on Abqaiq would slow average production there from 6.8 million barrels a day to roughly a million barrels for the first two months postattack, a loss equivalent to approximately one-third of America's current daily consumption of crude oil. Even as long as seven months after an attack, Abqaiq output would still be about 40 percent of preattack output, as much as 4 million barrels below normal—roughly equal to what all of the OPEC partners collectively took out of production during the devastating 1973 embargo.

THE ABQAIQ SCENARIO was only one of many considered by the Reagan-era disaster planners, in part because Saudi Arabia's oil system is so target-rich. Any oil extraction, production, and delivery system relies on a large, mostly exposed exoskeleton. Add to that the topography of eastern Saudi Arabia, where the vast oil fields are located—an ocean of sand broken by shifting dunes, all of it sloping gently into the Persian Gulf—and you have a security consultant's worst nightmare. Taking down Saudi Arabia's oil infrastructure is like spearing fish in a barrel. It's not a question of opportunity; it's a question of how good your bang men are and what you give them to work with.

Saudi Arabia has more than eighty active oil and gas fields, and more than a thousand working wells, but half of its proven reserves—12.5 percent of all the known oil in the world—is contained in eight fields, including Ghawar, the world's largest onshore oil field; and Safaniya, the largest offshore field in existence. One element that made Pearl Harbor such an attractive target in 1941 was so much American firepower, air and sea, boxed in such a small space. Even if a Japanese bomb missed its target, it was likely to find something worth blowing up. Tactically, the Saudi fields offer much the same sort of target environment. One scenario concluded that if terrorists were to simultaneously hit only five of the many sensitive points in Saudi Arabia's downstream oil system, they could put the Saudis out of the oil-producing business for about two years.

Once it's out of the ground or the seabed, Saudi oil moves through roughly seventeen thousand kilometers of pipe: from well to refinery, from refinery to onshore and offshore ports, within the kingdom and without. Much of that pipe is above ground. The buried part lies an average of three quarters of a meter below the surface, often in land occupied by nomadic tribes. A camel for transport, a spade, and a cordless drill are enough to sabotage a section of pipe. But if you want to step up the damage, there's no want of explosives in the explosive Middle East. A sack of fertilizer, a bucket of fuel oil, and a stick of dynamite would do the trick.

The kingdom maintains a huge inventory of pipe, which makes a single saboteur no more threatening than a gnat, but multiple saboteurs operating in concert at broadly spaced intervals throughout the oil web would create a plague of gnats as unpleasant and diverting as—and far more destructive than—the clouds of gnats that settle on Sunday picnics. Pipes, though, are the least of the problems.

A typical Saudi oil well produces about five thousand barrels a day of runny gunk: an unusable mixture of oil, dissolved gases, sulfur impurities, and salt water pumped into the well to create sufficient pressure to force the gunk out. From the wells, oil is pumped to one of five gas and oil separation plants maintained by Saudi Aramco, Saudi Arabia's state oil company. In vast, bulbous spheroids, a pressure step-down process releases most of the dissolved gases, while a second process takes out the salt water. The remaining sour crude is piped on to one of five stabilization facilities, where the pressure is further stepped down and oil is held in storage tanks pending desulfurization.

From a system engineer's point of view, all this movement, from the well through the refining process, is a ballet of connectivity. The stabilizing towers where the sulfur is neutralized, the spheroids where pressure is reduced and other impurities are siphoned off, the storage tanks where the oil is held between processing and shipping are, in effect, cathedrals of the industrial process. Terrorists and saboteurs tend to view the world differently. To them, the architectural features of downstream production offer one very attractive thing: virtually unimpeded line-of-sight targeting, just like the World Trade Center towers on a clear day.

There's also the distribution and delivery side. The Saudi oil system is divided into northern and southern producing areas. Northern oil gets refined at multiple locations, then piped to one of two terminals along the Gulf—Ju'aymah and Ras Tanura—and from there out to offshore loading platforms and mooring buoys located in water deep enough to handle oceangoing oil tankers.

All petroleum originating in the south is pumped to Abqaiq, about forty kilometers inland from the northern end of the Gulf of Bahrain, for processing, and from there on to Ju'aymah or Ras Tanura, or via the East-West pipeline over twelve hundred kilometers across the Arabian peninsula and the mountainous spine of western Saudi Arabia to the terminal at Yanbu on the Red Sea. (Another route out of Abqaiq, the seventeen-hundred-kilometer Trans-Arabian pipeline that runs to Sidon, on the Mediterranean coast in Lebanon, is mothballed as I write, as is the Iraq-Saudi pipeline, shut down in 1990 following the Iraqi invasion of Kuwait.)

Whatever the terminal, whichever the coast, the choke points are too many to count. At Ju'aymah the most likely point of attack would be the metering platform located eleven kilometers offshore. Four underwater pipelines feed crude oil and bunker fuel to the platform from onshore storage tanks. The platform, in turn, feeds five single-point mooring buoys, located still farther offshore, each capable of transferring 2.5 million barrels of oil and other fuel per day to tankers.

On an average day, about 4.3 million barrels of oil leave Saudi Arabia via the Ju'aymah terminal. Destroy the surface-metering equipment and control platform, inflict significant damage to half the mooring buoys and moderate damage to the onshore tank form, and loading capacity at Ju'aymah would be reduced from those 4.3 million barrels to somewhere between 1.7 and 2.6 million barrels two months out. Restoring full capacity might take as long as seven months.

A commando boat attack would do the job. Then and now, the waters surrounding the arid Arabian peninsula remain, vessel for vessel, one of the most dangerous navigable sites on earth, a place where even case-hardened destroyers like the U.S.S. *Cole* can be sunk by a Zodiac, a couple hundred kilos of plastique, and a crewman resolved to meet his maker.

Ras Tanura pumps slightly more oil than Ju'aymah—4.5 million barrels of sustainable daily export—and it offers a wider variety of targets and more avenues of attack. Ras Tanura's Sea Island facility, 1.5 kilometers east of the north pier in the Gulf, handles nearly all the terminal's export oil; Platform Four handles half of that and is the only one of the four to have its own surge tanks and metering equipment, in the latter case under the platform. (The others use equipment and surge tanks onshore.) As with Ju'aymah's metering platform, a commando attack on Platform Four by surface boat or a Kilo-class submarine—anything is for sale in the global arms bazaar—would be devastating.

Sea Island is fed by a complex of tanks, pipelines, and pumps that is further connected by pipe to Ju'aymah for added flexibility. This onshore complex is vulnerable to terrorist attack by ground and air: Ras Tanura sits about a hundred kilometers from the northern tip of Qatar, a hotbed of Islamic fundamentalists.

Yanbu, on the Red Sea, is more immune to attack, the engineers concluded, but happily there's no need to go after it. (I'm thinking like a saboteur here, just as the CIA trained me to do. One of the benefits of having spent a career as an agency case officer in some of the world's most volatile regions was a thorough education in how to destroy things.) You need only interdict the roughly nine hundred thousand barrels of Arabian light and superlight crude that are pumped daily to Yanbu to put the terminal out of business, and to do that, you simply take out Pump Station One, the closest to Abqaiq. Why? Because Pump Station One sends the oil uphill, into the al-Aramah mountain range, so it can begin its long journey across the peninsula. Without a working pump behind it, the oil flows in the wrong direction.

Even the short pipe run from Abqaiq to the Gulf terminals is not without opportunity. At Qatif Junction, a few kilometers inland from the coast, a manifold complex directs the flow of oil to Ras Tanura or Ju'aymah, or to the dormant Trans-Arabian pipeline. Inflict heavy damage on the complex and you'll stop the oil in its tracks for months. Unlike the off-the-shelf pipes that connect the terminals and processing facilities, the manifolds and pipe junctions at Qatif Junction would require custom fabrication to replace.

The assessments by the disaster planners were downplayed, for fear of rocking global oil markets, but you can bet they are not the only people to have calculated how much damage could be done to the Saudi petroleum chain—or the global money chain—by an expedient as relatively simple as blowing one of Abqaiq's stabilizing towers, or Ras Tanura's Platform Four, or the East-West pipeline's Pump Station One to smithereens. (Or, of course, all three.) A single jumbo jet with a suicide bomber at the controls, hijacked during takeoff from Dubai and crashed into the heart of Ras Tanura, would be enough to bring the world's oil-addicted economies to their knees, America's along with them. Indeed, such an attack would be more economically damaging than a dirty nuclear bomb set off in midtown Manhattan or across from the White House in Lafayette Square.

⸆

PROMOTERS OF ALASKAN, Mexican Gulf, Caspian, and Siberian oil sound like a broken record when they point out that the United States has been weaning itself from Saudi oil. They argue that Saudi Arabia accounts for only roughly 8 percent of U.S. crude oil consumption. They also argue that three of our four main oil suppliers are in the Western Hemisphere: Canada, Venezuela, and Mexico. True enough. But what they forget to mention is that Saudi Arabia sits on 25 percent of the world's proven reserves, maybe barrel per barrel the cheapest oil in the world to extract. More important, the Saudis own half the world's surplus production capacity—two to three million barrels a day. Take the Saudi surplus out of play, and the market loses its stability and liquidity. It may not seem like much oil, but the surplus capacity is what keeps the world's oil markets from going on a facedown roller-coaster ride during periods of crisis. In other words, no matter what country you buy your oil from, Saudi Arabia determines world price by how much oil it chooses to produce.

It was Saudi Arabia that broke the back of the 1973 OPEC embargo (though not before it enriched itself by tens of billions of dollars). As the Iranian revolution segued into Iran's protracted war with Iraq, the Saudis again used their surplus capacity to keep the oil flowing to the industrialized West. By 1979–80, the Ju'aymah terminal on the Persian Gulf was shipping about nine million barrels of oil daily, twice its normal output.

The same thing occurred during the 1990–91 Gulf War. The Saudis, backed by a couple of other Gulf states, produced an extra five million barrels a day, making up for the loss of Iraqi and Kuwaiti oil. Without its surplus capacity, the price of a barrel of oil likely would have soared to over a hundred dollars.

On September 12, 2001, less than 24 hours after the attacks on the World Trade Center and the Pentagon, the Saudis put on the market an extra nine million barrels of oil, going mostly to the United States. As a result, oil prices stayed low, and U.S. inflation spiked marginally in spite of the single most devastating terrorist attack in history. Take that same liquidity out of play with twenty pounds of plastique, and all bets would be off.

A DECEMBER 2000 study by the International Monetary Fund looked at the effect of a hypothetical five-dollar-per-barrel rise in the price of oil. Gross domestic product in the United States and most European countries would decline .3 percent on an annual basis. Financial markets would fall, but not to disastrous depths. Nations with a net export of crude oil would grow in wealth; those with a net import would fall. The Far East would suffer particularly because it produces so little oil of its own.

But all that was calculated on what would have been a then roughly 20 percent rise in the price of crude, a mild bump as economic catastrophes go. The terrorist attack on the Abqaiq oil facility envisioned by the Reagan-era scenarists would remove as many as 5.8 million barrels of crude a day from world markets, double the three million barrels a day taken out of production during the OPEC oil embargo, almost double the daily amount lost to the revolution in Iran and the subsequent Iran–Iraq war, and almost one-fourth the current average daily consumption.

What does history tell us about the effects of such a loss? Well, Americans saw double-digit annual inflation only ten times in the last century, four if you exclude the effects of the two world wars: in 1974, in the wake of the OPEC embargo, when inflation soared to 11 percent; and in 1979–81, when inflation topped out at 13.5 percent. By 1981 the price of a barrel of crude had hit $53.39, and regular gasoline was selling at U.S. service stations for over $2 a gallon.

The OPEC embargo sent the stock market plummeting. By the time the Standard & Poor 500 bottomed out in September 1974, it had lost 47.7 percent of its value in twenty-one months, almost exactly equal to the 47.8 percent lost in the twenty-eight months beginning in March 2000 as the dot-com bubble burst. Between

1980 and 1982, the index gave up another 27.1 percent of its value as the unrest in Iran and Iraq rocketed oil to staggering highs.

Inflicting selectively heavy damage on the Abqaiq oil-processing center would almost certainly duplicate those inflation figures and send stock indices plunging again. A coordinated attack on Abqaiq, Ras Tanura's Platform Four, and the East-West pipeline's Pump Station One, just to pick and choose from dozens of potential targets, would increase both effects exponentially while leaching the last bit of elasticity from the global oil-supply chain. The U.S. Strategic Petroleum Reserve would only help prop up international markets for several months. Unless alternative sources of oil quickly kicked in after that, we'd be in virgin territory—a kind of economic equivalent of the postnuclear-holocaust world of Nevil Shute's 1957 bestseller, *On the Beach*.

So what exactly would happen to the price of oil? I've surveyed contacts in the oil industry, but no one could come up with even an approximate figure. Apparently, good econometric forecasts on this kind of scenario don't exist. They tell me, though, that initially we could count on seeing oil hit $80 or $90 a barrel, based on supply and demand. But this does not factor in the panic that would ensue— wild speculative buying. And then there is the wild card of run-of-the-mill disruptions occurring at the same time, like in Nigeria or Venezuela. Now we have oil selling at way over $100 a barrel. But what if chaos in Saudi Arabia slopped over the border into the other Arab sheikhdoms that collectively own 60 percent of the world's oil reserves? My contacts won't even touch that one, but my guess is that we'd see oil at $150 a barrel or a lot higher. It wouldn't take long for everything else to follow suit: economic collapse, world political instability, and a level of personal despair not seen since the Great Depression.

Incidentally, Osama bin Laden has a more modest price expectation for Saudi oil: $144 a barrel. Take that multiple over the current market price, carry it back fifty years or so to the time when the West became dependent on Arab oil, and work forward from there— and you would have a wealth transfer on the order of $76 trillion from the industrial economies to the Muslim world, about $1.5 trillion a year. It wasn't until 1985 that the accumulated debt of the United States exceeded $1.5 trillion; 1985 was the first time the U.S. government budget topped the $1.5 trillion mark.

FOR THE REAGAN-ERA disaster planners who assessed the vulnerability of the Saudi oil infrastructure, Iran was the obvious threat. Another decade and the shifting winds of geopolitics would bring new worries: chaos in Iraq, for instance, spilling across the border into Saudi Arabia. The given, though, was that any threat to Saudi Arabia's petroleum production would come from outside the kingdom. Saudi Arabia was America's anchor in the Arab Middle East. It banked our oil under its sand. Losing it would be like losing the Federal Reserve. Even if the Saudis did turn anti-American, said the argument, they would never stop pumping oil, because doing so only would end up cutting their own throats. Or at least this was the assumption.

But all that was before the morning of September 11, 2001. Before fifteen Saudi citizens and four other Arabs commandeered four commercial airliners and flew them and their passengers into the buildings of New York and Washington and the farmland of Shanksville, Pennsylvania. Before Osama bin Laden became the most popular Saudi in history. Before *USA Today* discovered that, during the summer of 2002, nearly four in five hits on a clandestine al Qaeda website came from inside Saudi Arabia. Before it became known the Saudi ambassador's wife in Washington had been sending money, no doubt unintentionally, to the hijackers. The equations have changed. One report sent to the United Nations Security Council indicated that Saudi Arabia transferred half a billion dollars to al Qaeda in the ten years beginning 1992. Old assumptions are off the table. And the new realities are far from comforting.

Five extended, dysfunctional families own about 60 percent of the world's oil reserves, but the Al Sa'ud of Saudi Arabia control more than a third of that: potentially one in every five barrels the world consumes. This is the fulcrum that the global economy teeters on. Meanwhile, the mosques of Saudi Arabia preach a hatred of the West and the non-Islamic world that is as vitriolic as anything heard in Iran at the height of the ayatollahs. The kingdom's mosque schools have become hothouses of militant Islam, the breeding grounds of Sunni terrorism. Bali, Kenya, Bosnia, Chechnya, and Lower Manhattan all point back to these schools, to the Saudi state.

Terrified that the fanatics will one day come after them, the Al Sa'ud shovel out protection money as fast as they can withdraw it from their Swiss bank accounts. Never forget that it is the Al Sa'ud who ultimately sign the checks for these mosque schools. They fund militant Islamic movements in the Middle East, Africa, Central Asia, and Asia for the same reason. It's hush money to divert Muslims' attention from the money the Al Sa'ud are stealing against the day when they will have to flee the desert for their palaces strung out along the Riviera; their penthouses glowing against the night skies of Paris, London, and New York; their mountain aeries bathed by the cool evening breezes of Morocco. The House of Sa'ud, after all, knows what the West is beginning to learn: Horrors are out there waiting worse than Osama bin Laden; worse even than Khalid Sheikh Muhammad, the purported mastermind of September 11, who was finally grabbed in Pakistan in early March 2003. The Al Sa'ud know one other thing as well: They are hanging on by a thread, presiding over a kingdom deeply torn between past and present, and dangerously at war with itself.

That's why the disaster scenarios created during the Reagan years still matter. That's why we in the West—Washington, D.C., in particular—have to face up to our part in cultivating the virus that has infected Saudi Arabia. And that is why we must consider putting to sleep the host, the House of Sa'ud, if it can't or won't cure itself. At the very least, we will have to consider seizing the oil fields.

Will it come to that? I don't know. No one does. The future is never certain. Maybe the talk out of Riyadh about democratic reforms is more than cover fire. Maybe the U.S. war on Iraq will undermine all the old assumptions once more. All bets are off if Islam rises up en masse against the West and its infidel agents. But I've spent enough years in the Middle East to know that in a place like Saudi Arabia, things flow naturally toward their most combustible mix.

There's already more than enough rage against the West and against the House of Sa'ud. It's in the air in Riyadh and Jeddah's bazaars: the conviction that all the oil money has corrupted the ruling family beyond redemption, that the Saudi leaders have defiled the faith by allowing U.S. troops into the kingdom. Getting rid of the American military presence might help, but the brief against the ruling family runs further than the United States. On the street, the Al Sa'ud are reviled for failing to protect fellow Muslims in Palestine and Iraq and for standing by helplessly as Islam is humiliated. At the beginning of a new millennium, many Saudis believe that their country would be better off and the faith purer if everyone went back to the desert and lived off of dates and camel's milk.

The years I spent serving my country as a CIA officer in places like Lebanon, the Sudan, northern Iraq, and the Muslim states of Central Asia taught me something else. They showed me the human carnage and suffering that always seem to follow when America puts its head in the sand or when dollar signs blind us to what's in front of its nose. Saudi Arabia is no abstraction. It's a powder keg waiting to explode. If that happens, it could carry me and you, our savings and security, with it.

For a quarter of a century, I've been trying to understand the root causes of violence in the Middle East. I didn't begin this search after September 11, and I certainly didn't undertake it with an eye to Saudi Arabia and its crude oil. I wanted to know more about the Muslim Brothers: who they were, how they operated, why the U.S. had made common cause with the Brothers in such far-flung places as Yemen and Afghanistan. The harder I looked and the closer I got to answers, the more I realized that my search was leading me down two roads—to Riyadh and to Washington—and to the oil that connects them.

To ME, the immediate issue is threefold:

- Can the Wahhabis, the Shi'as, the Muslim Brothers, and everyone else in Saudi Arabia who wants to bring down the Al Sa'ud lay their hands on enough firepower to do so? That might sound easy, but believe me, it isn't.
- Is the House of Sa'ud beyond redemption or protection as a ruling authority?
- Does Washington have the capacity to see the Saudi kingdom for what it is? Or does it have its hand so deep in the Saudi wallet that it won't see and won't act?

Take the rage in the mosques and streets of Saudi Arabia; add weapons and a willingness to use them, not just against Western terrorist targets but against the House of Sa'ud and the petroleum infrastructure that supports it; continue to look the other way while it all happens; and we can take the last half century of oil-fired industrial prosperity and kiss it g-o-o-d-b-y-e.

But it all begins, as Part I of this book does, with firepower. That's why I found myself on the Israeli Riviera one sunny day in the spring of 2001.

Part I
Speak No Evil

1/We Deliver Anywhere

Caesarea, Israel—April 7, 2001

THE MARBLE PALACE perched amid the olive trees above the sea looked like a lot of other posh resort hotels I'd seen around the Mediterranean. The shiny new Mercedes and canary yellow Ferrari parked out front fit right in. I knew that if I poked around a little, I'd find a casino somewhere on the premises.

It didn't take me long, though, to notice that a couple things were out of place: the pack of little blond boys running around on the front lawn, shouting in Russian, and the young girls wearing identical bandeau bikinis, reading glossy Moscow weeklies by the pool. When the bellboy greeted me in Russian, I knew I had landed on one of those Russian beachheads I'd heard so much about. Since the collapse of the Soviet Union, the Russian mob, Russians fleeing the Russian mob, and just plain rich Russians had been setting up all along the Riviera, including Israel's coastline. The fancier the place, the better. Money never seemed to be a problem. And they liked to keep to themselves.

I was actually in Caesarea to see a Russian, someone I'd known only by reputation. Yuri, as I will call him, was a merchant of death.

He had made a colossal fortune in the early 1990s trading small arms for African oil. Over the last several years, with capital under his belt and the free run of Russia's state-arms-trading firm, Rosvoorouzhenie, he'd branched out and started peddling arms everywhere. Supposedly, Yuri could put his hands on almost any piece of Russian hardware, from a MIG-31 to a T-80 main-battle tank. But he did have his professional ethics. When a competitor floated the rumor that Yuri was moving weapons-grade uranium, Yuri had him squashed like a Volga tick. It was one thing to earn an honest living fueling civil wars in West Africa, but something entirely different to deal in the nasty stuff.

I saw Yuri come out of the elevator. Dressed in a pair of pressed Levi's, suede Italian loafers, and a diaphanous white linen shirt, he could have passed for a well-heeled tourist. Slim and sandy haired, he looked younger than his forty-five years.

We settled in a restaurant where Yuri waited glumly for his coffee. My chitchat about the weather, Caesarea, whatever I could think of that might keep the conversation from sinking into silence, barely got a nod out of him. I stopped talking and took a closer look. His waxy yellow skin told me he hadn't been spending his time on the beach or the links. To judge by the spiderweb of broken blood vessels in his cheeks, he liked to relax with a bottle of vodka.

My business with Yuri, if you want to call it that, was to do a favor for a friend who wanted to know if Yuri was interested in financing an oil contract, a perfectly legitimate one. My friend figured that the Russian, with all his loose cash, might want to get out of the arms trade and clean up his reputation.

As soon as Yuri finished his second espresso, I popped the question. I was halfway through it when he held up his hand to stop me. "You're on your way to Syria, our friend tells me," he said.

He was right. The next day I was flying to Amman, Jordan, and from there to Damascus. The borders between Syria and Israel had been closed ever since Israel's independence over half a century earlier. You had to touch down somewhere else before setting foot in Syria.

"I'm in the market for Syrian oil," Yuri said. "I'll take as much as they'll give me. And you know what? I'll pay two dollars above market price."

That was a curveball I hadn't seen coming. I didn't need to be a professional oil trader to understand that Yuri didn't have legitimate Syrian oil in mind—no one pays two dollars a barrel over world market for any oil. What Yuri was after, I had little doubt, was sanction-busting Iraqi oil, currently selling for a discount of ten to fifteen dollars a barrel in Syria. It was impossible to nail down the exact amounts involved—Syria obviously didn't publish figures— but I'd seen estimates that put the total trade above $3 billion a year, a business big enough to attract Yuri and lots of other vultures of the global economy.

Iraq was glad to have another market for its illicit oil, even at a steeply discounted price. It was thanks to smuggled oil that Saddam Hussein had stayed afloat since the end of the Gulf War. Saddam used the revenues to feed and equip his elite troops and intelligence services—his brutal praetorian guard. The clandestine trade in oil had started as soon as the last American M-16 fired its last round in February 1991. At first the oil moved via small barges hugging either side of the Persian Gulf coast and traveling at night, thereby avoiding detection by the American fleet. Iraq then started smuggling it out by truck, mostly to Turkey and Iran. I had seen miles-long truck convoys when I was in Kurdistan in 1994 and 1995. Syria came late to the game but was more than making up for that in sheer volume. Most oil went through an old pipeline to the Syrian port of Baniyas. Some came in by truck.

With all the revenue from Iraqi oil sold outside the United Nations–imposed oil-for-food regimen, Saddam did quite nicely. Not only could he pay for the forces that kept him from being overthrown, he had even started reequipping his regular army. Shipments of new Russian goodies were arriving every day. There was also enough money left over to keep Saddam's inner circle, including his vicious son Uday, who ran the oil business, from worrying about a shortage of Cuban cigars, sports cars, and prostitutes. The Iraqi in the street never saw a penny of it.

Syria didn't do badly, either. By selling the illegal Iraqi oil on its domestic market, Syria freed up the oil it pumped from its own fields to sell abroad at world prices. The country's oil exports rocketed from 320,000 to 450,000 barrels a day. Syria, of course, denied that the increase had anything to do with Iraqi oil, insisting against all evidence that the extra 130,000 barrels were squeezed out of its own fields. The fact is, Syria was making hundreds of millions of dollars a year off illicit Iraqi oil. For a country whose economy had been about to crater, that was a godsend.

As for the commission agents and traders—the WD-40 of this lovely end run around the United Nations sanctions on Iraq—there was plenty of money to treat themselves to new estates in Saint-Tropez or on Spain's Gold Coast. Maybe that's what Yuri was after: He seemed to have taken a liking to sweeping views of the Mediterranean.

The problem with Iraqi oil wasn't buying; it was unloading. Although the trade in Iraqi crude was an open secret, Syria didn't want to give anyone the chance to make a case by seizing a tanker full of the stuff. Syria never knew when some powerful congressman might hammer the State Department and the navy, forcing them to do something about the oil. With the screws turned, it wouldn't take the navy long to find a Syrian oil tanker on the Mediterranean. Sobered by such an ugly prospect, Syria wouldn't allow a drop of Iraqi oil to be exported. Yuri would have to come up with a damn serious sweetener to change Syria's mind. Illegal oil trading isn't my thing, but curiosity is, so I played along. They'd taught us at Langley that involvement is the first step to understanding.

"How are *we* going to make any money if we pay two dollars more than we have to?" I asked.

Yuri cut me off before I could continue. "Leave the numbers up to me." He didn't say anything for a minute, probably deciding how much he could risk telling me. Like espionage, the oil and arms business is run on a strict need-to-know basis: Give up only what you have to.

"What I'll tell you is this," Yuri went on. "I intend to wrap up my offer in a nice, neat package. I'm talking about PMU-300s. Tomorrow I could put my hand on twenty TELs and a hundred pencils. You open the door in Damascus, and I'll convince the Syrians this is a deal they can't refuse."

Now things were starting to get interesting. In the arms lingo, a TEL is a transporter-erector-launcher, and a pencil is a missile, but this wasn't just any TEL. The PMU-300 is a sophisticated Russian mobile surface-to-air missile system. I wasn't surprised Yuri was offering it for sale—he sold Russian arms for a living. What did surprise me was that he was pitching it here in Israel. Technically, Syria and Israel are at war. Syria's possession of PMU-300s would upset the balance of force between the two countries. I couldn't imagine Israel would be pleased to find out that sophisticated arms were being sold to its archenemy on its own soil, one sunny morning halfway between Tel Aviv and the Lebanese border. Then again, money helps disguise a lot of unpleasant truths.

I wasn't going to buy illegal Iraqi oil, and I wasn't going to buy arms for Syria, but I was closing in on the answer to a question I'd had for a long time. If Yuri was prepared to sell PMU-300s from a luxury resort hotel in Caesarea, armed with an international cell phone and a fat Rolodex, what else could he sell? And to whom? You don't need to be ex-CIA to know that globalization isn't just about Diesel jeans, Sony PlayStations, and Mercedeses. What I intended to find out was exactly how globalized the shady side of the arms business had become.

In all my years in the CIA, I saw very few borders you couldn't get arms through, around, or over. ███████████████████

██

██

██

██

Through the 1990s, arms were coming across the Amu Darya, the river that separates ex-Soviet Central Asia from Afghanistan, in raft loads. A few Stinger surface-to-air missiles found their way into the former Soviet Union. One errant Soviet-designed missile even made it to Mambasa, Kenya, where it misfired trying to bring down an Arkia Israeli Airlines passenger jet in late November 2002.

Western Europe hasn't been immune, either. On September 2, 2001, two young North African immigrants decided they'd had enough of France, or at least French authority. Armed to the teeth, they launched a military assault on the Beziers municipal office. After gunning down a mayor's aide with a Kalashnikov assault rifle as he sat in a car, they fired a rocket from a Russian-made launcher at an empty police car, which exploded in flames. They tried to do the same to a second police car—this one with four gendarmes inside—but the grenade turned out to be a dud. The police were left shaking their heads. Buying military munitions on the black market, it seemed, was easier than buying dope. Ten years ago an enterprising French criminal would have been lucky to put his hands on an unregistered handgun, and it would have cost a fortune. Today he could buy a Kalashnikov for five hundred dollars in one of Paris's ghetto suburbs, or a rocket launcher and grenade for three hundred. Don't forget: France has one of the most restrictive gun laws in the world.

Still, there had always been exceptions, borders that even the Yuris of the world couldn't violate. Listening to him now, I wondered if that was still the case.

Facts in the arms business aren't easy to come by. Arms dealers run a closed shop. They don't talk to journalists or researchers, put out a trade journal, or register with the chamber of commerce. To find out what's going on, you almost have to enlist an arms dealer— recruit him as an agent to take a look where you can't. During the first half of my career, the CIA put a high premium on such assets.

Sleeping with the Devil

Sniffing down the trail of Semtex, SA-7 shoulder-fired surface-to-air missiles, and Kalashnikovs was part of the job, just as following the money had been for the Watergate investigators. No longer.

That attitude changed completely in the 1990s, when the CIA's Office of General Counsel started to put in overtime worrying about arms dealers "graymailing" the agency. A mild form of blackmail, graymail works like this: An arms dealer will volunteer his services to the CIA, claiming he's a patriot who wants to run out the bad guys in the business. He provides a couple of tantalizing tidbits about some deal or another, but they end up being dead ends because the arms dealer is really after an insurance policy. He's counting on using the CIA as an umbrella that will cover him for anything he does, legal or illegal. If one day he's unfortunate enough to get caught selling arms to an embargoed country like Syria or Iran, he can falsely claim that his CIA handler (someone like me) had given him a go-ahead. Since CIA officers undercover cannot testify in court, the arms dealer walks.

Was it a legitimate worry? Sure. Arms dealers don't go into the business because they're patriots. But intelligence gathering is like investing in the market: You can stick your neck out and take your losses with your gains. Or you can clip T-bill coupons with the AARP bluehairs, clearly Langley's preference.

To give you an idea of how crazy it got, not too long before I resigned from the CIA in December 1997, I had the opportunity to recruit an arms dealer who, like Yuri, sold Russian weaponry in the Middle East. It was at a time when the CIA was beginning to understand what a disaster the old Soviet strategic-weapons labs and testing facilities were. Stocks were missing everywhere. During a routine visit to a former Soviet weapons site called Vozrozhdeniye, on an island in the Aral Sea, we found weaponized anthrax lying on the ground. Anthrax! The site was unguarded, and anyone could have picked it up. That's the kind of thing I wanted to turn this arms dealer loose on.

Times were hard in the arms trade. Supply and demand had gotten out of whack. My guy was happy simply to have the CIA pay his travel and expenses. He would do his business on the side—legitimate, he assured me—while giving me a heads-up when things like anthrax were being put on the market. I thought this operation would be fairly clear-cut, and inexpensive, too, but as soon as my bosses heard what I intended to do, the hand wringing started. At first they flatly refused to let me meet the guy. They relented only when I agreed to drag along a lawyer from the general counsel's office.

You can imagine the chill that put on the operation. Informants, by nature, work in the dark. Turn a government lawyer's spotlight on them, and they scurry back to their rat holes. The seventh floor at Langley had its priorities, though. If the guy tried to play us, the CIA brass wanted to be able to produce the lawyer in court. No one seemed to care that, in the end, we wouldn't learn a damn thing about the anthrax at Vozrozhdeniye or any of the other stuff missing from the ex-Soviet strategic-weapons sites. After I resigned, I heard that the informant was dropped—terminated, as it's called in the business—and the CIA went back to treating arms dealers like the clap, closing the best window we had into the international arms market and the deadly scourge of proliferation.

In Caesarea, face-to-face with a true titan of the arms trade, I wasn't about to let another opportunity slip by. More than anything else, I wanted to hear what Yuri could tell me about Saudi Arabia and arms.

By 2001 anyone who understood anything about Saudi Arabia knew it was circling the drain. Per capita income over the last twenty years had fallen by more than 60 percent. Birth rates had soared to among the highest in the world. Meanwhile, the royal family's grotesque corruption and thousand-and-one-nights lifestyle had started to take a real toll on the Saudi street. Popular preachers all over Saudi Arabia were openly calling for a jihad against the West—a metaphor, I assure you, that includes the royal family. Signs were mounting that the place was beginning to crack wide open. In 1995 the National Guard barracks was bombed, killing five Americans. Under a year later, a second terrorist attack on a U.S.

military barracks in al-Khobar killed nineteen U.S. servicemen. In 2000 two Saudi security officers hijacked a Saudi commercial jet bound for London and forced it to land in Baghdad. "We are just ordinary people, and we are calling for the rights of the Saudi people, such as decent education, decent health, and other services," one of the hijackers told officials when the plane put down in Iraq.

What I didn't know and was trying to angle Yuri into telling me was whether anyone had the ability to translate all this discontent into activity, like overthrowing the Al Sa'ud, the semisedentary, unworldly Bedouin clan that traces its lineage back to the eighteenth century. To do that, they would need arms, and a lot of them.

The Saudi government probably spends more per capita than any other country in the world on arms. (It acknowledges only that it spends 13 percent of its gross domestic product, but half of its revenue is earmarked for the military.) That's basically without having to provide for its own external defense; U.S. carrier groups and F-15 combat air patrols over the Gulf take care of that. (And the U.S. still manages to spend less than 4 percent of GDP on the military.) Also, Saudi Arabia has never fought in any Arab-Israeli war, from 1948 until today. In fact, the Al Sa'ud's military hasn't fought a war since the 1930s. To understand the significance of its spending on arms, look at the French for comparison. Although France has a modern, combat-ready mobile army that fights in a handful of African bush wars and participates in peace missions all over the world, it spends only 2.57 percent of GDP on its military.

So where does Saudi Arabia's defense money go? A lot disappears down the depths of corruption, but an equal amount goes for personal protection of the royal family. The Saudi National Guard, as well equipped as the best army in the world and as well paid, is probably the most expensive bodyguard service in the world. Every time you fill up your car with gas that has its beginning as Saudi crude—and statistically, that should be about one in every five or six times you pull up to the pump—you're contributing something like a dollar toward keeping Saudi royal heads attached to their necks.

Over the years I served in the Middle East, I always accepted on faith my government's comfortable assumption that with all the money the Al Sa'ud have dumped into arming their bodyguards, they could keep themselves (and our oil) safe, including preventing average Saudis from acquiring heavy weapons, the kind they would need to unseat the regime. Now I was beginning to have my doubts.

Yuri probably knew as much about dirty arms trading as any man alive. But why should I expect him to give me a quick refresher course? If he'd wanted to teach, he would have stayed in Moscow and found a job at a school. I'd have to convince him that he stood to make some money. Since I wasn't in the arms business, I'd need to invent some story, weave it out of whole cloth. Involvement may be the first step to understanding, but to become involved, you sometimes have to be "creative" with the facts.

"New subject, Yuri," I started tentatively. "I need some small stuff, you know, plastic explosives, rocket launchers, rifles."

Yuri's eyes flickered. The "stuff" I was talking about had made him a fortune in West Africa. He couldn't dismiss it out of hand.

Before he could answer, I lowered my voice and went on: "I need it delivered inside Saudi Arabia."

Yuri waited for what seemed like an hour before answering. He was sitting across the table from an ex-CIA officer whom he had just met. He must have figured he'd already given away too much about his business. Was I still working for the agency? Had I come to the Israeli Riviera to drag him into some dirty game and entrap him?

"I myself won't touch it," Yuri said at last with a zippered smile. "But if you're serious, I'll give you the number of an associate in Moscow. He's done it before."

"Done what before?"

"Delivered weapons inside Saudi Arabia. Like Domino's, he delivers anywhere, anytime. Even to the crazy Vahabis."

"Vahabis" is the way Russians end up pronouncing "Wahhabis."

"You're talking about pistols, rifles, ammunition?" I asked.

"Yes, and the big stuff, too. You got the cash, he's got the hardware."

Sleeping with the Devil

I shouldn't have been surprised. Six months later, someone would kill five people in the United States with weaponized anthrax, the same stuff left lying on the ground at Vozrozhdeniye, but this time in a form so sophisticated, it would take a Department of Defense lab something like five years to replicate. As I write this, a shipment of dismantled Scud missiles was recently discovered hidden on an unflagged North Korean freighter headed for Sana', the Yemeni capital. Were the missiles—probably manufactured in North Korea—meant for Yemen, a U.S. ally in the eerie calculus of the Arab world? Were they intended for overland shipment to Iraq, which Yemen supported in the last Gulf War? Or were they a private-placement purchase, using Yemen as a port of convenience? Maybe for some militant splinter group, say, with its own launcher buried in the Arabian desert? All allies are of convenience in the Middle East, and it was, after all, Yemeni nationals who helped bin Laden blow a hole the size of a semi through the armored hull of the U.S.S. *Cole*. Chances are we'll never know the whole truth. Maybe even Yuri couldn't ferret it out. But in the meantime, any of those possibilities seems as likely to me as any other. You want the big stuff these days, you can get it delivered right to your door, or theirs.

2/Circling the Drain

I NEVER CALLED Yuri's contact in Moscow, and I'll probably never find out for sure whether his network actually could deliver arms inside Saudi Arabia. But my gut tells me he could. And if not him, then someone else.

Anyhow, I'd already suspected Russian arms dealers were operating inside the kingdom's borders. They probably had been since the collapse of the Soviet Union in 1991. In the early 1990s, Osama bin Laden's main supply sergeant was Victor Bout, a former Russian military officer who had served in Angola, where he got involved in arms trafficking and oil. Like Yuri's associate, Bout had a reputation for delivering anything, anywhere, including the nasty stuff. Through a company called Air Cess, which owns one of the largest privately owned jet-transport fleets in the world, Bout works the toughest markets—Iran, Liberia, Angola, Sierra Leone, Iraq, and Serbia—taking advantage of out-of-the-way airports like Sharjah, in the United Arab Emirates, and Burgas, Bulgaria. The word was that for the right price, he could find you anything, maybe even a nuke delivered to downtown Riyadh. Although Bout's connections to bin Laden were exposed in the press, he continues to operate out of Dubai, Saudi Arabia's main depot for contraband and shady financial transactions. Dubai is where most of the money for the September 11 attacks was banked.

Bout is mostly bullet-proof because the Russian external intelligence service (the SVR) is part owner of Air Cess. What's more, Russian arms trafficking has become almost a legitimate business: Saudi defense minster Sultan bin 'Abd-al-'Aziz tried to get into it. Sultan even hosted a visit to Saudi Arabia by the head Rosvo-orouzhenie, Russia's state arms marketer.

I also didn't need Yuri to tell me that the kingdom's 4,431-kilometer land border and 2,640-kilometer shoreline are indefensible. Since before recorded history, Bedouin nomads and smugglers have wandered freely back and forth across the Arabian peninsula, unchecked and uncontrolled. Gold smugglers from India still sail up the Gulf and clandestinely unload their shipments every night. And we already knew Yuri's crazy Vahabis could get their hands on weapons. They did just fine arming themselves in 1979, when they stormed the Mecca's Great Mosque.

Loose arms and open borders are never a good sign, but they don't necessarily mean that a country is about to slip into a civil war or go under. What you need to bring down a regime like the Al Sa'ud is a readiness of its citizens to pick up those arms and use them, to fight and die for their beliefs, in this instance against a heavily armed, well-paid, and very extensive palace guard. Up until September 11, a lot of Middle East watchers, me included, didn't think the average Saudi fit that description. We all had hard-wired in our brains the stereotype of young, oil-rich brats screaming at their Filipino servants to take the wrappers off their candy. Fighting and dying for anything as abstract as a belief seemed beyond their range of probable actions.

September 11 undid that stereotype for me. The fifteen Saudi hijackers were all the proof I need that the kingdom has a reservoir of young men who won't flinch when faced with death, whether that entails flying planes into skyscrapers or blasting away at the Al Sa'ud or Saudi Arabia's oil infrastructure with heavy weapons. Militant Islam has energized young Saudis like we never thought possible.

Sleeping with the Devil

What about the Saudi royal family's army of guards, with all of their tanks and airplanes—surely they're up to taking care of the fanatics? That's another myth that will take an event as momentous as September 11 to kill. But let's look at the available evidence. Saudi Arabia's grim sheriff, Interior Minister Na'if, cares only about protecting the Sa'ud's grip on power, at the expense of everything and everyone else. ████████████████████████████████

██

████████████████████████

██

██

████████████████████ To make his point, Na'if went out of his way to avoid FBI director Louis Freeh. When Freeh showed up in Saudi Arabia to put some teeth into the investigation of the bombing of the U.S. barracks at Khobar, Na'if stayed on his yacht anchored off the coast in the Red Sea, near Jeddah. Freeh met with two low-ranking security officials in the internal security service, neither of whom knew anything about Khobar. The parallel would be for Na'if to come to Washington and be hosted by Freeh's driver.

It wasn't like Na'if had the diplomatic sense to keep his hate for Americans out of the press. After September 11, at the worst possible time, Na'if said that the United States, "the great power that controls the earth, now is an enemy of Arabs and Muslims." In fact, things were a lot worse than even the most rabid Saudi bashers suspected. ████████████████████████████████

██

██

██

██ Al-Rajhi is the managing director of the al-Rajhi Banking and Investment Corporation, which runs nearly four hundred branch offices in Saudi Arabia and abroad. Founded in 1987, it is one of the richest banks in the kingdom, contributing to charities like the International Islamic Relief Organization (IIRO), which funneled money to bin Laden and other militant Saudis.

No one could do anything about Na'if, including King Fahd. Na'if ran the Interior Ministry like his own personal reserve. As Fahd's full brother, Na'if is a "protected" prince and can't be fired, even as he steps up his private war against the United States and extorts money from militant Wahhabis. I often wondered why Na'if hated the U.S. so much. █████████████████████

███

███

███████████████████████████████████████

██████████████████████████

Louis Freeh has never gone on the record about Khobar and Na'if, but I suspect he wasn't surprised. He'd seen worse. By the mid-1990s, Qatar was hosting ten al Qaeda terrorists now on the most-wanted list. When Freeh received a rock-solid report showing conclusively that al Qaeda's most lethal operative, Khalid Sheikh Muhammad, was among those being harbored by the Qatar government, Freeh sent a *démarche* to the Qatari minister of foreign affairs, asking that Qatar honor its commitment to turn Muhammad over to the FBI.

Freeh particularly wanted to put away Muhammad because he was the uncle of Ramzi Yousef, the man who planned the truck-bombing of the World Trade Center in 1993. Muhammad had also planned to blow up eleven American airliners over the Pacific. He even practiced on a Philippines airliner, killing a young Japanese passenger on a flight in late 1994. One of Muhammad's associates arrested in the Philippines credits Muhammad with being an early backer of hijacking airplanes and running them into U.S. buildings including the CIA headquarters. Freeh's request to the Qatari minister leaves no doubt that he considered Muhammad a psychotic murderer.

"Muhammad's suspected involvement in terrorist plots clearly threatens U.S. interests," Freeh wrote in a letter shown to me by a high-ranking Arab intelligence official. "His activities in Qatar threaten your government's interests as well. Indeed, you indicated during our meeting that he may be in the process of manufacturing an explosive device that would potentially endanger the lives of the citizens of Qatar. In addition, you indicated that Muhammad has over twenty false passports at his disposal."

Qatar's response? Although Muhammad was an employee of the Qatari government at the time (ironically, he was working in the public water works), the administration claimed they could not find him. In fact, they secretly whisked Muhammad out of the country, keeping an FBI squad cooling its heels in a Doha hotel. Freeh's dismay must have turned to anger when he found out that Qatar had dumped $23,938,994.20 between 1997 and 1999 into a Washington law firm close to the White House and another $689,805.16 into a K Street public-relations firm to buff up its image and cover its flanks while it served as a holding tank for some of the world's most dangerous people. The icing on the cake was when the American ambassador in Doha—the man charged with convincing the Qataris to turn over Muhammad—later went to work for the Qataris. Muhammad himself won time to start master-minding 9/11.

What does Qatar have to do with Saudi Arabia, aside from the fact that it shares a border with the kingdom and has a population similarly weighted toward a militant, fanatical interpretation of Islam? Consider this: When Khalid Sheikh Muhammad was run to ground in Pakistan in March 2003, he was in the company of Mustafa Ahmed Hawsawi, a Saudi conduit for the September 11 hijackers drawing from accounts in the United Arab Emirates. According to a Gulf security official I talked to, Hawsawi crossed over from the kingdom to carry out the transfers to the hijackers. In other words, there are no hard-and-fast borders to this terror network. Osama bin Laden flies no national flag over his cave, wherever that might be. Anger against the West and particularly the United States spills all over the Land of Islam. But there are groups that all the signs keep pointing to—the Wahhabis, the Muslim

Brotherhood, and al Qaeda, of course—and there's one place that serves more than any other as the principal backer: Saudi Arabia.

The Clinton administration, by the way, didn't give a damn that its own FBI director got stood up in Qatar. It didn't even complain to the Qatari foreign minister, who wandered in and out of the White House as if he worked there. I was once asked to vacate the office of Al Gore's national security adviser so the vice president could meet with the foreign minister when he showed up unannounced.

But Na'if alone wasn't the problem. The House of Sa'ud and the kingdom it rules basically hit the mute button beginning in the mid-1990s, and it hasn't let up since. In 1996 the Saudi government simply declined Sudan's offer to turn over Osama bin Laden. Riyadh's explanation? Bin Ladin was too popular in Saudi Arabia; his arrest would incite a revolution. Since September 11, not a single indictment or even a useful lead has come out of Saudi Arabia. So thorough has been the lockdown that the FBI has not been allowed to interview suspects, including the families of the fifteen Saudi hijackers. Long after September 11, Saudi Arabia refused to provide advance manifests for flights coming into the U.S., a basic and potentially fatal breach of security.

If Saudi Arabia were even remotely a free and open country, the U.S. press might be able to tell us why Na'if is at war with America; but with few exceptions, American journalists are not issued visas to visit the kingdom. The few who visit find themselves closely controlled by the secret police. Don't look for much illumination from the supposedly new and improved FBI, either. The bureau's Riyadh office is, or at least was until recently, staffed with two Muslim agents, but not because they had special access to the Arab street. The FBI was far more interested in demonstrating how "in touch" it was with Saudi sensitivities. Perish the thought that we might risk insulting the Al Sa'ud by sending an infidel to watch them.

Sleeping with the Devil

FOR MOST AMERICANS, September 11 was both a national horror and a geopolitical awakening. It was almost impossible to absorb that fifteen of the hijackers were Saudis, the citizens of a country we'd always been told was our best ally in the Middle East, after Israel. But in the fall of 2002, when Saudi Arabia started to lead the Arab campaign against a war in Iraq, mainly because it was worried about its own stability, Americans began to come around to the fact that they'd been lied to about Saudi Arabia. A decade earlier, during the Persian Gulf War, the Saudis opened their door to U.S. forces. In 2002 America found itself begging Qatar to provide a communications base for our invading forces. As if Americans needed more evidence, perhaps two-thirds of al Qaeda prisoners being held in the Camp Delta prison facility at the Guantanamo Naval Base in Cuba—"the worst of the worst," according to Secretary of Defense Donald Rumsfeld—were said to be Saudi nationals.

Every day seemed to bring damning new revelations about Saudi Arabia, many connected to the royal family: The wife of the Saudi ambassador to the United States had handed out money that found its way to two of the 9/11 hijackers. A raid on the Hamburg apartment of a suspected accomplice of the hijackers had turned up the business card of a Saudi diplomat. The two hijackers who arrived in Los Angeles were met by a Saudi working for a company contracted to the Ministry of Defense. Other Saudis fed the ATM machines for the hijackers. When NATO forces raided the offices of the Saudi High Commission for Aid to Bosnia, founded by Prince Salman, they found before-and-after photos of the destroyed U.S. embassies in Kenya and Tanzania and of the World Trade Center (when it still stood), and of the U.S.S. *Cole,* as well as files on the use of crop-duster planes and materials for forging official U.S. identity cards. In November 2002 the Saudi embassy in Washington gave the finger to the State Department and federal law officials, providing a new passport for the wife of a suspected al Qaeda sympathizer and slipping her and her five children out of the U.S. after she was subpoenaed to testify before a federal grand jury.

As the facts against Riyadh mounted, the Saudis couldn't refute them. Instead, they reacted heatedly. In a rare press appearance at the kingdom's Washington embassy, Adel al-Jubeir, a foreign policy adviser to the crown, complained: "We have been assailed as the kernel of evil, the breeding ground of terrorism. Our faith has been maligned in ways that I did not expect Americans to ever do." In the meantime, Na'if continued to pretend that Saudi Arabia had nothing to do with the attacks. A year and a half later, there still hadn't been a single Saudi arrest that helped us get to the bottom of September 11.

Frankly, none of this should come as a surprise. The Saudi judicial system looks as if it were designed by Ghengis Khan. Saudi Arabia tops the world in public beheadings. (The venue for many of them is a Riyadh plaza popularly known as Chop-Chop Square.) The kingdom's secondary schools and universities have become the West Point of global terrorism. Its public-decency police force, the muttawa, has zero interest in stopping Saudis from plotting righteous murder abroad. It tends to more important matters, like forcing store owners to shut down during prayer times and beating women on the arms and legs when their robes are too short. In March 2002 it blocked the exits from a girl's school on fire in Mecca because the girls weren't properly covered; fourteen died. Foreign workers are virtually without rights in Saudi Arabia. No one in the kingdom, national or visitor, can practice any religion but Islam. Anyone caught putting up a Christmas wreath is lashed.

Even the U.S. State Department had to admit things weren't so good in the kingdom when it came to religion. It considered putting the kingdom on a blacklist of nations that restrict religious freedom, including Iran, Iraq, China, Burma, Sudan, and North Korea. The department's "International Religious Freedom Report for 2002" cited detentions of Christians, confiscation or censoring of Bibles, and harassment of Christians by the country's religious police. In the end, though, it just couldn't bring itself to do anything so extreme.

Things are even worse than they seem. Saudi Arabia doesn't

have what we would call a rule of law. Look inside a Saudi passport: It states that the holder "belongs" to the royal family. A Saudi commoner is chattel, a piece of property no different from an Al Sa'ud's Jeddah palace or his Rolls-Royce Silver Cloud. There are no rights in the kingdom, just as there isn't a parliament or a constitution.

Things might be better if Saudi Arabia were some romantic kingdom ruled by a wise, benevolent king and a royal family with a sense of noblesse oblige. But it isn't. Starting at the top, King Fahd is close to brain-dead, incapacitated by a 1995 stroke. This became clear late that year when Fahd shit in his pool during physical therapy, in front of his family. Crown Prince 'Abdallah supposedly fills in for Fahd, his half brother, but he has no real power. He is mistrusted and despised by the senior princes—the cabinet ministers—and his authority is checked at every opportunity.

Fahd's favorite wife, Jawhara al-Ibrahim, and her spoiled, megalomanic son 'Abd-al-'Aziz—Azouzi, or "deary," as Fahd calls him—actually run Saudi Arabia. Jawhara alone has twenty-four-hour-a-day access to Fahd. She decides who will see him and who won't, which decrees he will see and which he won't. For all practical purposes, she sets the general course of Saudi internal and external policy. For all we know, she states how much oil will be pumped or completely cut off.

Dementia, palace intrigues, and jealousy are only the start of the Al Sa'ud story. The Al Sa'ud are as violent and vengeful as any Mafia family. The first Saudi to write a book critical of the kingdom was kidnapped in Beirut and presumably murdered in the early 1970s. I learned, after I left the CIA, that in the mid-1990s, Na'if was behind at least two attempts on the life of Muhammad al-Masari, the leader of the London-based Committee for the Defense of Legitimate Rights. Surely that ought to be reason enough for al-Masari to join others in taking up arms against the Al Sa'ud—Osama bin Laden, for example. In another case, 'Abd-al-Karim Naqshabandi, a Syrian who irritated a member of the royal family, was beheaded on the streets of Riyadh in 1996, despite the pleas of human-rights activists from around the world. The charge: sorcery. Anything can be a capital crime in Saudi Arabia if it serves the interest of a Saudi don.

Like royals anywhere the Al Sa'ud are enormously resistant to change. They don't want to admit to the rot in the Kingdom. In particular, they don't want to talk about the fact that Fahd's stroke has set the country adrift, allowing corrupt princes to make fortunes in illegal ventures, from selling visas and alcohol to stealing property. They also do not want to talk about the fact that the importation of foreign labor has resulted in large numbers of young Saudis out of work, encouraging them to spend their time in the mosque being indoctrinated for jihad and righteous murder.

Every Saudi prince receives a substantial allowance, but since none can ever have enough money, many supplement their royal allotments through bribes on construction projects (mostly from the bin Laden family), arms deals, and outright theft of property from commoners. Besides visas, they also sell liquor and narcotics. In July 2002, Na'if bin Sultan bin Fawaz al-Shaalan was indicted by a Florida grand jury on charges that he used his personal plane to transport two tons of cocaine from Caracas to Paris in 1999. That incident surprised even me: I've known the Shaalan family for over a decade. Until then, they'd managed to avoid infection by the kingdom.

Sleeping with the Devil

Stories of Al Sa'ud profligacy are legion, but Fahd's youngest son, Azouzi, broke the mold when he built himself a sprawling theme park outside Riyadh because he was "interested" in history. He has told visitors that the park cost $4.6 billion. The property includes a scale model of old Mecca, with actors attending mosque and chanting prayers twenty-four hours a day. Also on the property: replicas of the Alhambra, old Mecca, and Medina, and half a dozen other Islamic landmarks. True to form, Azouzi seized the land the park was built on.

But he's only following family tradition. When King Fahd's family visits the palace at Marbella, they spend on average $5 million a day in the local stores, so much that shopkeepers want to name a street after the king. Yet as much as the Al Sa'uds love the objects money buys—diamonds, yachts, palaces, planes—they love human flesh more. Put simply, the Al Sa'ud are obsessed with sex, everything from prostitutes to little boys. Incidentally, Interior Minister Na'if has sex on the brain, too: He spends his spare time consulting with doctors about a cure for his impotence. It's apparently affected his wife, Maha, who has a severe anger-management problem. In 1995, on a visit to Orlando, she assaulted a male servant, accusing him of helping steal $200,000 in cash and jewelry. As Maha beat the servant bloody in front of the off-duty sheriff's department deputies assigned to her security detail, no one raised a hand. She had diplomatic immunity. The lesson didn't go unnoticed. Six years later, also in Orlando, another Saudi princess was charged not only with beating her servant but pushing her down a flight of stairs. This princess didn't get off so lightly, despite the Saudi embassy's claim that she was protected by diplomatic immunity. Police charged her with aggravated battery, then tacked on grand theft for snatching $6,000 worth of electronics from her former chauffeur.

But I was talking about sex.

THE SAUDIS ARE PROBABLY the most sexually repressed people in the world. Women are kept out of reach of men until the day they marry. After that joyous occasion, the husbands keep their wives locked up at home until the day they die. Only 5 percent of women work. A woman cannot drive. If she needs to go somewhere, a male first cousin, brother, or father has to chauffeur her. Even then she is allowed to go only to gender-segregated malls, restaurants, and swimming pools. If she's ever unfortunate enough to be caught in the act of adultery, she's stoned to death, along with her lover. It's easier for a young Saudi man to hitchhike to Afghanistan than to hook up with a young Saudi girl.

Like men anywhere, though, Saudi men won't take no for an answer. One desperate trick they've resorted to is writing their cell-phone number on a piece of paper and taping it to the back window of their car. It looks as if the car is for sale. But the owner's fantasy is that some brazen Saudi girl will call to introduce herself. With something like 380,000 young unemployed Saudi males, you can imagine all the cruising going on, waiting for that lucky phone call. Filipina and Indonesian servants in the kingdom live in constant fear of rape. Since foreigners work and live in the kingdom at the whim of their Saudi sponsors, the servants are afraid to go to the police. No one has any idea how much rape goes on in the country. Those statistics aren't published, but if sexual frustration were gold, the Saudis wouldn't need all that oil.

Saudis with money also don't have to take no for an answer. In the early 1970s, when the petrodollars started flooding in, enter-prising Lebanese began smuggling hookers into the kingdom for the princes. Since the women were posing as Middle East Airlines flight attendants and were driven directly to the royal palaces, the muttawa couldn't do anything about it. Having established a beach-head in the kingdom, a lot of the Lebanese pimps branched out into interior decorating and construction. Since no one in the royal fam-ily knows how to balance a checkbook, the Lebanese became fabu-lously rich. More than a couple went back to Lebanon and built political careers with their fortunes.

Sleeping with the Devil

Saudis who can't tap in to the stream of royal prostitutes take multiple wives, the younger the better. It's common for seventy-year-old Saudi men to marry girls in their early teens. Other rich Saudis simply go whoring abroad. You need only take a flight out of the Gulf to see the robes come off and the cigarettes and the liquor come out: These gentlemen are on their way to a party. Spend a night visiting popular clubs on France's Côte d'Azur or in Monte Carlo, and you'll find young Saudi men (and women) staying up all night, enjoying every moment of their freedom. London's red-light districts and call-girl services cater largely to Saudis and other Gulf Arabs.

Stories about Saudi whoring get a snicker in the American press and preachy editorials about women's rights, but everyone seems to be missing the point: Saudi Arabia spends a staggering percentage of its GDP on sex. If we're donating a dollar to the royal family's bodyguards every time we fill up the tank with gasoline that began as Saudi crude, we're probably donating half again as much for Saudis to get laid.

Needless to say, the royal family spends the lion's share. You can find their rutting palaces along the Mediterranean, all built to entertain prostitutes. Being of royal blood, a Saudi prince couldn't make do with some drab *garçonnière;* he needs all the comforts of home. Legend has it that King Fahd's administrator for the palace near Antibes once made a proposal to the government that is still talked about in France today: to move the Paris-Nice railroad track away from the palace. It didn't matter that the existing line didn't run all that near the palace, or that moving it would cost millions. Fahd, the administrator explained, would be annoyed to hear even the distant sound of passing trains while strolling in his garden. The French officials shook their heads in disbelief—they knew the king hadn't visited his Antibes palace in over a decade.

IN THE EARLY 1970S, the Al Sa'ud's Riviera frolicking came to an abrupt end after Fahd lost in one sitting a reported $6 million at a Nice casino and was photographed with a phalanx of young beauties. The royal family had to find a new playground. As soon as King Hassan of Morocco heard that the Saudis were in the real estate market, he phoned Riyadh to offer up Morocco. Hassan had no choice; he was stone-cold broke. With no oil of his own and the remittances from Moroccans working in Europe just not cutting it, how else could he afford the upkeep on his twenty palaces?

So it was that King Hassan allowed dozens of Saudi princes to build secluded estates in Morocco, many in the ruggèd mountains around Tangier. The area, called the Rif, was wild and lawless—a perfect place to hold an orgy or go on a drinking binge, away from the prying eyes of the Wahhabis back home and the Western press in Europe's old watering holes. A journalist trying to get a story or picture risked being kidnapped or having his throat cut. When I was in Morocco, the CIA picked up a rumor that a Saudi prince with well-placed friends in Washington had bitten off the breast of a young Moroccan girl in a drunken frenzy. King Hassan swiftly had the incident covered up. The girl's family was paid off, and she was told she would keep her mouth shut or spend the rest of her life in jail. The strong-arm tactics worked; the incident never saw the light of day.

In return for Morocco's delicate diplomacy, Saudi Arabia and the Gulf Arabs dumped loads of money into the country. It's impossible to calculate precisely how much, but there are tantalizing hints. In 1998 Saudi defense minister Sultan secretly bought Société Anonyme Marocaine de l'Industrie du Raffinage (SAMIR), Morocco's oil refinery, for $420 million. The transaction was handled through a cascade of nominees, shelf companies, and middlemen to keep Sultan's name out of the press. Saudi Arabia also poured almost a reported billion dollars into the huge Casablanca mosque. But that was merely the public face of Saudi aid.

Sleeping with the Devil

IF YOU'VE FOLLOWED THIS devil's logic so far, then it's a small step to the conclusion that we in the West and the Saudi rulers themselves are in serious trouble. All the ingredients of upheaval are in place: open borders, the availability of arms, political alienation, the absence of a rule of law, a completely corrupt police force, a despised ruling class, plummeting per capita income (and fabulously wealthy rulers to remind the poor exactly how poor they are), environmental degradation, surly neighbors, and a growing number of young home-grown radicals who care more about righteous murder than they do about living. The kingdom's schools churn out fanatics faster than they can find wars to fight. Burma, Vietnam, Cambodia, Nicaragua, Angola, Somalia, and Sierra Leone succumbed to chaos under less volatile conditions. Why should Saudi Arabia escape this fate?

3 / A Consent of Silence

WITH THIS KIND of rot, you'd think that every map in official Washington would have a red flag planted on the dot labeled "Riyadh" to remind the bureaucrats that Saudi Arabia is on life support. The truth is just the opposite. As I write this in early 2003, Washington still continues to insist that Saudi Arabia is a stable country, that its central government is in undisputed control of its borders; its police and army are efficient and loyal; and its people are well clothed, fed, and educated.

Let's start with the State Department. It is more responsible than any other government bureaucracy in Washington for spreading the big lie about the kingdom. To listen to Foggy Bottom's spin, you would think Saudi Arabia was Denmark. Just look at the way it handled visas for Saudis. By law, the State Department has overseas responsibility for visas; it issues them in our embassies and consulates. The 1952 Immigration and Nationality Act is clear about eligibility. The section of the law related to granting tourist visas, Section 214(b), reads: "Every alien shall be presumed to be an immigrant until he establishes that to the satisfaction of the consular officers . . . he is entitled to non-immigrant status." In other words, a foreigner who has no reason to return home—he's unemployed, unmarried, and broke—isn't eligible for a visa. The presumption is that he will remain in the U.S.

According to the law, all fifteen Saudis who took part in the 9/11 attacks should have been turned down for visas. With male unemployment in the kingdom hovering around 30 percent, and with per capita income in a free fall, Saudis should be presumed immigrants (unless they are royals or their retainers). Since most Saudis could work part-time at a 7-Eleven and make a better living than at home, they are an inherent risk of remaining in the U.S. Simply put, they don't meet the qualifications of the law. But it's worse than that.

Right through September 11, 2001, Saudis were not even required to appear at the U.S. embassy in Riyadh or the consulate in Jeddah for a visa interview. Under a system called Visa Express, a Saudi had only to send his passport, an application, and a fee to a travel agent to get a visa. The Saudi travel agent, in other words, stood in for the American government. A short wait, and any Saudi who had the money for a flight was on his way to New York—to disappear like a diamond in an inkwell or to run his airplane into a skyscraper. In other words, in issuing visas to fifteen unemployed Saudis, the State Department broke the law. Sure, four other hijackers got into the U.S., but did we have to make it so easy for the majority of the assault force to take its positions?

Then there's the question of State having zero political sense. Osama bin Laden is a Saudi by birth. Saudi citizens blew up the National Guard facility in 1995 and the Khobar barracks in 1996. Two Saudis hijacked a plane to Baghdad in 2000. Saudis almost certainly were behind the attack on the *Cole*. Saudis were involved in hundreds of other terrorist attacks, from Chechnya to Kenya and Tanzania. How much more evidence did the State Department need to figure out that Saudis were the world's new terrorists and needed to be tightly screened and interviewed? The way they ran Visa Express, Osama himself could have slipped through.

Sleeping with the Devil

It wasn't only visas, though. The State Department gave the Saudi rulers a pass on almost everything. It shielded the Saudis from human-rights groups. It supported them in the World Bank and the International Monetary Fund. It dismissed the National Guard and Khobar attacks as aberrations. Take, for instance, the State Department's 1999 report: "Patterns of Global Terrorism." The section for Saudi Arabia reads: "The Saudi Arabian Government, at all levels, continued to reaffirm its commitment to combating terrorism." Having set a tone of dissembling, the report goes on: "The Government of Saudi Arabia continued to investigate the bombing in June 1996 of the Khobar Towers." We know the last was a whopper. Na'if never lifted a finger to get to the bottom of it. But a lot else was going on in 1999 that State didn't want us to know about. That year Na'if released from prison two clerics who had issued fatwas to kill Americans. One of them, Safar al-Hawali, inspired bin Laden. At the same time, the fifteen Saudi hijackers were apparently being recruited and indoctrinated in Saudi mosques. So much for Saudi Arabia's "commitment."

State never told the truth to Americans heading to Saudi Arabia. Dependents of American citizens were never advised to leave. Saudi Arabia was never warned to cooperate on terrorism. When I used to say to my State colleagues that the kingdom might one day collapse, they would sneer, "There are no problems," then fling at me the old Saudi line: "The royal family is like the fingers of a hand. Threaten it, and they become a fist." Catchy, to be sure, but the reality is that when the Al Sa'ud are threatened these days, they pony up more money for the fanatics, and State hands out more visas.

State not only turned a blind eye to Saudi Arabia's radical Islamic foreign policy, it occasionally abetted it. State knew that Saudi Arabia's plan to run gas and oil pipelines across Afghanistan, from Central Asia to Pakistan, would help the Taliban stay in power and ensure that bin Laden had a safe haven. Nonetheless, State went along, even encouraging an American company, Unocal, to participate.

I got a short course in Afghan pipeline politics on February 4, 1997, when I was introduced to ███████████████████████ ████ for the Afghan pipeline. He had been sent by the State Department and the National Security Council to give me an update on Unocal's scheme. In spite of the ongoing civil war and the Taliban's tightening grip on Afghanistan, Unocal intended to proceed with both pipelines. It calculated that running a gas pipeline from Turkmenistan to Pakistan was going to cost $2 billion. A parallel oil pipeline would add another $2.5 billion. Putting this kind of money in a country in the throes of a civil war seemed to me like a risky investment. I asked ██████ if Unocal was nervous.

██████ looked at me for a couple of seconds as if I were a dim bulb. "With U.S. government guarantees and the World Bank putting up the money, no," he said. "We're not stupid enough to do this on our own."

██████ was right when he said Unocal wasn't alone. J. P. Morgan and Cambridge Energy Research had prepared a study on government-to-government payment structures in order to secure a World Bank loan. Unocal also roped in former U.S. ambassador Bob Oakley, one of Saudi Arabia's best friends in Washington. A slew of corporate giants were promised a piece of the action, including Fluor Daniel. Unocal had official blessing.

A week later, on February 13, 1997, ██████ was in Afghanistan talking to the Taliban. They demanded that Unocal build a road from Torghundi to Spin Boldak and invest money in the Kandahar schools—no doubt mosque schools. I have no idea whether Unocal ever built the road, but if it did, I wonder if bin Laden used it to escape.

Even after the 1998 attacks on the U.S. embassies in Kenya and Tanzania, organized by bin Laden from Afghanistan, Saudi Arabia continued to aid his host, the Taliban. In July 2000 *Petroleum Intelligence Weekly*, the bible of the international petroleum industry, reported that Saudi Arabia was sending as many as 150,000 barrels of oil a day to Afghanistan and Pakistan in off-the-books foreign aid. This tactic—sending free oil in lieu of cash—

was an established Saudi precedent. Turkey, Pakistan, and Morocco were similarly helped in the early 1990s, and Bahrain was getting its own daily 150,000 barrels in an acknowledged aid deal. We can only guess what motivated the House of Sa'ud to spend all this money when it was running a crippling deficit. According to press reports, beginning in the mid-1970s, Saudi Arabia poured over $1 billion into Pakistan to help it develop an "Islamic" nuclear bomb to counter the "Hindu" nuclear threat from neighboring India. The House of Sa'ud managed to keep that bit of foreign adventurism hidden from its American allies until well into the early 1990s.

Covert Saudi Arabian aid to the Taliban, which amounted to hundreds of millions of dollars, continued right through the attacks on the World Trade Center and the Pentagon. Still the State Department didn't protest. So I guess I shouldn't be surprised that State was waiving visa interviews right through September 11, 2001. You want to see the U.S.A.? Fine, drop us a postcard when you get there. And by the way, have a bang-up time.

The CIA let State take the lead in this waltz. No stranger to Washington politics, the CIA decided that the safest bet was to ignore Saudi Arabia by cleverly pretending it was a U.S. domestic problem, and thus by statute not in its jurisdiction. CIA directors had picked up long ago that the door to the Oval Office was always open to Saudi ambassador Bandar bin Sultan and not to them. While the country's chief spymasters waited for months to get a face-to-face, all Bandar had to do to see the president was hit the speed dial. The joke in the directorate of operations during the Clinton years was that if the director would only take his cue from Bandar and show up with a box of the president's favorite Cuban cigars, he would be invited back more often. Years later, Clinton's first CIA director, Jim Woolsey, would tell me that when a nut flew a plane into the White House, the joke at 1600 Pennsylvania Avenue was that it was Woolsey trying to get in to see the president. Incidentally, Woolsey was one of the few CIA directors to come out and tell the truth about the kingdom.

Bandar was not someone to be joked with, even by the president's CIA director. If Bandar suspected the CIA was undermining the kingdom in any way, he would complain to the president, then let loose a pack of rabid K Street lobbyists on the agency. Let's say some case officer in Berlin decided to "pitch" a Saudi diplomat, or try to recruit him to spy for the CIA. Recruited, the Saudi would be able to tell the CIA what, for instance, the religious-affairs section of the embassy in Berlin was doing, like maybe funding terrorist cells in Hamburg. Instead, assume the Saudi turned down the pitch and reported it to Riyadh. The case officer would hear the crystal breaking all the way from Berlin. As soon as the president put down the phone and recovered his hearing from Bandar's screeching, there'd be a call from a lobbyist, maybe one of the president's old political chums. "Mr. President," the lobbyist would purr into the phone. "We really must keep a better eye on those cowboys out at Langley. You know we have this big Boeing deal coming up, and if Bandar . . ." Act Three opens twenty-four hours later with the young case officer on an airplane back to Washington to start his new job: handing out towels in the CIA's basement gym.

Cowed by the same unspoken fears, the CIA's directorate of intelligence avoided writing National Intelligence Estimates on Saudi Arabia. It knew that NIEs—appraisals drawn from across the intelligence community, including the CIA, the Defense Intelligence Agency, and elsewhere—often find their way onto the front pages of U.S. newspapers and from there on to Bandar's breakfast tray, next to his fresh rose, croissant, and cup of Earl Grey tea. The directorate also knew the president hated reading bad news about the kingdom. It was one thing for Rwanda to go in the toilet, but not his good friends the Al Sa'ud. So I guess the CIA was on to something when it treated Saudi Arabia like a domestic problem.

So what do the Saudis have on the president, or the State Department? I'll start by saying I don't believe in conspiracies; I don't think Washington has ever been able to keep a secret. It's something a lot more subtle and insidious. It's what I call a consent of silence, or, more politely, deference. (A circumlocution preferred by certain ex-ambassadors to Riyadh who have chosen to turn a blind eye to the kingdom's dissolution.) It all begins with fast money, a category in which I include cheap oil. Saudi Arabia has lots of money and lots of oil. The country also proved over and over that it was willing to spend it, as well as open the oil spigots anytime we asked. With a national capital addicted to fast money and cheap oil, complaining about the situation was considered bad form, like pissing in the village well. No one wanted to hear it, and no one wanted to do anything about it. The only people willing to tell the truth were on the political fringe, and they were smugly dismissed as cranks.

4/Saudi Arabia—
Washington's 401(k) Plan

I f you've ever spent serious time in the Middle East, you know it's virtually impossible to pick up a tab. What usually happens at the end of dinner is that your Arab friend pretends he's going to the bathroom but veers off to corral the maître d', pull him out of sight, and pay. It's done so smoothly, you don't notice a thing. Another trick is for your friend to make sure you end up at a restaurant where he knows the owner: Then there's no way you can pay. Among Levantines, this ritual about who pays for dinner is a sign of hospitality; rarely does it involve any sort of quid pro quo. For the Saudis and rich Gulf Arabs, it's a matter of buying and selling people. If you hold yourself out as an alpha dog, you have to pick up the tab to remind the other dogs where they fall in the pack.

During the lead-in to the Gulf War, I was in Paris and got to see this money ritual up close. One night I invited four prominent Kuwaiti opposition leaders to dinner at the Ritz Hotel, maybe Paris's fanciest. (Princess Diana and Dodi Fayed had their final tryst there before they died in a car accident later that night.) The Ritz was normally too pricy for my CIA expense account, but the gritty charm of my usual Paris dives would have been wasted on the Kuwaitis. They may not have been royals, but they were fabulously rich.

As we were about to order, the Kuwaiti minister of petroleum, 'Ali Al Sabah, entered the restaurant, pulling in his wake a score of retainers. Passing our table, he nodded vaguely to my Kuwaiti friends, then stopped dead in his tracks when he caught sight of me. Normally, Gulf Arabs keep to themselves when they go out at night in cities like Paris and London. I was definitely out of place.

The petroleum minister came over to find out who I was. Shaking hands around the table, he pointedly came to me last, trying to make believe I was the furthest thing from his mind. I gave up only my name. *Make the bastard work to find out what I do for a living,* I thought to myself.

"And what brings you to Paris?" he finally asked.

The minister swallowed hard when I told him I worked at the American embassy. In those dark days before Coalition Forces gathered, stumbling across an American official meeting with the opposition was certain to ruin a Kuwaiti oil minister's day. Not only did Kuwait's ruling elite wonder if it was going to get its kingdom back; it was uncertain it would be allowed to rule even if it did. Having overrun Kuwait with nary a peep of opposition, Saddam Hussein might bypass the Amir and cut a deal directly with the Kuwaiti people to share power—the same people I was having dinner with. But that could happen only if the United States went along. Hence, the interest in *moi.*

The minister paused and then did what he knew best—threw money at the problem. With a crooked finger, he summoned the maître d'. "These gentlemen are my *honored* guests," the minister said loudly enough for half the restaurant to hear. "Give them *anything* they ask for."

Before the maître d' could get away, the minister grabbed him by the arm. "And for my American friend, your *best* bottle of Bordeaux."

For a split second, I considered telling the esteemed oil minister that while the Amir might be able to buy and sell the U.S. Treasury, our air force could still turn his sandbox into molten glass. I couldn't, though; I had to think about my guests. A tussle over the check with the minister of petroleum would have caused them problems for years on end. As for the Bordeaux, halfway through dinner, I faked my own trip to the bathroom to check the wine list. It set back the Sabah something like $5,200, hardly worth a blink in Kuwait City.

Saudi Arabia's seduction of Washington worked the same way: They paid, we took, and everyone politely averted their eyes. It all began with a lesson the Saudis learned at San Clemente, California, after the 1968 presidential election: America might be the most powerful nation on earth, but its leaders couldn't say no.

ADNAN KHASHOGGI is almost a cartoon of the Saudi wheeler-dealer: a sometime venture capitalist and arms middleman, ridiculously rich (in fits and starts), and unapologetic for it. One day Khashoggi turns up in the newspapers accused of obtaining $64 million in illegal loans from the collapsed Bangkok Bank of Commerce. The next day he's in the New York society columns, attending charity balls in the Hamptons and donating millions to help American farmers.

The son of the personal physician of Ibn Sa'ud, who founded the modern Saudi kingdom in 1932, Khashoggi was serving by the mid-1970s as middleman on an estimated 80 percent of all arms deals between the United States and Saudi Arabia. From Lockheed alone, he pocketed $106 million in commissions from 1970 to 1975. Other defense contractors contributed hundreds of millions more during the decade. Northrop officials told a Senate subcommittee looking into foreign payments by U.S. corporations that it had given Khashoggi $450,000 to bribe Saudi generals into buying the company's wares—an allegation that didn't prevent the Reagan administration from using Khashoggi as its own middleman during the Iran-Contra fiasco. (Having served as basically a pimp for the Shah of Iran in the 1970s, Khashoggi knew how to cut a dirty deal as well as anyone.)

In the late 1970s Khashoggi made a splash by trying to donate nearly $600,000 to three prestigious Philadelphia-area colleges—Swarthmore, Haverford, and Bryn Mawr—to establish a Middle East studies program that would create understanding and sympathy for the Arab point of view. That plan fell apart after the Northrop bribe charges surfaced. Undeterred, the civic-minded Khashoggi jumped back into higher education in 1984 with a $5 million gift to American University, on Massachusetts Avenue in D.C., halfway between the White House and the Beltway. AU had planned to honor Khashoggi's money by naming the school's new sports center and convocation hall after him, but administrators changed their minds in the wake of the Iran-Contra hearings. Even universities have consciences, apparently.

By January 1987, when *Time* put Khashoggi on its cover as the prototype of the new international operator, he was a regular at Marbella, the jet-set-hot retreat on the Spanish Riviera, where he maintained a five-thousand-acre estate. Other addresses included Paris, Cannes, Madrid, the Canary Islands, Rome, Beirut, Riyadh, Jeddah, Monte Carlo, a 180,000-acre ranch in Kenya, and a $30 million, thirty-thousand-square-foot apartment on Fifth Avenue in New York with a pool overlooking the spires of Saint Patrick's Cathedral. To get to and among his many homes, Khashoggi had his choice of the 282-foot yacht *Nabila*, the same one used in the James Bond movie *Never Say Never Again;* a DC-8, where he could rest on a ten-foot-wide bed beneath a $200,000 spread of Russian sable; two other commercial-size jets; twelve Mercedes stretch limos; and so on. (*Time* estimated the cost of Khashoggi's lifestyle at $250,000 a day in early 1987, servants included, or a little over $91 million a year, roughly a quarter of the annual budget of Haiti, a nation of seven million people.) At Marbella, there was a small warehouse devoted to nothing but the Saudi's wardrobe: over a thousand handmade suits alone, cleaned, pressed, encased in plastic, and ready to be shipped to any golden shore where their owner might happen to wash up for a few nights or more.

None of this normally would make the slightest difference to us as Americans. We all grew up with stories about the fabulous wealth of Arab sheikhs and their viziers. It started to make a difference, though, when the money slopped over into Washington or, rather, San Clemente. In late 1968, days after Richard Nixon won the White House, Khashoggi was one of the first to fly out to congratulate the president-elect. He didn't forget to pass on the regards of Interior Minister Fahd—the prince who'd sent him to San Clemente and the current brain-dead king. When Khashoggi got up to leave, he "forgot" his briefcase, which happened to be stuffed with $1 million in hundreds. No one said a word. Khashoggi went back to his hotel to wait for a telephone call. The phone never rang. It never would. A couple days later, and Khashoggi knew the trick had worked: Washington was for sale. Like original sin, that changed everything.

You won't find that tale in the history books. You can barely find anyone still alive to confirm or deny it. Having paid out so many bribes in his life, even Khashoggi probably doesn't remember it. I heard the story from a source who was directly involved. Is it true? I don't know. But it's taken as gospel inside the palaces of Riyadh and Jeddah. Thanks to that story and a lot of others, Saudis believe Washington is no different from Rabat, Paris, London, or any other capital that has its hand out. And if anyone had any doubts, Nixon's first visitor in the White House was Fahd. Nixon put him up at Blair House, the official White House guest residence strictly reserved for heads of state. See: It was all about money.

Five years later, when Nixon Treasury Secretary William Simon set out for Riyadh hoping to sell T-bills and bonds to a kingdom newly awash in petrodollars, he was armed with talking points like a pitchman making cold calls. "Investment directly with the U.S. Treasury can provide great convenience and protection against the adverse movements otherwise likely to face an investor when placing or liquidating large investments," read one of the slides prepared for Simon.

The idea was to get the Saudis to underwrite the U.S. budget deficit. Eager to become America's lender of last resort, with all the leverage that implied, the Saudis took the bait and happily swallowed it. Soon William Simon and Secretary of State Henry Kissinger had cooked up another scheme: the Saudi–U.S. Joint Commission on Economic Cooperation, which would create an infrastructure for "the new Saudi Arabia," one modeled on the United States. The Saudis jumped on that one, too, and the commission worked after a fashion, a miracle considering Saudi Arabia is a theocratic tyranny without property or individual rights. But the only important thing was that the Saudis paid for everything—U.S. salaries, Saudi salaries, living expenses for American commission workers detailed to Saudi Arabia, the whole shooting match, depositing over $1 billion in a U.S. Treasury account.

Washington knows fast money when it sees it, but it had never seen anything like this. The cookie jar was bottomless. It wasn't long before the Saudis were spreading money everywhere, like manure on a winter's field. The White House put out its hand to fund pet projects that Congress wouldn't fund or couldn't afford, from a war in Afghanistan to one in Nicaragua. Every Washington think tank, from the supposedly nonpartisan Middle East Institute to the Meridian International Center, took Saudi money. Washington's boiler room—the K Street lobbyists, PR firms, and lawyers— lived off the stuff. So did its bluestocking charities, like the John F. Kennedy Center for the Performing Arts, the Children's National Medical Center, and every presidential library of the last thirty years. The Saudis even kicked in a quarter of a million dollars on a winter sports clinic for disabled American veterans.

Saudi money also seeped into the bureaucracy. Any Washington bureaucrat with a room-temperature IQ knows that if he stays on the right side of the kingdom, some way or another, he'll be able to finagle his way to feed at the Saudi trough. A consulting contract with Aramco, a chair at American University, a job with Lockheed— it doesn't matter. There's hardly a living former assistant secretary of state for the Near East; CIA director; White House staffer; or member of Congress who hasn't ended up on the Saudi payroll in one way or another, or so it sometimes seems. With this kind of money waiting out there, of course Washington's bureaucrats don't have the backbone to take on Saudi Arabia.

What's going on here? The way I look at things, it amounts to an indirect, extralegal tax on Americans. Saudi Arabia raises the price of gasoline, then remits a huge percentage to Washington, but not just to anyone. A big chunk goes to pet White House projects; part goes into the pockets of ex-bureaucrats and politicos who keep their mouths shut about the kingdom. And a lot goes to keeping our defense industry humming in bad times. Add it all up, and Saudi Arabia is one of Washington's biggest hitters.

Washington likes to describe all this with an inoffensive, neutral economic term: recycling petrodollars. But it's plain old influence peddling. And by the way, the Saudi tax is a lot more efficient than the IRS. The Saudis do both the collecting and the spending, keeping Washington's visionless bureaucrats out of it. The General Accounting Office and the Office of Management and Budget would only demand some pointless accounting for all that money.

THE SAUDI ARABIA of today isn't the gold mine it was in the 1970s and early '80s, when it had more cash than sand. Back then the huge remittances to the U.S. didn't put a dent in the Saudi budget. That all changed when the Gulf War ate up Saudi Arabia's entire budget surplus. Since then the country has been living off credit and begging for money. But Riyadh knew it couldn't back out, couldn't quit running a parallel IRS. Pissing off Washington's power elite was as dangerous as pissing off its fanatics.

Here's an example. Throughout the nineties, Americans (and Europeans) consistently paid less for Saudi oil than Asians paid, on the average of $1.00 a barrel. In 2001, prices split sharply, with Americans reportedly buying Saudi oil for $4.83 less a barrel. That's an effective discount of $2.8 billion a year—a discount off Asian markets at least. And in September 2001, in the wake of the September 11 attacks, the price disparity between American and

Asian markets surged to a reported $9.66. Oil analysts I talk with dismiss the notion that Saudi Arabia has in place a program to sell discounted oil to the United States. Oil markets are extremely complicated, they tell me, and there are logical market reasons that Asians from time to time pay more for Saudi oil. Asians, for instance, willingly pay a steep premium in order to secure their oil supplies, even buying higher priced spot contracts when markets are volatile. There are other considerations, like transportation costs and varying market structures, the fact that Asia produces almost no oil of its own, and the fact that Saudi Arabia is invested in U.S. downstream production. These factors alone, the oil analysts tell me, are what accounted for the wide price differences between Asian and Western markets in September 2001. As one analyst told me, "It's simply that Asia pays a surcharge for its oil. There is no Saudi discount for oil going to the U.S."

Be that as it may, the point is that Saudi Arabia has consistently forgone making enormous profits in tight markets, such as occurred after September 11. If the Saudis had taken even a little of their oil off the market on the afternoon of September 11 instead of pumping more, it could have made billions gouging Americans. The same thing happened in 1990 when Saudi Arabia and its Gulf allies opened their taps, making up for the five-million-barrel-a-day output lost from both Iraq and Kuwait. Had they wanted, they could have kept oil hovering above $100 a barrel and walked away from Desert Storm with a lot of money rather than a gaping deficit.

The reason that Saudi Arabia has forgone huge profits on its oil sales is because it does not want the United States to forget who is its most reliable supplier. Not only has it paid a lot to hold that position, it has turned a deaf ear to increasingly shrill Asian complaints about the "Asian premium." As I write, Russia has plans in place to build pipelines east across Siberia, which one day might cause Saudi Arabia to lose its Asian market. The bottom line is that what the Saudis really care about is driving home the message to Washington that it needn't worry: Sure, we've lost control of our country, and our citizens are slaughtering yours, but you can depend on us to keep your cars on the road and your houses warm. And, by the way, you'll feel better if you don't think about the unpleasant reality that your oil bank is sitting on dangerously shifting sands.

The Saudi oil subsidies didn't fall on Washington like some weird, benevolent meteorite. The business landscape is filled with such deals, each of them pointed reminders that even apocolyptic acts of terrorism needn't get in the way of business. In 1997, Saudi Aramco set up a joint venture with Texaco, Inc., later joined by Shell Oil, to refine roughly eight hundred thousand barrels of Saudi crude a day. In 1998 the same three companies joined to form Motiva Enterprises, one of the largest oil-refining and marketing companies in the United States. AT&T got into the game with a $4 billion contract to expand the Saudi telecommunications network. Even Lucent Technologies, a collapsed star of the U.S. high-tech stock-market bubble, landed a July 2001 contract worth $240 million to improve mobile-phone service.

In May 2001, the Saudi Higher Economic Council approved long-term contracts with American oil companies worth "tens of billions of dollars," according to the Saudis, to provide desalinization and power-generation plants and to develop the kingdom's natural-gas resources. A few months earlier, the Saudi Arabian General Investment Authority issued a license to a consortium of U.S. contractors to build three thousand new schools in the kingdom, at a cost of $3.5 billion. Allah alone knew where the Saudis were going to get all the money, but that didn't seem to be bothering anyone on either side of the Atlantic. The point was that we couldn't do without our Saudi fix.

It's not just that Saudis spend boatloads of money in the United States. Spending boatloads of money was part of the deal from the very beginning: The U.S. would buy the House of Sa'ud's oil and provide protection and security, and the Saudis would buy their weapons, construction services, communications systems, and drilling rigs from the U.S. All this recycling, to judge solely by the numbers, was a dream come true. Collectively, two-way trade between Saudi Arabia and the United States grew from $56.2 million in 1950 to $19.3 billion in 2000.

Money only goes so far, no matter how much you have to spend. Professional sports are full of filthy-rich owners who can't buy a title for love or money. What has made the Saudi money so effective is that it is well targeted, and in Washington especially, the Saudis have hooked up with a culture that seems willing to do almost anything to get it.

Call it a poetic coincidence. But right as the Carlyle Group was getting into its annual investor conference at Washington's Ritz-Carlton Hotel on September 11, 2001, American Airlines Flight 77 slammed into the Pentagon, only two and a half miles to the south. If United Airlines Flight 93 had hit the White House, its presumed target, the Carlyle attendees would have felt the shock, and it was a group fairly hard to shock. At the meeting were the group's senior counsel James Baker, secretary of state in the Bush I administration; then Carlyle chairman Frank Carlucci, Ronald Reagan's last secretary of defense and national security adviser before that; and Shafiq bin Laden, representing the Bin Laden Group—one of the world's largest construction companies—but far more famous today as Osama bin Laden's brother. The gathering was the perfect metaphor for Washington's strange affair with Saudi Arabia.

Named for the luxurious Manhattan hotel where the private investment company was dreamed up in 1987, the Carlyle Group has had a long and profitable relationship with the Al Sa'ud family. In 1991, as one of its first big coups, Carlyle paved the way for Prince al-Walid bin Talal to purchase nearly $600 million in Citicorp stock. A nephew of King Fahd, Prince al-Walid was named the world's sixth richest person by *Forbes* in 2001, with assets of roughly $20 billion, most of that through his Riyadh-based Kingdom holding company.

Prince al-Walid has a knack for saying what's on his mind. Shortly after the September 11 attacks, the prince flew to New York City to donate $10 million to the Twin Towers Fund, set up by New

York mayor Rudy Giuliani to aid the families of the victims. Al-Walid couldn't resist offering the helpful advice that the United States needed to "reexamine its policies in the Middle East and adopt a more balanced stance toward the Palestinian cause." Apparently, the Carlyle Group forgot to tell him that New York City is overwhelmingly pro-Israel, and that Americans don't like being reminded about living off Saudi charity and putting our foreign policy up for sale. But Rudy Giuliani didn't need the Carlyle Group to remind him of the realities of American politics. He immediately told the prince what he could do with his check. And in case you've been sailing the Galapagos Islands without a ham radio for the last three years, the White House never offered to return the $2.8 billion oil subsidy in solidarity with Giuliani.

One thing certain about Carlyle's management: It never missed an opportunity to make money. Tap into the uninterrupted flow of Saudi oil and arms, the Carlyle thinking went, and you couldn't go wrong. Look at a couple of Carlyle deals, and you get the point. For much of the 1990s, the defense contractor BDM International, in which Carlyle then had a controlling interest, received $50 million annually to provide training and operational and logistical services for the Saudi Arabian National Guard, the Al Sa'ud's bodyguards. (Carlyle sold its stake in BDM to TRW in late 1997.) Until shortly after the 9/11 attacks, Carlyle also served as adviser to the royal family on the Economic Offset Program. In the official literature of the kingdom, the Economic Offset Program encourages foreign investment in Saudi Arabia and helps to ensure that a critical percentage of its oil revenues remain there. Unofficially, and more accurately, the program assures that a percentage of all arms sales to the Saudis are siphoned off into fees and commissions to businesses owned almost entirely by royal family members.

Carlyle has also made a fortune through buying up small defense contractors and flipping them to defense giants like Boeing, Lockheed Martin, and TRW International, a major weapons provider to the Saudis. Along the way, it bought its own arms business, United Defense, America's eleventh largest defense contractor. As the world's largest consumer of U.S.-made armaments, Saudi Arabia virtually makes the secondary market for American fighter planes, missiles, tanks, armored vehicles, and other weaponry and supporting services. Saudi Arabia was also the second largest consumer, after the U.S. military, of the Bradley Fighting Vehicle, which was for many years the mainstay of United Defense's product line.

In Washington, to bring up the "revolving door" between government and business is like discussing incest in the family. But Washington's franchise players head straight for the Carlyle employment office as soon as they're out of the government.

In addition to serving as a professional home for James Baker and Frank Carlucci, Carlyle also employs Arthur Levitt, former head of the Securities and Exchange Commission; William Kennard, who chaired the Federal Communications Commission during the second Clinton administration; Afsaneh Beschloss, former treasurer and chief investment officer of the World Bank and wife of historian Michael Beschloss, a regular on PBS's *The NewsHour with Jim Lehrer;* and Richard Darman, who ran the U.S. Office of Management and Budget under the first president Bush and, during the Reagan administration, served as assistant to the president and the Treasury deputy secretary. Just to prove that Carlyle is truly an international conglomerate, former British prime minister John Major serves as chairman of Carlyle Europe.

No one in Washington has better contacts or has worked them more effectively than Frank Carlucci. In addition to his posts as defense secretary and national security adviser, Carlucci was deputy director of the CIA from 1978 to 1980, after a stint as ambassador to Portugal. He also competed on the Princeton University wrestling team with Donald Rumsfeld and has stayed friendly with him in the years since. ███████████████

██

██

██

██

Sleeping with the Devil

In 1972 Carlucci was deputy to Caspar Weinberger at Richard Nixon's Office of Management and Budget when a new White House fellow named Colin Powell, on loan from the U.S. Army, reported for work. Eight years later, when Ronald Reagan made Weinberger secretary of defense, Powell became his senior military adviser. In 1987 Carlucci, who had been serving as assistant to the president for national security affairs, succeeded Weinberger as secretary of defense, and Powell stepped into Carlucci's slot as national security adviser. (Carlucci likes to call himself Powell's godfather.)

Carlyle did its own godfather schtick for George W. Bush as well. Back in 1990, when the future president was wandering the Lone Star State in search of a career, Republican insider Fred Malek found Bush a slot on the board of a Carlyle subsidiary: Caterair, an airline-catering company. A decade later, when Bush II was governor of Texas, the state teachers' pension fund invested $100 million with the Carlyle Group.

Carlyle's most famous adviser is George Herbert Walker Bush, the forty-first president of the United States. Greatly admired among the monied classes in Saudi Arabia and Kuwait for their leadership in the Gulf War, Bush and John Major have traveled frequently to both places on Carlyle's behalf, opening the doors to some of the world's most well-heeled investors. Indeed, even as his son was campaigning for the presidency in 2000, Papa Bush flew to a posh desert compound outside Riyadh to discuss Saudi–U.S. business relations with Crown Prince 'Abdallah. Carlyle insists that Bush was not carrying the investment firm's portfolio on the trip, but it could not have escaped the notice of his superwealthy hosts that G.H.W. Bush is a trusted and highly valued Carlyle senior adviser—with that son making a run at the White House.

Like many advisers to high-powered equity firms, G.H.W. Bush is compensated for his time, reputation, and Rolodex with shares in the investments he helps to generate. Bush is also allowed to plow back into Carlyle investment funds money he earns by giving speeches on the firm's behalf—generally in the $80,000-to-$100,000 range for each speech. Again, Carlyle is a private entity, and Bush I a private citizen. No reporting of total take is required or expected, but it would strain credulity to think that the former president has earned less than the mid-seven figures from his decade-old association with the investment firm, the bulk of that either directly or indirectly from Saudi Arabia. Anything less would be almost disrespectful.

Because Carlyle is privately held, only its principals know how much of its money—$13.9 billion under management as of November 2002—comes from Saudi investors. The Bakr bin Laden family had a piddling $2 million invested in the Carlyle Partners II fund, a portfolio that includes United Defense and other defense and aerospace companies. With embarrassment spreading on both sides, Carlyle and the bin Ladens parted company in October 2001, some five weeks after the World Trade Center and Pentagon attacks. About a dozen other Saudis are thought to still be investors in the group.

Carlyle is also not required to reveal annual compensation to its partners, or their net share in the firm. An article in the March 5, 2001, *New York Times* estimated that Jim Baker's share might then have been worth in the vicinity of $180 million, but that was arrived at simply by dividing the firm's eighteen partners and one outside investor into the estimated total equity of $3.5 billion. (That was before Carlyle took half the stock in United Defense public, reaping what was said to be a nearly $700 million profit.) You can be certain the Carlyle Group is no penny-ante game. When Frank Carlucci resigned as chairman in November 2002, former IBM CEO Lou Gerstner stepped into his slot.

It was a Carlyle partner who confirmed to me the detail work on Azouzi's $4.6 billion palace. I was in southern France in August 2002, visiting a friend who keeps a small sailboat near Cannes. We had just moored when we spotted a man on a brand-new yacht next to ours that was flying an American flag. As it happened, my friend knew him. He said the man worked for the Carlyle Group. We struck up a conversation across the water and got to talking about Saudi Arabia. At the first opportunity, I asked about Azouzi's palace.

Sleeping with the Devil

The man knew about it, adding that he'd recently been in it. As soon as he'd confirmed the price tag on the amusement park, he asked why my interest. When I told him I was writing a book on Saudi Arabia, he went below deck, suddenly seasick.

FOR A CITY of supposedly dull bureaucrats, Washington is endlessly inventive about tapping into Saudi funds. Between his stints as secretary of defense and vice president, Dick Cheney served as CEO of Halliburton, a frequent beneficiary of Saudi construction projects both during and after his tenure. In late 2001, with Cheney a step from the presidency and his old company reeling from accounting scandals, Halliburton landed a $140 million contract to develop a new Saudi oil field. The company's subsidiary, Kellogg Brown & Root, also placed a successful $40 million bid with two Japanese partners to build a new ethylene plant there.

Like the Saudis, Cheney has shown a sharp interest in Central Asian oil, both privately and publicly. As Halliburton chairman, Cheney defended Heydar Aliyev against charges that the Azerbaijan strongman routinely violated human rights, while simultaneously castigating the Clinton administration for its "failure . . . to recognize the strategic asset of the oil and gas business." Cheney also helped put together a 1993 deal between Kazakhstan and Chevron as he was serving on the Kazakhstan Oil Advisory Board.

As Halliburton chairman, Cheney was instrumental in securing a $489 million in loan guarantees from the Export-Import Bank for the scandal-plagued Tyumen Oil Company, or TNK, a Russian entity formed to exploit the oil reserves in the Caspian Sea region. According to the *Moscow Times,* the bulk of the Ex-Im Bank loan guarantee, $292 million, was to go for buying equipment from Halliburton to develop TNK's Samotlor oil field. Halliburton also has a major engineering contract with the head of the Caspian Consortium, BP Amoco.

As vice president, Cheney has made sure that the Ex-Im Bank

stays in friendly hands. The bank's new chairman, Philip Merrill, was assistant secretary general of NATO during the Bush I administration and is a close personal friend of both Dick Cheney and his wife, Lynne. Although her official résumé omits the fact, Lynne Cheney worked in the early 1980s for one of Merrill's publications, *Washingtonian* magazine. Merrill was sworn in to his new Ex-Im Bank post in early December 2002 at an invitation-only ceremony at the Cheneys' official vice-presidential residence.

During the dark interregnum of the Clinton years, Donald Rumsfeld and Colin Powell joined former secretaries of state Henry Kissinger (Nixon and Ford) and George Shultz (Reagan) and other luminaries as company directors of Gulfstream Aerospace Corporation, the luxury jet manufacturer purchased in 1990 by an investment team headed by Teddy Forstmann, cochairman of Bush I's failed 1992 reelection campaign. Their job was basically the same as Bush I's with Carlyle—opening doors to governmental and super-wealthy private clients, including the Saudis and the Kuwaitis, where all four men have star drawing power. In 1998 Forstmann rewarded his directors by letting them cash in—at $43 a share—stock options that they had purchased at anywhere from $3 to $28 a share. Kissinger's take for a mere five months on the board was $876,000 after expenses, Thomas Toch reported in the December 21, 1998, *New Republic*. Shultz took home $1.08 million and Rumsfeld $1.09 million, while Powell pocketed $1.49 million.

In November 2000, not long before he was nominated to be secretary of state, Powell received as much as $100,000—one report said $200,000—for a half hour of off-the-cuff remarks at Tufts University in Massachusetts. The speech was paid for through a Tufts speakers fund endowed by Issam Fares, the deputy prime minister of Lebanon. Virtually every penny Fares owns traces back to his dealings with Prince Sultan, the Saudi defense minister, and Turki bin 'Abd-al-'Aziz, another brother of King Fahd. Powell at least had a good precedent to go by. The first president Bush basically stiffed his own ambassador during a state visit to Paris by spending time at Fares's elaborate digs on the Île Saint-Louis.

Sleeping with the Devil

There's also plenty of space for the Saudis and their fat contracts in the boiler rooms of Washington. Over at Qorvis Communications, which was earning roughly $200,000 a month to buff the Saudi image in the U.S., it took three partners over a year after the 9/11 attacks to decide that being the mouthpiece for a state that supports terrorists might be a bad career move. The law firm of former Texas Republican congressman Tom Loeffler was not similarly stricken by conscience. Fund-raising chief for Bush II's first gubernatorial race and finance cochair of his presidential campaign, Loeffler might be as close to the Bush White House, including Dick Cheney, as anyone in Washington. In late 2002, the Saudis approached Loeffler Jonas & Tuggey, waving a $720,000-a-year retainer to represent the kingdom's interests. Tom Loeffler, the firm's founder and senior government affairs partner, accepted the money. What's the point of access if not to profit from it?

IN A DIFFERENT MORAL CLIMATE, all this chumminess among Washington, America's corporate boardrooms, and Riyadh plus the rest of the Arab world might be at least cause for alarm: Economic incentives exist in every direction for President Bush and his advisers to close their eyes to the contamination in Saudi Arabia. In a sense, though, no one can be blamed for being too close to the Saudis, because finding a high-ranking former U.S. government official who isn't at least tangentially bound to Saudi Arabia is like searching for a teetotaler at a Phi Gam toga party.

Brent Scowcroft, national security adviser in the Bush I administration and a longtime intimate of the older Bush, runs the Scowcroft Group, which markets intelligence services and market analyses to multinational corporations, including oil and other energy companies. The company's literature notes the group's "extraordinary regional expertise" in the Middle East and its "strong ties to key decision makers." Scowcroft also sits on the board of Pennzoil–Quaker State. Incidentally, Scowcroft is an intimate of Bush's national security adviser, Condoleezza Rice, and of CIA chief George Tenet, giving them both advice on how we can "improve" our intelligence in the Middle East.

In another case, Lawrence Eagleburger, secretary of state in the Bush I administration, joined Halliburton's board of directors while Dick Cheney was doing time as the company's CEO.

Henry Kissinger heads up Kissinger Associates, which counts among its corporate clients Boeing and Atlantic Richfield/ARCO, as well as many others doing business in Saudi Arabia. Like Scowcroft, Eagleburger, Rumsfeld, Powell, and all the others, Kissinger won't have his integrity questioned. He also won't stop exploiting his ties to Saudi and other Arab leaders—all those years of shuttle diplomacy and Camp David confabs—or sucking on the massive tit of petrodollars. On the sunny banks of the Potomac, if you retire with a high enough title, you get to have it both ways. (Woe be to any lowly government functionary who dares to point this out. If there's one thing the status quo hates, it's a whistle-blower.)

So pervasive and intricate are the client ties to Saudi Arabia in Washington that the two people named to head up the National Commission on Terrorist Attacks—Kissinger and Vice Chairman George Mitchell, the former Senate majority leader—both resigned their positions before the hearings got under way, rather than divulge their own client lists. To find a commission head free of the client taint, George W. Bush finally nominated former New Jersey Governor Thomas Kean, the president of Drew University, whose only lasting Washington connection is that he's an alumnus of the same exclusive D.C. prep school that educated Al Gore and President Bush's two younger brothers, Neil and Marvin. At the time he was nominated, it should be noted, Kean was also a director of Amerada Hess, the petroleum goliath that has joined forces with a Saudi oil company to develop Central Asian oil fields, but more about that in a few paragraphs.

Even Louis Freeh, the former FBI director, is said to have seriously considered an offer to work for the Saudis after he retired from the bureau in 2001. If so, he must have awakened every morning since 9/11 thanking God and fate that he instead took a job with MBNA, the credit-card giant.

At the corporate level, almost every Washington figure worth mentioning has served on the board of at least one company that did a deal with Saudi Arabia, and practically every deal with the Saudis grows opaque, lost in some desert sandstorm back near the well heads where all the money sprang from.

Until it was purchased by Northrop Grumman in late 2002, TRW counted among its board members former CIA Director Robert Gates and former Undersecretary of State and Ambassador to Japan Michael Armacost. National Security Adviser Condoleezza Rice was, for many years, a board member of Chevron, which merged in 2001 with Texaco. Chevron Texaco is a partner with Saudi Aramco in both Star Enterprise and Motiva Enterprises. In the weird way of these interlocking corporate and government webs, oil is quite possibly being transported to the U.S., even as you read these words, via the oil tanker that Chevron named for Rice.

ChevronTexaco—whose board members include Carla Hills, former secretary of housing and urban development (under Gerald Ford) and former U.S. trade representative (under George H. W. Bush); former Louisiana senator J. Bennett Johnston, who made a specialty of energy issues in Congress; and former Georgia senator Sam Nunn, who served most notably as head of the Senate Armed Services Committee—also has joined forces with Nimir Petroleum to develop Kazakhstan oil fields thought to contain upward of 1.5 billion barrels of oil. Nimir, in turn, is owned by the bin Mahfouz family. A 1999 audit conducted by the Saudi government is said to have found that the National Commercial Bank, partially owned by the bin Mahfouz family, donated at least $3 million to charities, some of whose money may have found its way into bin Laden's networks. One of the charities, Blessed Relief, counts 'Abd-al-Rahman bin Mahfouz among its board members. 'Abd-al-Rahman's father, Khalid bin Mahfouz, couldn't even enter the United States in the early 1990s because of an indictment and involvement in the BCCI international-banking scandal.

Elsewhere in the Riyadh–Washington interface, Nicholas Brady, secretary of the treasury under the first President Bush, and former George H. W. Bush assistant Edith Holiday serve on the board of Amerada Hess along with Tom Kean. Amerada Hess has teamed with some of Saudi Arabia's most powerful royals to exploit the rich oil resources of Azerbaijan. In 1998 Amerada Hess formed a joint venture, Delta Hess, with Saudi-owned Delta Oil to exploit petroleum resources in Azerbaijan. Houston-based Frontera Resources Corporation joined the Azerbaijan hunt the same year, teaming with Delta Hess. Among Frontera's board of advisers: Lloyd Bentsen, the former Texas senator, ex–secretary of the treasury, and 1988 Democratic vice-presidential candidate; and yet another former CIA director, John Deutch. (If ex-CIA directors didn't exist, America's corporate boards would have had to invent them.)

Here, too, the trail gets complicated. Delta Oil was formed in the early 1990s by fifty wealthy Saudis, including Crown Prince 'Abdallah, according to a May 1999 report by the U.S. embassy in Riyadh. The greatest among equals, though, appears to be Muhammad Husayn al-Amoudi, a Saudi who operates out of Ethiopia, where he oversees a conglomerate with tentacles in construction, banking, oil, and mining. The al-Amoudi and bin Mahfouz families have formed several partnerships, including Delta-Nimir, an oil venture that joined forces with Unocal in 1994 to develop oil fields in Azerbaijan. Like the bin Mahfouz clan, the al-Amoudis have been accused of giving money to Osama bin Laden, in this case through the family-controlled Capitol Trust Bank of London and New York.

We'll probably never sort out whether Saudi Arabia's charities knowingly funded bin Laden. In all probability, they were a lot like American-Irish pub keepers in New York, handing around a tin can for the IRA: Most of the money ended up feeding orphans and widows back in the old country, but some of it no doubt ended up buying guns and explosives. That doesn't let anyone off the hook, though. The Saudi government and Washington never demanded an accounting, letting the believers among the Al Sa'ud and the Wahhabi militants send money to bin Laden through unwitting fronts. If it was easy money for the faithful in Washington, it was easy for the faithful in Riyadh and Jeddah, too.

EVEN WASHINGTON'S COMMONERS started to look at Saudi Arabia as their supplemental 401(k) plan. Aware that government bureaucrats can't retire comfortably on a federal pension, the Saudis put out the message: You play the game—keep your mouth shut about the kingdom—and we'll take care of you, find you a job, fund a chair at a university for you, maybe even present you with a Lexus and a town house in Georgetown.

Walter Cutler, former U.S. ambassador to Saudi Arabia, is president of the Meridian International Center in Washington. Established to "promote international understanding," according to its website, the center has been generously supported by Saudi donors. Board members include a who's who of Congressional and Cabinet wives: Mrs. Spencer Abraham, Mrs. Ken Bentsen, Mrs. John Breaux, Mrs. Jon Corzine, Mrs. William Frist, Mrs. Charles Hagel, and Mrs. Patrick Leahy, to parse only the first half of the alphabet.

Edward S. "Ned" Walker, Jr., a former assistant secretary of state for Near Eastern affairs in the Clinton administration and an ambassador to Tel Aviv and Cairo before that, presides over the Middle East Institute, also in Washington. Founded in 1946 to promote understanding of the Arab world, the institute operated in 2001 on a budget of $1.5 million, $200,000 of which came from Saudi contributors, according to Walker. The institute's board chairman is Wyche Fowler, Jr., the former Georgia senator and ambassador to Riyadh in the second Clinton administration. Other board members include former Defense Secretary James Schlesinger and former FBI and CIA Director William Webster.

American journalists have provided example after example of American diplomats and other State Department officials who left their Middle East posts, signed on with some Saudi-backed entity or another, and began carrying the party line to op-ed pages, learned conferences, and anywhere else that would have them. Why not, with the Kissingers, Scowcrofts, Powells, and Carluccis setting such a splendid example? The little people need to eat, too. They eat less, but the rules are the same: See no evil. Hear no evil. Speak no evil.

Prince Bandar, Saudi Arabia's longtime ambassador to the United States, once told an associate that he is careful to look after American government officials when they return to private life. "If the reputation then builds that the Saudis take care of friends when they leave office, you'd be surprised how much better friends you have who are just coming into office," Bandar observed, according to a *Washington Post* source. When you're rich and arrogant enough, you can buy the luxury of candor.

Just to make sure no one is tempted to complain too much, Saudi Arabia keeps possibly as much as a trillion dollars on deposit in U.S. banks—an agreement worked out in the early 1980s by the Reagan administration, in yet another effort to get the Saudis to off-set the U.S. budget deficit. The Saudis hold another trillion dollars or so in the U.S. stock market.

On the compulsory one-to-ten scale of economic catastrophe, having the Saudis withdraw all their U.S. bank deposits and vacate the stock market is probably only a six, well below the Saudis turning off the oil spigot or having the spigot blown to bits—the ten-point, apocalypse-now disaster. But it all begins to suggest that someone might have someone else by the short hairs.

5/Pavlov and His Dogs

IN 1994 CIA headquarters brought me back to Washington after a two-year stretch in Dushanbe, Tajikistan, the remotest, poorest patch of hardscrabble on earth. Frankly, I was happy to come home and kick back for a while. I'd had enough of cold showers, military rations, and the bedtime lullaby of tank fire, and I needed a break before going to one more godforsaken part of the world. That is, until I started looking around Washington for a place to rent.

When I signed up with the CIA in ▓▓▓▓ I could afford Washington, even an apartment in Georgetown. Back then you could still go out a couple of times a week without having to spend the rest of the week eating pork and beans. This had all changed by 1994. Rents in Georgetown had gone through the ceiling. All the local places I had hung out in were gone, replaced by trendy French cafés, boutiques, and cigar bars. If you had a family and wanted to lead anything like a middle-class life in Washington, you were looking at Virginia's exurbs, maybe an hour's commute away.

I was about to give up and settle for someplace outside the Beltway when I happened on a house in Palisades, a neighborhood just outside of Georgetown. The house was on a month-to-month lease, but that didn't matter. It was the perfect size: three bedrooms, two baths, and a lawn, more than adequate for me and my family. Better still, it was maybe five minutes by car to headquarters in Langley, Virginia. In fact, it was close enough for me to ride my bicycle to work: a straight shot across the Potomac River on Chain Bridge to Route 123, a hard pump for about half a mile up a hill, then an easy pedal right up to the CIA's front gates. It not only saved buying a second car; I got a good daily workout in the bargain.

One night I was on my way home and noticed a convoy coming up Route 123 from the Potomac, led by a Chevy Suburban 2500 with flashing lights. At first I thought it was the president—he's the only official in Washington who gets that kind of protection. But right before the convoy got to me, it turned in to a gated estate. The enormous iron gates opened, and in a second the cars disappeared down a tree-lined driveway. Only then did I notice that I was riding in front of the estate of Prince Bandar, the Saudi ambassador to the U.S. Because the limo windows were fashionably smoked, I could only guess it was Bandar coming home.

The next day I asked about Bandar's status and was told that he alone of all ambassadors got official State Department protection. The Suburban must have belonged to State. Even back then, the incident seemed to encapsulate something important about Bandar, Washington, the CIA, and the peculiar relationship between Saudi Arabia and the United States. Here I was on my bicycle, a CIA official supposedly charged with protecting America's national security, passed on the road by the Saudi ambassador with his U.S. government protection, who then pulled into his estate overlooking the Potomac—the best piece of property in Washington. Ten of my houses could have fit inside his.

But it was a lot more than that. Bandar could wander into the White House and around Congress for a chat anytime he liked. It took me weeks to get an appointment with a low-ranking staffer in the National Security Council, and I'd be lucky to get even a few minutes. Bandar was an A-list Washington party guest. He could pass a sensitive message to anyone in the government or the press whenever he liked—on the opening night of the Kennedy Center;

at a sit-down dinner in the house of Katharine Graham, the late publisher of the *Washington Post*; or at the Cosmos Club. Bandar was a Washington player; I—the CIA—wasn't.

Bandar's convoy, his sprawling house, the special access, the no-limits lifestyle: They were all a constant reminder of the way Washington really ran. Forget the crap about democracy, about the capital of the free world. Washington was a company town, and Bandar had a seat on the board. If you wanted to move into even the outer reaches of his orbit, you had damn well better play by his rules.

EVERY ARRANGEMENT as cozy as the U.S.–Saudi embrace needs someone with a foot in each camp: well connected at either end of the line, able to move comfortably in two cultures, expansive enough to make people seek out his company yet attentive to all the details that get results at the end of the day. For the Washington–Riyadh axis, that person is Bandar bin Sultan bin 'Abd-al-'Aziz. Prince Bandar ranks low on the royal-gene charts—although his father is the Saudi defense minister, his mother was a mere house servant—but Washington has always cared more about money than bloodlines.

Ever since he was named the Saudi ambassador to the U.S. in 1983, at age thirty-four, Bandar has been winning friends and influencing people for the Al Sa'ud. A daredevil fighter pilot in his younger years, a Muslim with a taste for single-malt scotch and Cuban cigars, and an envoy with an always open wallet, Bandar has proved himself a franchise player, working both the public and private sides of diplomacy. As the Saudi military attaché to the U.S., he scored a stunning coup in 1981 by convincing Congress to approve the sale of AWACs early-warning aircraft technology to Saudi Arabia, over the near-hysterical objections of AIPAC, the powerful Israeli Washington lobby. Later, as ambassador, Bandar paid down the kingdom's debt by secretly placing $10 million in a

Vatican City bank as reported in 2002 by the *Washington Post*. The money, deposited at the request of then CIA director William Casey, was to be used by Italy's Christian Democratic party in a campaign against Italian communists. In June 1984 Bandar ponied up the first of $30 million from the royal family so Oliver North could buy arms for the Nicaraguan contra rebels.

It's on the personal front that the affable Bandar truly shines. When George H. W. and Barbara Bush flew to Saudi Arabia in late November 1990 to visit the troops massing there to take Kuwait back from Iraq, Bandar's wife, Princess Haifa, invited the Bushes' newly divorced daughter, Dorothy, and her children to celebrate Thanksgiving at Bandar's Virginia farm. When the president and Bandar met in Riyadh several days after Thanksgiving, Bush is said to have embraced the prince with tears in his eyes, proclaiming, "You are good people." (The tears are by Bandar's own account.)

A visit to the Bush summer home in Kennebunkport, Maine, earned the prince the affectionate family sobriquet "Bandar Bush." Bandar reciprocated by inviting Bush to hunt pheasant on his estate in England. For good measure, Bandar also contributed an even $1 million to the construction of the Bush Presidential Library in College Station, Texas. At Bandar's suggestion, King Fahd sent another $1 million to Barbara Bush's campaign against illiteracy, just as he had donated $1 million to Nancy Reagan's "Just Say No" campaign against drugs.

Prince Bandar is not the only Saudi with an acute interest in presidential libraries and the like. Back in October 1983 Adnan Khashoggi—the arms merchant and future Iran-Contra middleman—footed the $50,000 bill at a New York City benefit for Jimmy Carter's presidential repository in Atlanta. Six months earlier, the former president and future Nobel Peace Prize winner had sung the kingdom's praises at a Saudi trade conference held in Atlanta. Much more recently, in late 2002, Prince al-Walid kicked in $500,000 to help launch the George Herbert Walker Bush Scholarship Fund at Phillips Academy, Andover—alma mater to George

Sleeping with the Devil

W. Bush as well. A year earlier, you'll recall, Rudy Giuliani had turned down Prince al-Walid's attempted $10 million gift.

Press accounts portrayed Bandar as largely on the outside during the Clinton years, passing melancholy weeks locked up in his humble Aspen mountain cabin (fifty thousand square feet, thirty-two rooms, sixteen bathrooms, assessed value $55 million). It's true that the two men have differences of style: Bandar is proud of his flyboy military past; every time Clinton tries to march on a parade ground, he looks as if he should be carrying a saxophone, and the thought of him hunting anywhere is plain scary. Clinton had his own back-door connection to Riyadh: a friendship with Prince Turki, the former head of the Saudi intelligence service, dating back to their undergraduate days at Georgetown University. But it's just as likely that White House aides worked hard to keep the president and Bandar apart. The last person Bill Clinton needed to spend more time with was a fabulously rich Arab with a wandering eye.

But Bandar was still his usual useful self. *Newsweek* reported that he played a role in convincing the Libyans to turn over two of its citizens suspected in the 1988 bombing of Pan Am Flight 103 over Lockerbie, Scotland. The magazine also wrote that Bandar helped to break down Saudi resistance to the FBI's investigation of the 1996 bombing of the Khobar Towers—an odd interpretation, since the investigation lingers on over a half decade after nineteen servicemen died there.

On the personal side, Bandar used his influence to convince King Fahd to donate $23 million to the University of Arkansas's new Center for Middle Eastern Studies, "a gesture of respect" for the Arkansas governor who had just been elected president. Clinton had been lobbying hard for the money since 1989, including a 1991 meeting with the Saudi ambassador and a November 1992 phone conversation with King Fahd only a week after he was elected president. The money finally came in two installments: an initial $3 million, followed by the balance two weeks after Clinton's inauguration: Timing is everything. As he does at the end of every administration, perceived friend or foe, Bandar also invited each of the Clinton Cabinet members out to dinner at a restaurant of his choice, private or public room, depending on their willingness to see and be seen.

With the Bush II administration, Bandar retook the White House as spectacularly as when the British burned it in 1814, turning himself into a permanently visiting head of state. His long service in Washington makes him the dean of the diplomatic corps, but it's his parties that everyone likes to talk about. In December 1997 Jimmy and Rosalyn Carter joined Bush Sr. at Bandar's Potomac River mansion to help celebrate the twenty-fifth anniversary of the prince's marriage to Princess Haifa. Two years later, when Nelson Mandela visited Washington, the Bandars feted him at a party in the McLean mansion that lasted until one in the morning and included an after-dinner performance by singer Roberta Flack.

Then there's Bandar's famous Rolodex. In April 2001 Yasir Arafat called Saudi Crown Prince 'Abdallah to complain after Israeli soldiers fired on a convoy ferrying officials of the Palestinian Authority. (Equal-opportunity favor-doers, the Saudis pick up Arafat's hotel tab whenever his entourage overnights in Washington—generally at the Ritz-Carlton, where the Carlyle Group was holding its annual meeting when American Airlines 77 slammed into the Pentagon.) 'Abdallah in turn called Bandar, who called Dick Cheney, who called Colin Powell, who once was Bandar's racquetball partner. (Powell and Bandar came to know each other back in the late 1970s through David Jones, then chairman of the Joint Chiefs of Staff and another of Bandar's racquetball buddies.) Within an hour of Arafat's call from Prince 'Abdallah, Powell was reading the riot act to Ariel Sharon in Tel Aviv. Tinkers to Evers to Chance was never so efficient.

In mid-2002, word leaked to the press that the semiofficial Defense Policy Board, chaired by the durable cold warrior Richard Perle, had endorsed an assessment that Saudi Arabia wasn't our friend when it came to terrorism. To be exact, the report called

Sleeping with the Devil

Saudi Arabia "central to the self-destruction of the Arab world and the chief vector of the Arab crisis and its outwardly directed aggression. The Saudis are active at every level of the terror chain, from planners to financiers, from cadre to foot-soldier, from ideologist to cheerleader."

Again Powell was on the phone within hours, this time assuring Bandar—and, through him, his principals—that such apostasy was not the official stance of the Bush II administration. To reinforce the message, Bush II invited Bandar down to the family ranch at Crawford, Texas, an honor usually reserved for the heads of state: Think Vladimir Putin in chaps and spurs.

In what could have been a delicious irony, the Defense Policy Board security breach is suspected to be the work of master leaker and Saudi handmaiden Henry Kissinger, who would later briefly head the blue-ribbon commission charged with investigating the intelligence lapses that allowed 9/11 to happen. He had to resign before taking up his duties, little doubt because he had Saudis on his client list.

Bandar once told an American reporter that the phrase "don't ask, don't tell" might have originated with a verse from the Qur'an: "Ask not about things which, if made plain to you, may cause you trouble." Maybe the verse should be carved over the front door of the State Department, too.

WHEN IT CAME OUT that Bandar's wife, Princess Haifa, had made charitable contributions that may have inadvertently helped two of the hijackers get settled in San Diego, Powell visited NPR's *Morning Edition* on November 28, 2002, to defend the prince and princess, although with faint praise.

"I have known Prince Bandar and Princess Haifa for many years," Powell told interviewer Michele Kelemen, "and I think it most unlikely that they would do anything that would support any terrorist organization or individual. But let's see what the facts are."

"Most unlikely"? "Let's see what the facts are"? Had the Bandarians broken ranks? Was the Bush administration sending a coded message? Perhaps, but Powell also might have been simply laying down a little cover fire for himself. In early March 2001 Princess Haifa hosted a lunch at her McLean digs for eighty of Washington's most prominent women, including the wives of Donald Rumsfeld, Chief of Staff Andrew Card, Treasury Secretary Paul O'Neill, and Supreme Court justices Clarence Thomas and Anthony Kennedy. The guest of honor: Alma Powell, wife of Colin.

So it goes in Washington, but to me the greatest surprise of the whole affair wasn't that Princess Haifa donated money that found its way to terrorists. Charitable contributions to the needy are an admirable obligation of Muslims, enshrined in the Qur'an; and Princess Haifa and her husband have Dumpsters of money to hand out. But how could anyone who counted not know that some of the money might end up with the soldiers of jihad? Let's get serious: When was the last time we asked Saudi Arabia to account for anything? It's just another sign that where Saudi Arabia is concerned, Washington stopped seeing the big picture long, long ago.

Whatever you think about Saudi charities—and I've already said that I think they might be overrated—they've been operating right under our noses for years. It's like the 9/11 attacks themselves: No one saw them coming because no one wanted to look. In March 2002, half a year before the breathless revelation of Princess Haifa's errant contribution, Treasury agents raided the northern Virginia headquarters of four Saudi-based charities: the SAAR Foundation, the Safa Trust, the International Institute for Islamic Thought (IIIT), and the International Islamic Relief Organization (IIRO). Also included in the raid was the local headquarters for the Muslim World League, an umbrella group funded by the Saudi government, which sent money and weapons to bin Laden. Gathering money scant miles from Bandar's Potomac River mansion, all five charities can point to a long line of humanitarian causes they have aided and supported. Treasury officials and other experts can also point to a long string of alarming associations.

Sleeping with the Devil

Testifying before Congress on August 1, 2002, Matthew Levitt, a senior fellow with the Washington Institute for Near East Policy, noted that Tarik Hamdi, an IIIT employee, had personally provided Osama bin Laden with batteries for his satellite phone, a critical link in the stateless world that bin Laden inhabits. IIIT and SAAR are suspected of helping finance Hamas and the Palestinian Islamic Jihad, home to some of the most accomplished suicide bombers in the Middle East. From 1986 to 1994, Muhammad Jamal Khalifa, brother-in-law of Osama bin Laden, ran the IIRO's Philippine office, from which he channeled funds to al Qaeda. Only excellent work by the Indian police prevented another IIRO employee, Sayyid Abu Nasir, from bombing the U.S. consulates in Calcutta and Madras. (Madras gets a little personal: I used to work there.)

Interviewed by PBS's *Frontline* about the problems with keeping track of Saudi money as it flows around the world, Prince Bandar said that the "money leaves Saudi Arabia, goes to Europe, and we can follow it; goes to the United States, America, and we lose contact with it." A good thing, maybe, for the Bandars. Princess Haifa's contribution to a Saudi who aided two of the September 11 hijackers added up to $130,000. Throw in $550,000 that a mysterious Saudi donated to a San Diego mosque that served as a forward base for the same two hijackers, and the money exceeds the roughly $500,000 the FBI estimates as the total cost of the 9/11 attacks. In other words, Bandar's—or some other Saudi's—"lost" money ended up paying for nineteen jihadis to massacre more than three thousand people. We'll never know whether it was lost money that went where it was supposed to go until the Saudis decide to assist with our investigation.

In October 2002 a U.S. delegation headed by Alan Larson, undersecretary of state for economic affairs, went to Riyadh, ostensibly to press the Saudis into increased surveillance of their countrymen's charities and financial networks. But as Jeff Gerth and Judith Miller reported in *The New York Times,* the story didn't end there: "In an illustration of the persistent quandary facing Washington, American and Saudi oil executives said Mr. Larson had another item on his agenda. He wanted to ensure, they said, that Saudi Arabia would pump millions of barrels of extra oil into the world market should there be a shortfall caused by an American-led attack on Iraq."

Don't ask, don't tell, don't know. Above all, speak no evil . . . and keep that oil flowing. The Saudis had it right all along.

RIYADH HOLDS UP a fistful of petrodollars, and Washington salivates. More and more, we're seeing the dual result of that Pavlovian conditioning: an almost pathological unwillingness on the part of U.S. government agencies to stare reality in the face, coupled with a massive money grab by those who do see that the House of Sa'ud is on its last wobbly legs.

But to focus solely on money, or even money and oil, is to miss the full complexity of the story. The marriage of Washington and the House of Sa'ud is far more textured. It winds its way through geopolitics, World War II, and the sometimes myopic struggle to contain communism. Franklin D. Roosevelt plays a part, as does the eighteenth-century tribal chief Muhammad Ibn Sa'ud. So does another eighteenth-century Arab, Muhammad ibn 'Abd-al-Wahhab and the archconservative thirteenth-century cleric Ibn Taymiyah. And so, finally, do the fruits of all the malignant seeds planted by Ibn Taymiyah: the Muslim Brotherhood.

To learn more about all this, I needed a history lesson and a tutor in the dark side of Islamic theology. I would have to travel to places that most Westerners would not willingly go.

Part II

Sleeping with the Devil

6/The Seduction

"FROM THE CAPITAL of Arabia, the chief town of the Nejd, the center of the Wahhabis, and a tent just north of His Majesty's palace, I send you greetings," twenty-nine-year-old Thomas C. Barger wrote to his young wife, Kathleen, back in Medora, North Dakota, on the last day of summer 1938. "There have been fewer than four dozen Europeans here, and I don't believe that many of them sent letters out."

Geology had landed Tom Barger in Riyadh. To the west of the capital, located roughly in the center of the kingdom, lies the Arabian Shield, a volcanic mountain range with peaks as high as nine thousand feet, stretching from Jordan, in the north, all the way south to the Gulf of Aden. (The last Arabian volcanoes went dormant only seven centuries ago; broad black lava beds, known as *harrahs*, can still be seen running down the mountainsides toward the Red Sea.)

Eastward, as the Arabian highland drops toward the Persian Gulf, the underlying volcanic mantle gives way to sedimentary rock formed from the remains of ancient aquatic plants and animals, left behind from prehistory when seas covered this lower land. As the waters receded and the earth's crust roiled and buckled, these sedimentary deposits were pushed deeper and deeper beneath the surface, and as that happened, the heat and pressure from above combined with the decomposition of the organic remains below to produce the fossil fuel we know as petroleum, black gold, oil.

Oil had been successfully brought out of the ground by drilling in 1859: Colonel Edwin Drake's famous little well at Titusville, Pennsylvania. Eleven years later, John D. Rockefeller incorporated the Standard Oil Company in Ohio, and oil was primed to become the new fuel of the industrial revolution. Before the century was out, Russia had joined the U.S. as the world's major producer. Indonesia, Romania, and Mexico all had fledgling oil industries by the start of World War I. Fighting was breaking out in Europe when oil was discovered in Venezuela and elsewhere in the Caribbean Basin.

Among the Persian Gulf states, Iran led the way. The first well there came in in May 1908. By 1913 a 135-mile pipeline tied the field to a refinery at Abadan, atop the Persian Gulf. The giant oil field at Kirkuk, in northern Iraq, was tapped in 1927. By 1935 it was delivering petroleum via a pair of six-hundred-mile pipelines to the Mediterranean coast at Tripoli in Lebanon, and to Haifa in what was then Palestine. Bahrain, the tiny island sheikdom in the Persian Gulf between Qatar and Saudi Arabia, came on-line in 1932 with help from the Gulf Oil Corporation. It was only a matter of time until eastern Saudi Arabia—geologically of a piece with western Iran, Bahrain, and southern Iraq—would join the party.

Tom Barger was part of the second wave of engineers and geologists sent by Standard Oil of California to make oil happen in Saudi Arabia. Working under a royal lease, the SOCAL team had already brought in the kingdom's first well to produce oil in commercially exploitable quantities: Damman Well Number Seven, near Dhahran, begun on New Year's Day, 1938. By September of that year, when Barger showed up in Riyadh, the prophecy was about to be fulfilled.

SOCAL, one of many offshoots of the court-ordered 1911 breakup of Standard Oil Company, would go on to become a principal in Aramco—the Arab-American Oil Company, formed to exploit and manage Saudi oil, the world's largest depository. Tom Barger would rise to CEO of Aramco in 1961, a post he would hold until 1969. And oil would upend almost everything about the capital, the kingdom, in some ways the entire Muslim world, and of course, the Western world, too, because oil, the West, Islam, and Saudi Arabia can never be wholly separated.

It is amazing to think how new Saudi Arabia is, given the hold that it has on the Western consciousness and the wallet of the industrial world. The Saudi Arabia that Tom Barger flew into in 1937 had been a united kingdom for only five years. As late as the mid-1920s, the vast interior of the Arabian peninsula existed in almost total isolation from the rest of the world—a place characterized not by oil and its riches but by poverty, religious xenophobia and fanaticism, and, at its heart, an almost impenetrable desert culture.

The Arabian coast had long been known to traders. A thin trickle of European explorers had tackled the peninsula's vast arid reaches in the nineteenth century. The holy sites at Mecca and Medina had been subjects of fascination in the West for centuries, but it wasn't until 1865 that the coordinates of Riyadh, the future capital of the future kingdom, were fixed on Western maps.

Syria, Iraq, Egypt, and the African Muslim states of Algeria and Morocco were all undergoing modernization to one degree or another in the years after World War I. Kuwait, on Arabia's northeastern border, had been packed with colonial intriguers for decades. Not so Saudi Arabia: It remained as it had been for centuries, a medieval Arab society rent by internal and external aggression.

Ibn Sa'ud had seized Riyadh on January 15, 1902, with an army of fewer than two hundred warriors and a raiding party of forty men. He was then in his early twenties. Intent on restoring a family dynasty that had been waxing and waning since the eighteenth century, he would spend the next two dozen years doing battle on all sides—against the dying remnants of the Ottoman empire, against competing Arab rulers, especially the Hashemites in Jordan, and finally, against his own supporters when they wouldn't honor his authority. He won control of Mecca in 1924 and of Medina the following year. Both had been part of a short-lived ancestral realm.

By 1927 Ibn Sa'ud sat atop a dual kingdom that covered most of the peninsula. Five years later, he combined the two parts into a single realm and named it for his family: Saudi Arabia. But even as first-world oil interests came calling, his capital remained an unelectrified city of some thirty thousand deeply isolated people, surrounded by a mud wall and almost never visited by foreigners.

Ibn Sa'ud's offspring, and their offspring, would become some of the world's richest people, famous from the casinos of Monte Carlo to the brothels of London for their profligacy; the lords of billion-dollar palaces, owners of the best thoroughbreds and yachts, donors of university chairs and college laboratories, buyers of influence in every capital of the West, ready to whisk around the world at a moment's notice on fleets of private jets. In the mid-1930s, though, during the dark years of the Great Depression, the king's minister of finance, Shaykh 'Abdallah Sulayman, was still hauling the national treasury around in a tin trunk. Revenues from taxes on livestock, cereals, fruits, trade, and other commodities, as well as other royal prerogatives, went into the trunk for safekeeping. When the king decided on an expenditure, he would write the recipient a chit, which 'Abdallah would, in due course, redeem from the trunk. When the trunk ran dry of riyals, 'Abdallah would simply disappear until the stores were built back up.

It was the many barren periods within the royal trunk that led 'Abdallah and his king to agree so readily to exploration terms clearly favorable to Standard Oil of California. The agreement granted SOCAL "the exclusive right, for a period of 60 years, to explore, prospect, drill for, extract, treat, manufacture, transport, deal with, carry away, and export" oil and oil products in an area of over forty thousand square miles, twice the size of France.

In return, the company promised to provide the Saudi government with an immediate loan of £30,000 gold or its equivalent (about $1.56 million in 2002 U.S. dollars), an "annual rental" of

Sleeping with the Devil

£5,000 gold, and an advance royalty of an additional £50,000 gold ($2.6 million), plus an identical payment once oil had been discovered in commercial quantities, as well as ongoing royalties when the business expanded. Acting on the king's behalf, 'Abdallah Sulayman signed the pact on May 29, 1933. The first two SOCAL geologists arrived four months later.

World War II, in a sense, brought Saudi Arabia into the world. Britain and Germany both vied for the kingdom's support, the Germans in part to use the peninsula as a back door for attacking Russia through its underside on the northern border of Iran. Officially neutral, the king favored the British, not from any long-standing love but because Britain and its colonies remained Saudi Arabia's principal food source.

Saudi oil, too, came to assume ever greater importance as other sources of petroleum were cut off during the war. The Japanese invasion and occupation of Burma and Indonesia closed two critical sources. After never extracting more than 5.1 millions barrels of oil annually through its first six years, Aramco ramped up to 7.8 million barrels in 1944 and nearly tripled to 21.3 million barrels in 1945. By then Saudi oil had become vital to the Allied cause.

Despite the kingdom's newfound—and largely unsought—importance on the global stage, it wasn't until February 14, 1945, that King Sa'ud, then in his mid-sixties, met his first Western head of state: Franklin Delano Roosevelt.

Roosevelt had been courting Ibn Sa'ud for several years, and not merely to secure oil for the war effort. FDR had his eye on the strategic value of the vast Saudi reserves for the postwar years, and he was well aware that he would have to overcome British dominance in the Middle East if he was going to make the Saudis America's new best friend in the Islamic world. On February 8, 1943, Standard Oil of California had written to the secretary of the interior, Harold Ickes, encouraging the Roosevelt administration to counter British influence by bringing Saudi Arabia under the umbrella of American lend-lease assistance. Ten days later, Assistant Secretary of State Edward Stettinius declared the kingdom of vital interest to the United States and extended direct and indirect aid that would eventually amount to almost $100 million.

Until the war, the American ambassador to Cairo had borne responsibility for the Saudi kingdom as well, but even before the lend-lease deal, the Saudis had been given their own chargé d'affaires, stationed in Jeddah. (From 1944 to 1946, the post was held by William Eddy, a onetime intelligence officer and experienced Arabist. In what would become the great tradition of the U.S.–Saudi relationship, Eddy would go on the oil dole after the war as a consultant to Aramco.)

Roosevelt sent his own personal envoy to Saudi Arabia in the spring of 1943. In the fall, the Saudis responded with two delegations. First Crown Prince Sa'ud and later Prince Faysal and his brother Khalid visited the United States, where they met the president and key members of Congress and the administration. The crown prince stayed for a month, with all the trappings of a state visit.

Just as the Saudis were leaving the capital, a group of American geologists was handing Washington a report on the future of oil. They predicted that the center of extraction would shift from Mexico and the Caribbean to the Persian Gulf region. Reserves there were far greater. Gulf oil wells were up to thirty times more productive than the average wells in Latin America and up to 150 times more productive than average wells in the U.S. And the proximity of the Gulf made transportation cheap, or would make it cheap once an oil infrastructure had been put in place. In the meantime, the fragile Saudi economy had gone into the tank. The lend-lease program was slow in arriving, and a relative trickle when it did. Muslim pilgrims fulfilling their obligation to visit Mecca provided the bulk of the country's prewar revenues. Fighting in both the Pacific and European theaters had severely curtailed that and cut off most of the kingdom's trade with the rest of the world.

In a February 7, 1944, telegram from Dhahran to his corporate masters in the States, SOCAL's Floyd Ohliger wrote, "food situation . . . regarded greatest urgency by his majesty as starvation conditions becoming widespread." A government warehouse in Jubail had about two thousand tons of foodstuffs for Riyadh, but government transportation was on the verge of collapse, "although some dates going from Hofuf by camel." SOCAL could help, Ohliger wired, but only by delaying construction on the vital oil terminal at Ras Tanura.

In January 1945, in a top-secret memorandum to then Assistant Secretary of State Dean Acheson, Wallace Murray, head of the Office of Near Eastern and African Affairs, provided a "description of the character and extent of the American national interest in Saudi Arabia, together with an analysis of the situation which makes it necessary for this government to consider what positive steps it must take immediately in order to afford adequate protection to this interest."

The United States wasn't alone, Murray noted, in having an acute interest in the kingdom and its oil. "If the Saudi Arabian economy should break down and political disintegration ensue, there is a danger that either Great Britain or Soviet Russia would attempt to move into Saudi Arabia to preserve order and thus prevent the other from doing so. Such a development in a country strategically located and rich in oil as is Saudi Arabia might well constitute a *causi belli* threatening the peace of the world."

The first priority of American policy, Murray argued, should be to safeguard and develop "the vast oil resources of Saudi Arabia, now in American hands under a concession held by American nationals." The memo doesn't envision the U.S. becoming the Saudi's primary petroleum customer; that would come later. The expectation was that the Western Hemisphere would continue to be largely petroleum self-sufficient. But by filling Europe's postwar oil appetite with Saudi oil, instead of oil from Venezuela, Mexico, and elsewhere in the Caribbean Basin, the United States could preserve its region's resources and maintain a reserve it could fall back on in times of military emergency.

Of more pressing importance, Murray wrote, "the military authorities urgently desire certain facilities in Saudi Arabia for the prosecution of the war, such as the right to construct military airfields and flight privileges for military aircraft en route to the Pacific war theater. . . . Thus far King Ibn Saud has declined to grant those facilities because of British objections, believed to arise from postwar political considerations."

Since 1940 Great Britain had pumped nearly $40 million into Saudi Arabia, to maintain stability and heighten its influence there. American lend-lease aid to the kingdom had been about $13 million, with another $13.4 million coming in the form of advances from the Arabian American Oil Company. To counter British influence and keep the Soviets at bay, Murray, who would become U.S. ambassador to Iran at war's end, recommended as much as $57 million in additional U.S. aid over the next five years. Otherwise, some other nation "might attain . . . a position in Saudi Arabia inimical to our national interest there."

In an enclosed letter dated December 11, 1944, and also stamped "top secret," Secretary of the Navy James Forrestal carried the argument still further:

> *The prestige and hence the influence of the United States is in part related to the wealth of the Government and its nationals in terms of oil resources, foreign as well as domestic. It is assumed, therefore, that the bargaining power of the United States in international conferences involving vital materials like oil and such problems as aviation, shipping, island bases, and international security agreements relating to the disposition of armed forces and facilities will depend in some degree upon the retention by the United States of such oil reserves. . . . Under these circumstances, it is patently in the navy's interest that no part of the national wealth, as represented by the present holdings of foreign oil reserves by American nationals, be lost at this time. Indeed, the active expansion of such holdings is very much to be desired.*

Sleeping with the Devil

The United States did have one great advantage with Saudi Arabia. Ibn Sa'ud had spent much of his life fighting tooth and nail to assemble his kingdom. He didn't want to cede control to a nation such as Great Britain, with a long colonial past and a proven appetite for interfering in the region. Confined by its own geography and defined for much of its existence by its isolationism, the United States seemed a better and safer choice for a backward kingdom just finding its feet in global matters.

For the Saudis, the question was how to approach the United States. In a letter delivered to the American minister at Jedda for transmittal to Roosevelt, Ibn Sa'ud and his ministers put forth their case with delicacy and remarkable coyness:

> *When the King sees the great nation of America content to have its economic activity in Arabia reduced and defined by its ally, Britain, America in turn will surely understand that Saudi Arabia may be excused if it yields to the same constraint from the same source, not merely to please an ally, but to survive. Without arms or resources, Saudi Arabia must not reject the hand that measures its food and drink.*
>
> *Unwilling as he is to entertain the thought, the King cannot but consider the possibility that American may lose interest in his distant land, after the war, as she has retired to domestic preoccupations after other wars. . . .*
>
> *The Saudi Arabian government therefore inquires whether there is an exit for our two nations from this confinement.*

Who was courting whom? Ibn Sa'ud had pulled all the right strings.

BY FEBRUARY 1945, it was time for the two leaders to meet. Already in the Mediterranean to discuss reparations and the possible postwar dismemberment of Germany with Winston Churchill and Joseph Stalin, Roosevelt steamed to the Great Bitter Lake in the Suez Canal after the Yalta Conference closed. On February 12 he met with Farouk I of Egypt aboard the U.S.S. *Quincy*, which had carried the president all the way from Norfolk, Virginia. Ethiopia's Haile Selaisse followed the next day. Meanwhile, at Jeddah on the Red Sea, Ibn Sa'ud and his party were boarding the U.S.S. *Murphy*, the first American warship to make port in Saudi waters, and setting sail for the Great Bitter Lake. On the fourteenth, the Saudi king came aboard the *Quincy*.

To accommodate Ibn Sa'ud, the ship's crew covered the bow with a large tent and set out a decorative chair and an assortment of rugs and seating cushions for the king and his traveling party. In accordance with Muslim custom, a live sheep was slaughtered daily on board and prepared for his meal. At a dinner thrown for officers and crewmen, the king spoke through an interpreter of his own military conquests. U.S. Navy Captain John Keating recalled Ibn Sa'ud quoting from the Qur'an: "First I am a warrior: Only then am I a king." At six foot four, he looked every bit the warrior.

Away from the festivities, aides showed Ibn Sa'ud newsreels that glorified U.S. military operations. The message was clear: If you need protection from your enemies, who better to have on your side than the world's preeminent military power? The reverse message—if you want oil in your future, who better to have on your side than Saudi Arabia?—didn't need asking.

In their talks aboard the *Quincy*, Franklin Roosevelt and Ibn Sa'ud put their common seal on many arrangements already in the works. America would have access to Saudi ports. It could construct the military air bases on Saudi soil, albeit with a lease limited to five years. Equally important, Aramco, dominated by SOCAL and other American oil companies, could begin building the Trans-Arabian pipeline to the Mediterranean. Roosevelt had hoped to gain the king's support for a Jewish state in the Middle East, but Ibn Sa'ud argued that it was the Germans, not the Arabs, who had harmed the Jews; and thus the Germans, not the Arabs, who should pay. Roosevelt ended up promising the Saudi king that the United States would consult equally with Jews and Arabs over any change in U.S. policy toward Palestine. He also vowed that America would not seek to occupy Saudi soil as the British had occupied so many of Saudi Arabia's neighboring countries. The latter point was key: Winston Churchill rushed to meet with Ibn Sa'ud as soon as he learned that Roosevelt had done so, but he was too late. The deal had been cut.

To commemorate the meeting, the two leaders parted with an exchange of gifts: a sheik's robe and solid-gold knife for Roosevelt, and harem outfits for wife Eleanor and their daughter, Anna, who had accompanied the president from Norfolk. FDR presented Ibn Sa'ud with a Douglas two-prop plane, to be delivered later, and an exact replica of his own wheelchair. The king, who suffered from an old leg wound, took to the chair immediately and rarely left it except to sleep, until his death in 1953 of obesity, lack of exercise, and general decrepitude.

Contemporary historians and other commentators tended to treat the meeting as an aside, and even modern historians are apt to give it short shrift. Yalta is where the action was. The war was winding down. Europe needed to be rebuilt; Germany and Japan, to be shaped into pacifist nations. But it was on the *Quincy*, not at Yalta, that the energy cornerstone of America's postwar industrial machine was laid.

Heavily invested in Iran and elsewhere, British and British–Dutch oil interests would continue to dominate the Middle Eastern trade in the years immediately following the war, but as the Saudi–U.S. relationship took root and spread, and as Saudi oil production grew—from 21.3 million barrels extracted in 1945 to 142.9 million in 1948 and over 300 million by 1952—all that would change.

With the United States, the Saudis had protection against Egypt, against their ancient enemies in Jordan, against the Shi'a and the Iranians and all the other intrigue and danger of the Arab world. With the Saudis, the U.S. broke European hegemony in the Middle East and set up a bulwark against communist influence in the area. Everything that would come to define the U.S.–Saudi relationship was there from the beginning: oil diplomacy, the inter-twining of government and corporate influences, the intermingling of public and private interests. The only thing missing was excessive greed, and that would take care of itself. The balance of global industrial-oil would have two clear termini: the U.S. and Saudi Arabia. People at either end would grow rich beyond all reckoning; and the second leg of the triangle that connects money and power, Islam and Christianity, terrorism and nationalism, would be complete.

THE FIRST LEG of that triangle had been set in stone two centuries earlier when Muhammad ibn 'Abd-al-Wahhab was expelled from the desert oasis town at Al 'Uyaynah, northwest of Riyadh.

Born at Al 'Uyaynah in 1703 or 1704, Muhammad was said to have learned the Qur'an by heart by the time he was ten years old. At twelve, he entered into a marriage arranged by his father and set off on a pilgrimage to Mecca. Soon thereafter he was in Medina, studying under 'Abdallah ibn Ibrahim ibn Saif, and from there he traveled far and wide, including to Kurdistan, Baghdad, and Basra, in what is now Iraq. In Basra, at the confluence of the Tigris and Euphrates rivers, 'Abd-al-Wahhab began preaching the message that would resound through Saudi Arabia to this day.

Islam, 'Abd-al-Wahhab told anyone who would listen, had lost its way. Islam was a monotheistic faith. The Qur'an strictly enjoined Muslims to refrain from imputing divine qualities to anyone other than Allah. Even the prophet Muhammad, founder of the faith, was only an ordinary man called by Allah to an extraordinary mission. Yet the evidence of polytheism was everywhere in the Muslim world: Muslims worshiped at the prophet's tomb. They went on pilgrimages to mosques built atop the tombs of saints, offered sacrifices, and prayed for the saints' intervention. Magicians, sorcerers, fortune-tellers—all ran afoul of the Qur'an. So did those who trusted their fate to talismans and amulets. 'Abd-al-Wahhab even went so far as to order his followers to cut down the few trees that lived on the peninsula because they were worshiped by pagans.

Sleeping with the Devil

Forced to leave Basra while he was still developing his message, 'Abd-al-Wahhab returned to Al 'Uyaynah and there launched his relentless puritan campaign. Islam could be made pure again, he preached, only by returning it to its purest form: the Qur'an and the Sunna, the code of conduct and acceptable views based on the prophet Muhammad's life. Anything introduced since—any practices instituted more recently than three centuries after Allah had delivered the truth through his prophet—was *bida,* an abominable innovation. Ostentatious living, gaudily decorated mosques, and excesses of style were insults to Allah and distractions from his word. By way of correction, 'Abd-al-Wahhab and his followers— the Wahhabis, as they became known—offered strict prescriptions that extended to the tiny details of everyday life. There was a Wahhabi way to sneeze, embrace, shake hands, yawn, kiss, dress, and so on. There was even a Wahhabi way of reinterpreting physics; strict Wahhabis believe the world is flat. (If this begins to conjure images of the Taliban rule in Afghanistan, there's a good reason.)

For the pagans who followed faiths established before Muhammad introduced the one true religion and the one and only god, there was no pity for their ignorance. For Muslims who refused to acknowledge the truth of 'Abd-al-Wahhab's teaching, there was jihad: holy war. The Wahhabis lived by the sword, and anybody who opposed them died by it.

Wahhabi intolerance finally got to be too much for 'Uthman ibn Mu'ammar, the ruler of Al 'Uyaynah. Facing opposition from his own people and fearing the wrath of powerful tribal chiefs—and unwilling, apparently, to have his guest put to death—'Uthman ordered 'Abd-al-Wahhab to leave his territory but offered him the choice of destinations. And thus it was that sometime in the late 1730s or early 1740s, Wahhab walked forty miles down the Wadi Hanifah to Dar'iya, near present-day Riyadh, and made the acquaintance of its ruler, Muhammad ibn Sa'ud, great-great-great-great-grandfather of Ibn Sa'ud. It was a marriage made in heaven.

For nearly two hundred years, the Wahhabis, Muhammad ibn Sa'ud, and his descendants would wage war across the width and breath of the Arabian peninsula. In 1801 a Wahhabi raiding party sacked Karbala, the site of the tomb of the prophet's grandson, Husayn, and one of Shi'a Islam's most holy shrines. In the course of eight hours, the Wahhabis massacred some five thousand Shi'a and destroyed Husayn's tomb, a horror and an insult the Shi'a have never forgiven.

It was the Ikwhan—the brethren of Wahhabi tribesmen—who helped Ibn Sa'ud capture the holy cities of Mecca and Medina; they battled the infidels, waged war against polytheists, humbled the idolators, and expelled the foreign opportunists and their lackeys until, after much back and forth, Ibn Sa'ud unified the conquests, named the vast bulk of Arabia after himself and his family, established Wahhabism as the state religion, and set out with his Wahhabi supporters to create an Islamic realm in the puritan tradition almost at the very moment that the discovery and exploitation of oil were on the verge of changing everything.

THE THIRD LEG of the triangle—the Wahhabis and the industrial West—has always been the wild card.

Externally, petroleum and the wealth it generated wrenched Saudi Arabia into the mid- and late twentieth century. The formation of OPEC in 1960 handed the House of Sa'ud a lever by which it could begin prying itself loose from its corporate masters in America. American politicians helped, too. For a quarter of a century after World War II, the United States, not Saudi Arabia, held the global surplus oil balance, largely by domestically storing vast amounts of petroleum bought abroad. By the mid-1950s, though, independent U.S. oil producers and American coal companies had had their fill of foreign imports. After trying and failing to stem the flow with voluntary restrictions, President Dwight Eisenhower imposed mandatory quotas on foreign oil imports in 1959. Fourteen years later, when Richard Nixon removed the import quotas, the U.S. had exhausted its surplus and become a net importer of oil. It didn't take long for the Arab world to punish America for its neglect.

On October 6, 1973, Syria and Egypt attacked Israel, kicking off the Yom Kippur War. Two weeks later, on October 19, OPEC announced a total embargo on oil exports to the United States, in retaliation for American and Western support of Israel during the war. The next day, Saudi King Faysal, whom American officials were convinced would never take part in an embargo against the West, joined it, bowing to pressure brought by a coalition of other Arab producers and the kingdom's Wahhabi Muslim clergy. Suddenly, the petrodollar spigot acquired new dimensions—you could open it up to make money, or close it off to make even more.

Within seven decades, Riyadh exploded from a mean compound of thirty thousand inhabitants to a sprawling metropolitan area of over four million people. Muslim and non-Muslim foreigners poured into the kingdom to work in the oil fields. At the same time, Saudis made wealthy by oil poured out of the country: to American universities (some two hundred thousand Saudis have been educated in American schools since the end of World War II), to London and Paris and Rome to shop for luxury goods, to playgrounds in every corner of the world.

Overnight, a medieval society seemed to become a modern one. Always under the surface were the House of Sa'ud's longtime supporters, their base, their strength, their brotherhood of warriors: the Russian arms dealer Yuri's "crazy Vahabis." For the Wahhabis, modernity was the one implacable enemy. In geology, when plates of the earth's crust move in opposite directions, earthquakes result. The plate tectonics of societies and cultures work the same way.

Even Ibn Sa'ud had been unable to fully control his puritan fanatics, especially the leaders of the Ikwhan. Some of those who wouldn't submit to his authority Ibn Sa'ud simply had mowed down; others he brought to Riyadh, where they were imprisoned until there was nothing of them to remember.

By the late 1960s, the fault lines that always existed between the moderation necessary to get along in the larger world—diplomatically, militarily, and economically—and the rigid puritanism demanded by the same faith had begun to pull dangerously apart. Ibn Sa'ud was succeeded upon his death in 1953 by his free-spending son Crown Prince Sa'ud. Other members of the royal family, along with religious leaders, wrested authority from the crown prince by 1958 and forced his abdication in 1964 in favor of his half brother Faysal, but the pattern of royal excess wouldn't disappear. Nor would the Wahhabis' insistence that Islam be purified. Ironically, it was the Israelis who showed them how.

On June 5, 1967, Israel launched a preemptive attack on Egypt, Syria, and Jordan, quickly and decisively defeating all three countries. From Jordan, Israel captured the West Bank and Jerusalem; from Syria, the Golan Heights; and from Egypt, the Sinai Desert. It was maybe the most humiliating defeat the Arabs had ever suffered, at least since they were forced out of Spain in 1492, just as Columbus was sailing for America. But for some Muslims, it was much worse. They had lost Jerusalem and the Dome of the Rock, the third holiest site in Islam.

At first Arabs reacted by pouring into the streets in outrage, protesting mostly against the U.S. Then they realized they had been betrayed by their own governments. All the arms they had bought over the years had done them no good. Why? Because so much of the money that was supposed to go into defense had ended up in the pockets of corrupt princes, politicians, and military officers. That's an old lesson, but there was a new one to be learned from the 1967 debacle. A much larger Arab force had been defeated by a relatively tiny state based on religious cohesiveness: Israel. Wouldn't the Arabs be stronger if they reorganized according to their own belief, Islam?

The Wahhabis, egged on by their Egyptian and Syrian fundamentalist mentors, took the lesson to heart. See, we told you so, they started to preach in the mosques; God conquers all. Anxious not to be conquered itself, the House of Sa'ud climbed aboard the bandwagon even before it was fully built. Beginning in the early 1970s, the royal family and charities administered by family members used their vast reservoirs of petrodollars to build a network of mosques and religious schools, in the kingdom and abroad, where a fresh generation of Muslim teenagers could be indoctrinated into the most violent and radical interpretation of Islam: intolerance to innovation, the imposition of Allah's law as it appears in the Qur'an, and death to the infidels occupying the domains of Islam.

Far from being a threat to American interests, the schools, or *madrasahs,* served them extravagantly. From the very onset of the cold war, U.S. strategists were determined to establish Saudi Arabia and its leaders as a kind of sacred bulwark against godless communism. Just as Saddam Hussein would later be demonized by American propagandists, so Ibn Sa'ud and his successors were lionized as defenders of the faith, guardians of the holy shrines, "the nearest we have to a successor of the caliphs," one breathless U.S. ambassador wrote of Ibn Sa'ud.

The Wahhabis relished their role as the voice of militant Islam: stern of demeanor, committed beyond Western understanding, willing to die for their beliefs. And the *madrasahs* were the place to recruit, a supermarket of spiritual warriors. In the 1980s the schools were the main breeding ground for the Islamic militants called to holy war against the Soviet invaders in Afghanistan. Armed with U.S.-supplied weapons, backed with U.S. money and logistic support, the "Arab-Afghans" drove the Red Army back to Moscow, crippled a superpower, and arguably changed the course of history—a success by every measure of warfare and geopolitics.

Trouble was, an infidel was an infidel, whether he wore a red star on his uniform and patrolled the streets of Kabul or supported the Jewish occupation of Arab soil. Militant Saudi Islam also proved more unwieldy than the computer models at the National Defense University and elsewhere had projected. Like kudzu, the impulse toward jihad began to wind its way around everything. Most alarming, the use of Arab "freedom fighters" in the crusade against communism combined Wahhabis and the Muslim

Brotherhood to create the perfect storm. No, it was worse than that. It was like mixing nitroglycerin in a blender. But it would take decades for America to feel the blast, and then Washington would pretend it had nothing to do with it. Even today many of the bright boys along the Potomac can't stop congratulating themselves on what a great deal we made with Saudi Arabia.

7/The Honeymoon

Amman, Jordan—February 1980

IT WAS THE TAIL END of dusk as the plane banked to land at the Queen Alia airport. I could just make out Amman in the distance, sitting out there on the edge of the Syrian Desert. Carved out of ragged limestone hills, it glowed like a garnet. It looked, well, biblical.

Too bad I wouldn't get to see much of it. Early the next morning, I was going on to Damascus to track down a Syrian major I'd met in India. Normally, the CIA wouldn't have risked sending me into a country like Syria to meet someone I barely knew, but he was an Alawite, the minority sect that had ruled Syria with an iron grip for the last ten years. The CIA knew virtually nothing about the Alawites. Clannish and closemouthed, they were as good as impossible to recruit as sources. Few had ever defected. It was a long shot that anything would come of the meeting, but the CIA thought it was worth the price of the ticket.

I had my own agenda. I was starting to get interested in the Muslim Brotherhood. Ideally, I would have asked for an assignment to Saudi Arabia, where so many of the Brothers were coming to roost even back then; I could have learned a lot by simply poking around. But Saudi Arabia was a closed society, shielded from the curious, and the State Department never would have let a CIA officer loose there for fear of offending the Saudis. Syria, I figured, wasn't a bad second choice. The Alawites, after all, seemed to have figured out how to deal with the Brotherhood, or at least keep it at bay. Learning how they did it was sure to tell me something, and my Syrian-officer connection seemed like a promising guide. I will call him 'Ali.

Before leaving India, I'd read everything I could about the Alawites. The majority of Syrians were Sunni Muslims, about 74 percent; the Alawites represented only 11 percent of the population. Nonetheless, the Alawites held every position that had anything to do with power. Hafiz al-Asad, the president, was an Alawite. So were the key army and air force generals. Every important job in Syria's half-dozen intelligence services was held by an Alawite. But more than anything, it was the handpicked midlevel Alawite army officers who prevented some Sunni colonel from attempting a coup.

Let's say a Sunni colonel needed to move one of his tanks across Damascus, maybe for repairs. He couldn't load it on a transport and send it off, as colonels in most armies around the world could. Before he could even pull the transport out of its shed, the colonel had to get the permission of the senior Alawite in his regiment. It didn't matter that the Alawite might be only a major or captain, or that his position had nothing to do with repairing tanks. The point was that Asad trusted the junior officer—the Alawite—and not the Sunni colonel. Answering to a subordinate didn't do much for the colonel's morale, but Asad went to bed at night relatively sure that the colonel wouldn't be tempted to detour his tank to the president's front door and knock it down with a 125-mm armor-piercing round. Alawite officers were something like political commissars in the old Soviet Red army.

Years later, a former Alawite officer would tell me a story to illustrate how finely tuned the system was. Late one night a second lieutenant commanding a forward position on the Golan Heights was surprised to hear his military landline ring. It was a little past four, and the front was quiet; there was no conceivable reason for headquarters to be calling. The lieutenant's curiosity turned to suspicion when the caller asked for his name. He demanded the caller identify himself. When he understood it was Asad on the line, the lieutenant almost knocked over the telephone leaping to attention. His initial thought was that he had unknowingly committed some hideous act of *lèse-majesté* and was about to lose his head. He calmed down as Asad asked a few questions about the front, but his astonishment rushed back when Asad asked after his two children—by name. Assured they were well, Syria's head of state said good-bye and hung up.

My Alawite officer friend swore that Asad hadn't checked the lieutenant's file before he called. As a young officer, he said, Asad had made it a habit to know all of his fellow Alawite officers by name, clan, and family, and those same officers carried him to power in 1970. When Asad rose to a position that gave him access to military personnel files, he read them all, including the Sunnis' and Christians'. Asad had a remarkable memory for detail. He could tell you all about an officer's training record, evaluations, and assignments. Knowing his officer corps inside and out was what kept Asad in power for thirty years, until he died in his bed on June 10, 2000. As we used to say in the CIA, Asad had "coup-proofed" Syria.

Needless to say, the system didn't make the Alawites popular, especially with Syria's Sunni majority. To make matters worse, the Sunnis questioned whether the Alawites were even real Muslims. Not much is known about Alawite beliefs; they have no canon. Alawite elders transmit their tenets orally from one generation to the next, but since an elder is usually in his wheelchair by the time he receives the truth, he's not inclined to chat about it. The little that is certain is Alawites believe in a sort of trinity—heresy to orthodox Muslims, who hold that Allah's power is indivisible. The Alawites' enemies also accuse them of many other ugly heresies, from drinking wine in the mosque to being a lost tribe of Israel.

Still worse, Asad was minister of defense when Syria and the rest of the Arab world were humiliated in the Six Days War of 1967. Syria's Sunni Muslims blamed Asad personally, alleging that if he had been Sunni, a true believer, he never would have let such a colossal defeat happen. As long as Asad was alive, he had this stinging accusation ringing in his ears. He knew that if he ever made a single concession to Israel—anything short of getting back all the land he lost during that war—the growing ranks of Islamic fanatics would accuse him of betrayal and, worse, apostasy. Asad knew early on what the West is beginning to sense: that the wave of Islam was going to be one hell of a ride.

Not surprisingly, Syrian Sunnis despise the Alawites and dream in the darkness of night about one day overthrowing them. Syria's Islamic fanatics, the Muslim Brotherhood, actually tried. In 1973, when Asad dropped a clause in the Syrian constitution that the president had to be a Muslim, Muslim Brother–inspired riots broke out all over the country. Asad was forced to restore the clause, but the damage was done. The Muslim Brothers started assassinating Alawites and even targeted their "Christian" allies, the Soviet military advisers who helped keep Syria a thorn in the West's side. On June 16, 1979, the Muslim Brothers attacked an artillery school in Aleppo, picking out Alawite cadets for execution. In 1980, in sympathy with the Iranian revolution, Syrians took to the streets again, demanding an Islamic state—one not headed by infidel Alawites.

Sitting at my desk in South India, the more I read, the more curious I grew about the Muslim Brothers. Back then I knew almost nothing about Islam, but from what I'd seen in Madras and elsewhere on the subcontinent, Muslims were relatively tame. Sure, they might riot and burn Hindu shops, but the outbursts rarely lasted over a day or two, and the discontent never turned into terrorism. India's Muslims weren't assassinating politicians or setting off car bombs, like the Brothers.

I asked headquarters for a backgrounder on the Muslim Brotherhood and got back a one-page regurgitation of what was already public. At least it was a decent primer on the group's history. The

Sleeping with the Devil

Muslim Brotherhood was founded in 1928 by an Egyptian, Hassan al-Banna, to purify Islam and rid Egypt of foreign influence. In 1947 it turned to violence, attacking Jewish-owned businesses in Cairo. A year later, the government banned the Muslim Brotherhood. "When words are buried, hands make their move," al-Banna was widely quoted as saying when he heard the news. On December 28, 1948, the Brothers made good on al-Banna's prophecy by assassinating the Egyptian prime minister. The government responded by cutting off the snake's head, killing al-Banna in 1949, but that only made the Brothers more fanatical. After al-Banna's successors made an attempt on Egyptian president Nasser's life in 1954, Nasser shut down the Muslim Brotherhood altogether, driving it underground and into exile.

Most of the Brothers ended up in Saudi Arabia, but not all. Some fled to Syria, where students returning from Egypt in the 1930s had founded a branch. Eventually, the Syrian government would grind that under its heel and send the Brothers scurrying again, most to the Saudis but some to West Germany (where they would establish the cells that set the stage for September 11). Others remained in Damascus and elsewhere in Syria, driven underground but not out of existence.

That was the extent of the available information. Based on headquarters' messages, I gathered that the CIA knew next to nothing about the Muslim Brotherhood. My assumption was that it didn't have a source, a spy, a plant, anything, anywhere in the organization. The agency clearly had no idea how the Syrian Brothers were organized or where they were getting their money, and frankly, I was surprised.

Even from remote India, I could tell the Brotherhood was spreading like a virus. Branches had popped up in sub-Saharan Africa, South Asia, and elsewhere, but Syria seemed to be the real problem. It could make or break a peace settlement with Israel. Officially, Washington wanted Asad gone—he was armed by the Soviet Union and sided with them in almost every international dispute—but if he were replaced by the Brothers, you could count on things getting a lot worse. If history was any guide, the Brothers weren't going to sit around Asad's palace smoking his Havana-leaf cigars; they would be at the front, leading an attack on Israel. How could the CIA not know whether the Brothers had any chance of taking over Syria? Not having a spy in the Brotherhood was as unthinkable as the pope not having a spy next to Martin Luther.

Then again, I'd been with the CIA only a couple of years and didn't yet understand the way things worked.

THAT NIGHT IN AMMAN I kicked back at the Intercontinental Hotel bar with a beer, confident I would succeed where my colleagues had failed. Once in Damascus, I would convince Major 'Ali to tell me all about the Brothers. He'd give me the hard facts, the ones that head-quarters didn't have. 'Ali might be an Alawite, but I figured that since his life was on the line, he would have made it his business to know about the enemy. (Did I mention I was young and naive?) Of course, I would have preferred to get the facts from a real, live Syrian Muslim Brother, but that seemed a long shot, since I had no idea where to find one.

The next morning before heading off for Damascus, I went to see Amman's chief, Tom Twetten. I had known Tom from when he was deputy in Delhi and I was in Madras. Slim and prematurely gray, Tom was friendly and competent. I suspected even then that he was on his way up, and he did go on to become the CIA's deputy director of operations. At the end of Tom's career, in one of those ironic twists of fate, his son-in-law was murdered when Pan Am 103 blew up over Lockerbie, Scotland.

Tom and I talked mostly about the mechanics of getting me into Syria. Headquarters had routed me though Amman in order to bypass the Damascus airport, which was closely watched by Syrian intelligence. If I took a taxi from Amman to Damascus, I could slip in and out of the country before the Syrians noticed, or so the plan went.

Sleeping with the Devil

When we finished, I asked Tom about the Syrian Muslim Brothers.

He shrugged. "The Jordanians give them money and refuge, but only because they hate the Syrians—'my enemies' enemy is my friend' sort of deal."

"What do the Jordanians say about them?" I asked.

"We don't press the Jordanians for details. And they don't volunteer anything. The Muslim Brotherhood isn't a target for us."

What Twetten was telling me was that he had no instructions to spy on the Muslim Brotherhood. CIA posts overseas are only supposed to spy on countries or terrorist groups that headquarters tell them to spy on. I can't tell you for sure, but the Soviet Union must have been Amman's number one priority, with China maybe a distant second. In practical terms, it meant that almost every case officer working for Twetten spent his days and nights chasing Soviet diplomats, hoping one might agree to spy for the CIA. In his spare time, an Amman case officer might take a Chinese diplomat out for lunch, but only if he couldn't find a Soviet. Since the Muslim Brotherhood wasn't a target, Amman wasn't supposed to waste time or money on them, not even a quarter for a couple of falafel sandwiches.

Twetten also had the problem of the CIA's white-as-rice culture. Back then—and this wouldn't change much, right up until I left the CIA in December 1997—most case officers were middle-aged, Caucasian Protestant males with liberal-arts degrees. If they had any experience, it was in the military. Few spoke Arabic, and the ones who did spoke it badly. (Spending all your time with Russian-speaking diplomats didn't do anything for your Arabic.) Since most Brothers spoke little English, a nearly insurmountable cultural and language barrier existed between the CIA and the Brothers. Even if Twetten had any incentive to go after the Brothers, the chances of one of his officers ever running into one, let alone being able to talk with him, let alone recruiting him, were close to zero.

Amman was the model for the rest of the Middle East. The Muslim Brotherhood—and radical Sunni Islam in general—was off the CIA's radar scope. Maybe a handful of analysts back at headquarters followed it in their spare time, but with no input from the directorate of operations and no spies in the Brotherhood, they had to draw on open sources, mostly journalists and academics, and they weren't doing so well themselves.

Ever since Nasser shut down the Muslim Brotherhood in 1954, finding a Brother to interview—a militant one, at least—had been nearly impossible. They'd buried themselves too deeply underground, and Saudi Arabia, which became the Brotherhood's patron after 1954, was a book as closed as the Brothers. Academics and journalists were rarely granted visas to the kingdom. The few who were couldn't get close to the Muslim Brotherhood offices, mosques, divinity schools, and *madrasahs*. In other words, militant Islam was a deep black hole. When Osama bin Laden emerged publicly in the late 1990s, for most Americans, he might as well have popped up out of hell.

In fairness, it wasn't all the CIA's fault. Until September 11, there wasn't a president who cared whether Langley spied on the Brothers. During the cold war, presidents lost sleep worrying about the Soviet Union and its nukes. A third-world dictator who ended up with a Brother's bullet between his eyes was near the bottom of the White House's list of gnawing worries. Basically, the CIA existed, and always had, to spy on the Soviet Union. Something like 60 percent or more of the CIA's budget was dedicated to giving the president a heads-up on whether those nukes were on the way. Every dirty war the CIA got involved in, from the Bay of Pigs to Angola, had something to do with containing communism. Sure, a president might have an occasional question about a place like South Africa or Japan, but as far as he was concerned, the rest of the world was a footnote.

That, at least, is the official explanation—which is to say, it's the one that official Washington wants you to believe. The real answer is infinitely more complicated. Yes, the Soviet Union was a distraction. And yes, the Muslim Brothers were hard to get to. But at the bottom of it all was this dirty little secret in Washington: The White House looked on the Brothers as a silent ally, a secret weapon against (what else?) communism. This covert action started in the 1950s with the Dulles brothers—Allen at the CIA and John Foster at the State Department—when they approved Saudi Arabia's funding of Egypt's Brothers against Nasser. As far as Washington was concerned, Nasser was a communist. He'd nationalized Egypt's big-business industries, including the Suez Canal. He bought his weapons from the Soviet Union. He was threatening to bulldoze Israel into the sea. The logic of the cold war led to a clear conclusion: If Allah agreed to fight on our side, fine. If Allah decided political assassination was permissible, that was fine, too, so long as no one talked about it in polite company.

Like any other truly effective covert action, this one was strictly off the books. There was no CIA finding, no memorandum of notification to Congress. Not a penny came out of the Treasury to fund it. In other words, no record. All the White House had to do was give a wink and a nod to countries harboring the Muslim Brothers, like Saudi Arabia and Jordan. That's what happened during the Yemeni civil war that got under way in 1962. When Nasser backed an anti-American government and sent troops to help it, Washington quietly gave Riyadh approval to back Yemen's Muslim Brothers against the Egyptians. As Tom Twetten said, the enemy of my enemy is always my friend: It's an ironclad rule in the Middle East.

If the CIA had spied on the Brothers, that would only end up exposing them for what they were—mass murderers who, if you gave them any thought at all, could be counted on to turn against us one day. If Tom Twetten or any other CIA officer in the Middle East were somehow to turn over a rock and tattle to Washington, his next job would be running the basement candy stand at Langley, maybe on the same shift as the Berlin case officer turned towel man who tried to recruit a Saudi diplomat.

THE CIA HAS REQUESTED THAT THIS SECTION—
RELATED TO FOREIGN FUNDING OF
THE MUSLIM BROTHERHOOD—BE DELETED.

██ In 1980 President Carter's national security adviser, Zbigniew Brzezinski, cut a deal with Saudi Arabia: America would match, dollar for dollar, Saudi money going to the Afghan resistance of the Soviet occupation. (To give you an idea of the money involved, in 1981 alone, Saudi Arabia kicked in $5.5 billion.) So far, so good. But if you read the fine print, you see that the bulk of the money went to the militant Muslim groups, including Abdul Sayyaf's.

Sayyaf, the head of the Ittehad-e-Islami, was a particularly dangerous man to give money and weapons to. While a student at Islam's oldest and best-known university, Cairo's al-Azhar, he was recruited into the Muslim Brotherhood. Afterward, just in case he hadn't completely absorbed the lesson of jihad and righteous murder, he did an apprenticeship with the Wahhabis in Saudi Arabia. His bloody tracts and sermons were public, but no one in Washington raised a yellow flag, let alone a red one, for fear of upsetting Riyadh.

If the Saudis and Pakistanis were partial to the Afghan Muslim Brothers, the wisdom in Washington said that was the price you had to pay if you expected them to do the dirty work. And if the Muslim Brothers were cold-blooded murderers and crazy enough to take on a Soviet armored column with small arms, all the better. Washington has always prided itself in fighting wars on the cheap. If success was a high Soviet body count per dollar, then the Muslim Brothers were a fabulous bargain.

It occurs to me that if John Ashcroft had been attorney general back then, I and everyone else who played a part in ████████ ████ and Afghanistan would have found ourselves on one of his al Qaeda lists. No doubt about it, we were aiding and abetting the people who would become our archenemies. Hell, I'd probably be writing this from a cage in Guantanamo Bay.

Sleeping with the Devil

I HADN'T FIGURED OUT any of this as I settled into the backseat of a dinged yellow 1965 Plymouth taxi that was going to make it to Damascus only if Allah willed it. All I knew was that Islam seemed like a calm sea—sunny and flat on the surface, but with all kinds of things going on below.

The Muslim Brothers seemed to be everywhere and nowhere. How else could they survive in a police state like Syria? How did they infiltrate themselves and their weapons from Jordan into Syria? And why weren't the Jordanians—or, for that matter, the Egyptians—telling us anything about them? The Muslim Brothers were one of those subterranean truths in the Middle East that we find out about only when they decide to surface. Today there's even a name for these places where the real truths (as opposed to the convenient ones) reside: the Arab basement.

The moment I saw Major 'Ali pull up in his Soviet-military UAZ jeep, I knew the detour through Amman and the day-long taxi ride had been a waste of time. Not only did he have two armed thugs in the backseat, but his chase car and follow car were packed with soldiers in full battle gear. One carried a belt-fed RPD machine gun, another a rocket-propelled grenade launcher that stuck out the window.

The major's Mad Max caravan accompanied us everywhere. When we pulled up in front of Damascus's main department store, his soldiers blocked the doors and cut off access to the parking lot so we could browse without someone popping us. When we lunched at a restaurant on the Barada River, they restricted the entrances, including the kitchen door. People had to wait to get in or out until we were done. All through lunch, one of 'Ali's gunmen stood directly behind him, cradling a locked-and-loaded Kalashnikov. Traveling with this circus, I never could have gotten in and out of Syria unnoticed.

The second day of my visit, I got around to slipping in a question about the Muslim Brothers.

"I don't know," 'Ali answered. "They're just crazy. The only thing they know is killing."

"Are they going to win?" I asked.

By way of an answer, 'Ali gave me a quick tour of Damascus's terrorist sites. The air force headquarters, which hadn't been completely rebuilt after the Muslim Brotherhood car-bombed it, was ringed with cement barriers and sandbagged positions. Both ends of the street in front of Asad's apartment were barricaded with concrete. It was the same with the Soviet embassy. Armored vehicles were patrolling the streets, and the police were stopping cars and pedestrians for random checks. Damascus might as well have been a concentration camp.

We drove next to old Damascus and a street named a Street Called Straight. It might have been straight when it was laid out by Alexander the Great's city planners, but now it wound through the old city's maze of shops, open-air spice stands, donkey carts, hawkers, itinerant vegetable sellers, and children running in all directions. It was late afternoon, and the place was packed with end-of-day shoppers. Some women wore head scarves; most didn't. You could barely hear amid the shouting. 'Ali swept his hands over the chaos. "Here are your Brothers."

When we got back to his apartment, he added, "Oh, we'll win, all right, but only with this." As he spoke, he slapped the pistol at his side.

I left Damascus the following day without 'Ali ever telling me anything about the Muslim Brotherhood. He also hadn't let slip a thing about his religion or how Asad had pulled off the miracle of holding on to power for so long. Although we got along well enough, 'Ali was as clannish as the rest of the Alawites. He had no intention of tutoring me or any other American official on what made Syria tick.

I'm sure headquarters concluded that sending me to Damascus had been a waste of a plane ticket and too much cab fare, but the trip hooked me on the Middle East, mostly thanks to the Muslim Brotherhood. They were still a complete mystery to me—a riddle to be solved. One thing did seem obvious. Even if Asad managed to rout the Brothers, they would not go quietly back into their caves.

INDIA PROVED to be a good rear base for keeping an eye on an increasingly volatile Syria, and for filling the gaps in my learning that 'Ali had declined to tutor me on. The Brothers tried to assassinate Asad on June 25, 1980. I don't know how close they got, but it was close enough to really piss him off. The following morning Damascus woke up to the whir of helicopters putting down at a military cantonment west of Damascus. The copters loaded up two companies of Asad's elite guard unit, the Defense Companies, then flew east to Palmyra's notorious military prison where Muslim Brothers were being held. Waiting guards threw open the doors, and the Defense Companies stormed in, moving from cell to cell, executing prisoners. The Brothers had only enough time to yell, "God is great! God is great!" Although something like five hundred Brothers died that day, the Brotherhood wasn't intimidated.

In February 1982 the Syrian Muslim Brothers seized Hama on the Orontes River, Syria's fourth largest city, with roots going back to the Bronze Age. When they started to cut the throats of Alawite officials and their families, Asad acted. He called in the Defense Companies again and ordered, "Level it." After a couple days of continuous shelling, the center of Hama was a smoldering pile of rubble. An estimated twenty thousand people were killed, including, presumably, most of the Brothers. Hafiz al-Asad wasn't happy to go down in history as the butcher of Hama or the man who destroyed a world-class historic city, but it was either that or run for it, along with one million other Alawites. The Brothers would never again pose a serious threat to Asad.

(An old Syrian joke has God sending the Angel of Death to Damascus to summon Asad to judgment. A few days later, the angel returns to heaven, battered and bloody, having been worked over by

Asad's notorious secret police. ("Oh no," God shrieks in horror, "you didn't tell them who sent you?")

Asad systematically removed anyone suspected of being a Brother from any institution that had anything to do with Islam. Every cleric, Friday prayer leader, soothsayer, corpse washer, and *madrasah* teacher was vetted and revetted. Even a long-forgotten, veiled reference to jihad was enough to land a cleric in jail or put him out of a job. Just as it had in the army, the system worked. By the time of Hafiz al-Asad's death, the Syrian Muslim Brotherhood existed in name only. There wasn't a peep out of anyone when another Alawite, Asad's son Bashar, succeeded him. The only Syrian Brothers left to complain were in exile, mostly in Saudi Arabia and Germany.

The second part to Asad's strategy will be familiar to any Mafia don. Asad knew he had to keep his friends close and his enemies closer, which meant never letting Saudi Arabia get out of sight. His brother Rifa't al-Asad, the commander of the Defense Companies, married the sister of Crown Prince 'Abdallah's wife. Closer to the jugular, Asad held the threat of terrorism over the heads of the Al Sa'ud. His intelligence services kept close ties with Palestinian terrorist groups who could strike at will inside Saudi Arabia, and he made it crystal-clear to the Al Sa'ud that if they backed a terrorist attack in Syria, they could expect a Palestinian attack in the return mail.

Asad also courted the Saudi Shi'a opposition. Although they make up only about 10 to 12 percent of Saudi Arabia's population, the Shi'a provide the critical labor for the oil fields in the Eastern Province. Almost as oppressed as Christians in Sunni-Wahhabi Saudi Arabia, the Shi'a are prone to violence. Asad allowed the Shi'a leaders to open up offices in Damascus and Beirut, as a reminder for the Al Sa'ud that he wasn't above blowing up their wells. It wasn't long before Saudi "charity" money for the Brothers inside Syria dried up.

So, Major 'Ali had been half right about taking care of the Brothers. Turning Hama into a landfill had blunted the Brothers' terror campaign. But it was Middle Eastern politics that did the trick: promising revenge; placing family, allies, and pawns in positions of power and influence; and above all, never compromising.

IF ONLY EGYPT, which spawned the Brotherhood, had done the same. Instead, it let things drift and paid the price. Even after Nasser banned the Brothers in 1954, al-Azhar University continued to crank out fundamentalist preachers. Modest neighborhoods in Cairo, such as Abdin—where Muhammad Atta, the presumed team leader of September 11, grew up—were heavily under the influence of the Brothers, as were parts of Alexandria and Assyut.

The world witnessed the bloody consequences on October 6, 1981, when Egypt's Islamic Jihad—another name for the militant wing of the Muslim Brotherhood—assassinated Anwar Sadat. I'll never forget watching the TV clips played over and over the next day. The brazenness of the attack, in broad daylight, in front of the world's press, in the middle of a military parade, oblivious of Sadat's bodyguards, suggested a group that would stop at nothing. They all knew they would die in the attack or be executed at the end of a show trial. But death wasn't a threat, and Sadat wasn't the end of it. In 1993 the Muslim Brothers, again under the name of the Islamic Jihad, tried to kill the interior minister and later the prime minister. In 1995 they tried to kill Hosni Mubarak while he was visiting Ethiopia. Two years later, the Brothers attacked the temple at Luxor, killing fifty-eight foreign tourists and four Egyptians.

And, of course, they attacked once more on September 11, 2001, in New York City and suburban Washington, D.C. I'll never forget watching those TV clips over and over, either. The press kept calling the attackers al Qaeda, thanks to Osama bin Laden's relentless publicity machine, but it was the Muslim Brothers through and through—the same crew we had used to do our dirty work in Yemen, Afghanistan, and plenty of other places. Only now *we* had become their dirty work, and Saudi Arabia their home.

8/Guess Who Came to Dinner

Khartoum, Sudan—January 1985

AFTER THE SADAT ASSASSINATION, I was determined to talk with a real live Muslim Brother. How else was I going to learn what made the Brothers tick? And if we didn't know what made them tick, how would we ever stop them? I didn't know it at the time, but I would get my chance two months later, in December 1981, less than twenty blocks from the White House.

One morning I was walking out of my Georgetown apartment building to go to Arabic class when I noticed that the new desk clerk—a very tall, slim black man in his early thirties—was reading a book in Arabic. I walked over and introduced myself. Khalid, as I will call him, was a Sudanese, a graduate student in comparative law. We talked for a long time, then struck a deal for him to tutor me in Arabic. I needed the practice, and he needed the money. He had brought his wife and children from the Sudan and was barely surviving.

For the next six months, we gave it our best, but I've got to admit that Khalid did my Arabic more harm than good. The problem was that he had a classical education in the language. Worse, he'd taken a degree in Islamic law. Even by the end, I couldn't hold a conversation with Khalid without his reminding me not to forget the complicated vowel endings that the man in the street never used. It was like Chaucer trying to teach modern English.

Lessons aside, we became friends. I helped edit Khalid's dissertation, taught him how to drive, and even gave him my clunker when I was assigned to Tunis for my second year of Arabic. It was the first car he had ever owned. At least once a week, I joined Khalid and his family for dinner in their apartment in Adams-Morgan, a racial mixing bowl north of Dupont Circle.

After I left for Tunis, Khalid and I lost track of each other. I had no idea what became of him until I was assigned to Khartoum in January 1985 and saw his picture in a local newspaper. The caption said he had been appointed as a judge to one of Sudan's new Islamic courts. I put down the paper and headed straight to his court. Nothing like running into an old friend in a sandbox like Khartoum.

The two religious policemen blocking the court's front door looked at me slack-jawed when I asked for Judge Khalid, explaining that he was a friend. It was rare to see a Westerner in Khartoum, much less have one show up at one of its notorious Islamic halls of justice. Inside, the anteroom was packed. The electricity was off. The place was hot and dark and reeked of sweat. I would have turned around and left if I hadn't heard a voice booming inside the courtroom. It sounded like Khalid, but I couldn't be sure. I'd never heard him raise his voice. He'd always come across as gentle, soft-spoken, and polite. Now he sounded downright possessed.

Abruptly, the yelling stopped. A second later, the crowd parted like the Red Sea, and out came Khalid with one of the policemen by his side, his *jalabiyah* sweeping the filthy floor. He came running over to me, straight-arming some innocent who wandered into his way, and gave me a hug.

"Let me finish up here," he said. "And then you come to my house for lunch." He changed his mind almost as soon as he'd finished speaking. "No, Mr. Bob, you stay, and we will start working on your Arabic again. You need it." He put his arm around me and pulled me into the courtroom with him. Mind you, I'd spent three years unlearning everything he had taught me, but I was curious to see who or what had made Khalid so mad.

He shooed away an old man sitting on the front bench so I could sit down, then went around and stood on his dais, winked at me, and resumed yelling as if nothing had happened. The audience stopped staring at me and listened raptly to Khalid.

The object of his fury was a small man dressed in dirty denims, a shirt that might have once been white, and a pair of cracked leather sandals. He had a rope for a belt and was standing inside a waist-high battered wooden enclosure that reminded me of a hockey penalty box.

The man never said a word. He wouldn't even look up at Khalid. It looked as though he didn't have a lawyer, and there was no jury, either. If the man's family was there, they weren't saying a thing. As Khalid went on, I understood that the man had been caught stealing a pot from an open-air market that morning.

Without warning, Khalid lowered his voice and handed down the man's sentence. "In the name of the merciful and compassionate, I find you guilty of theft. I sentence you to twenty lashes." With a nod from Khalid, the two policemen pushed their way back through the crowd, grabbed the man by both arms, and led him out of the courtroom.

As soon as they were gone, pandemonium broke out in the court. About half the audience was shouting that it had been a fair call. The other half was screaming and crying. Some of the latter must have been the man's relatives and friends. Everyone was trying to leave at the same time.

When I managed to get outside, I saw the condemned man tied to a tree, face flattened sideways against the bark. Someone had removed his shirt, and the two policemen, now cradling automatic weapons, stood on either side, making sure no one attempted to interfere. Khalid stood directly behind the man, the sleeves of his *jalabiyah* rolled up. His right hand, gripping a leather whip, was raised. He paused for maybe ten seconds. As he was about to strike, he intoned, *"Bismi ar-rahman, ar-rahim"*—"In the name of the merciful and the compassionate"—and brought the whip down with a force only a man of his size could attain. At every lash, the penitent spit out "God is great!" between his clenched teeth.

On the drive to Khalid's house, we didn't say anything for a long time. Khalid could tell I was uneasy. The entire spectacle went against everything he had learned about the law in America.

"You know, Bob, there is no choice in Sudan," he said at last in English. "We are a very poor, troubled country. If we ever let go of control, it's over for us—we will live like wild animals. The one thing people will ever understand and accept is the Qur'an. We will never enjoy the luxuries of your legal system. Please don't look at this as an American."

"How do you know what they want, the people?" I asked. It was a question any American would want the answer to.

"Please understand that the Sudanese are backward. They're just starting to understand what the Holy Qur'an is. Do you know what the ignorant do when they're sick? They rip out a page of the Holy Qur'an that they think has to do with their illness. They boil it in a pot of water until the ink bleeds away, and then they drink it, believing it will cure them. These people need a firm hand."

I let it drop. "How did you know that guy stole the pot?"

"My police saw him"—the judicial police assigned to his court. *Great,* I thought, Khalid was judge, prosecutor, defense, jury, and executor, all wrapped into one.

Although he had never said anything, I was starting to suspect Khalid was a Muslim Brother. He had studied under Sudan's Muslim Brotherhood guide Hassan al-Turabi when Turabi was dean of the law faculty at the University of Khartoum, a prime recruiting ground.

I never went back to Khalid's court, but I continued to see him as often as I could. I usually drove out to his one-story whitewashed house south of Khartoum. The house was testament to how poor even a judge was in the Sudan. We sat on synthetic Korean-made carpets; there was almost no other furniture. The glass in some of the windows was missing, and gusts of sand blew through. The kitchen sink never seemed to have running water, and Khalid's wife had to prepare dinner outside, drawing water from plastic buckets. It didn't seem to bother anyone, though.

I pressed Khalid to tell me about the Muslim Brotherhood. General Nimeri's regime had started to wobble in early 1985. It looked as if Khalid's old law dean might make a grab for power. The Muslim Brothers supposedly had a strong following in the army.

One evening I got tired of beating around the bush—elicitation obviously wasn't working—and I asked Khalid if he was a Muslim Brother.

Khalid had this endearing habit of smiling with his eyes. He flashed me a smile now. "I'm a Sufi, Bob," he said. "I really don't know anything about them."

What Khalid wanted me to believe was that a Sufi, an Islamic mystic, held a set of beliefs so diametrically opposed to a Brother's that he couldn't possibly be a Brother. Maybe, I thought, but I also noted that Khalid hadn't exactly denied it.

I got my answer late one night in March when there was a pounding on my door. It was after midnight, and I was asleep. When I opened the door, I found Khalid's wife. A scarf covered most of her face, but I could see she had been crying. "Khalid's been arrested," she said. "Please help me get him out. The children won't stop crying." Earlier that night, she said, the police had come and taken him away. She had no idea where he was being held.

I did what I could to reassure her and then drove her home. But that was all I could do. The next morning the news was splashed all over the newspapers: Nimeri had arrested the Muslim Brother leadership. Khalid must have been among them. Unless the Sudanese had made a highly unlikely mistake, he was a Brother after all.

When General Nimeri was forced from power in April 1985, the new government released Turabi and the Brothers, including Khalid. Turabi would come to share power with a pro-Islamic military government, partially realizing his dream of establishing an Islamic government in the Sudan. As for Khalid, he'd had all the excitement he needed and found himself a professorship at a Saudi-financed university.

I would never see him again. By the time he was released, I had already been pulled back to Washington thanks to the Libyan hit team that showed up in town to hunt CIA officers. I thought a lot about him, though. Here was a guy I'd spent the better part of a year with, a friend, but he couldn't bring himself to tell me he was a Brother. I was starting to sympathize with the CIA. The Brotherhood was a nut almost impossible to crack. But damned if I was going to give up.

IN LATE 1985, I was assigned to the CIA's new Counter-Terrorism Center and started to poke around headquarters archives to see if there was anything authoritative there on the Brothers. It wasn't easy. Although the purpose of CTC was to bring all CIA files and experts under one roof, no one followed radical Sunni Muslims. CTC had specialists for everything else, from the Japanese Red army to the German Baader-Meinhof Gang, but not one for the most adept terrorists of them all: the Muslim Brotherhood.

Post–9/11, it's easy to say what a mistake it was to leave out the Sunnis, but even back then I thought it was odd. After all, in 1979 Sunni fundamentalists took over the Mecca mosque, shaking the Sa'ud royal family to its bones. A special French police team had to be brought in to take the mosque back because the Saudi army refused to take orders. In the middle of it all, a Sunni fundamentalist mob burned the U.S. embassy in Islamabad. Militant Sunnis were a much bigger threat to the United States than the Japanese Red army, for God's sake, yet the CIA still didn't have a single source in the Brothers. The files I did find were stuffed with old newspaper clippings, a few analytical pieces, and cables from embassies.

What I did come across that was interesting was the trial of the Islamic Jihad members who assassinated Sadat. It was especially instructive on how the Islamic Jihad had wormed its way into elite units of the Egyptian military and through the tight security screen surrounding the October 6 parade. Via an elaborate recruitment of key people, they smuggled into the barracks boxes of ammunition to load their Kalashnikovs; live ammunition wasn't supposed to be within miles of the parade. It underscored the importance of having someone bless such an act. For Sadat's assassination, that person was 'Umar 'Abd-al-Rahman, the blind sheikh currently in jail in the United States.

What really struck me was the way the Islamic Jihad cited a thirteenth-century Syrian cleric to justify the murder. Ibn Taymiyah was born in 1263 in Harraan, near what is now Urfa in Turkey, but spent most of his life in Damascus, where his father had fled from the Mongols. Ibn Taymiyah's numerous polemics and other writings attacking orthodox theology had made him one of the most controversial figures of his day. In 1306 an Islamic court imprisoned him for his heresies, and he spent most of the rest of his life behind bars, in Cairo, Alexandria, and Damascus. He died in 1328. That much was relatively easy to find, but why had Ibn Taymiyah become, in essence, the patron saint of the Brothers? And what did the writings of a cleric who had been dead for more than 650 years have to do with the present slaughter in the Middle East?

More and more, these seemed to be vital questions. A tide of history was playing out under our noses, and we were looking everywhere but the right place for the reasons.

In 1986 some exiled Syrian Muslim Brothers in Germany knocked on the door of the U.S. embassy in Bonn, thinking America might be thrilled with their latest plot to take down Hafiz al-Asad. As I described in *See No Evil*, I jumped at the chance to meet them, but other than finding out they had an SA-7 buried at the end of the Damascus airport, ready to shoot down Asad's plane, I didn't learn a whole lot about them. I didn't need to fly out to Germany to know they wanted to kill Asad. A year later in Beirut, I got my chance to spend some quality face-to-face time with a Muslim Brother. I even got a couple of quick lessons in jihad.

In April 1987 I'd been in Beirut almost a year when I heard about a Syrian Muslim Brother living in East Beirut named Zuhayr Shawish. My first thought was: What is an Islamic fundamentalist doing living in a strictly Christian enclave? Just as quickly, I reminded myself that the Lebanese Christians were at war with Syria and needed all the friends they could get, even a Muslim fanatic who preached that the East's Christians should be fed to the Red Sea's sharks along with the Jews. It was Tom Twetten's rule again. I arranged to meet Shawish.

I checked around about Shawish. At one time he had been a fairly well-known figure in Syria, even a member of parliament. When the Syrian government cracked down on the Brothers, he was forced to leave. After a detour through Saudi Arabia and a few other places, he landed in Beirut in the early 1980s and now ran an Islamic bookstore, or at least that was what he told people. (If Shawish was making a living selling Qur'ans to Christians, he was one hell of a salesman.)

Meeting him wasn't going to be easy. I couldn't walk into his bookstore and introduce myself as his friendly neighborhood CIA agent. Even if the United States was the nominal ally of the Lebanese Christian Maronites, Shawish had no reason to talk to the CIA or any other American official. It was probably a toss-up whether he hated the CIA, Israel, or the Alawites more. What I needed was what the CIA calls cover for action—another of those lies woven out of whole cloth.

I came up with the idea that I would pose as an American of Lebanese heritage, a Muslim who had grown up in the United States. That would explain my flawed Arabic and my ignorance about Islam. The cover was weak as rooster soup, but that's the best I could do.

The part of East Beirut that Shawish lived in was one of the most exposed neighborhoods on the Green Line, the no-man's-land that separated Christian parts of the city from the Muslim side: a short, clear sniper shot from Hizballah's front line. As soon as I turned down Shawish's street, I gunned the Peugeot. A heavy metal gate was already opening from the inside as I pulled up in front of Shawish's house. It closed behind me as soon as I was inside.

Shawish's house was dark as a grave. Fifty-gallon drums stuffed with sand blocked all windows and doorways. Sandbags and boxes of books filled the few remaining spaces. The electricity was off; it probably had been in that part of Beirut for months. It looked like Shawish couldn't afford a generator, or maybe he just didn't care.

I was shown into another dark room where I found Shawish sitting on a tattered rug, his legs crossed under him, reading by candlelight. A flannel cloak and layers of robes covered him, but I could tell he was a large man. With his salt-and-pepper beard and the cracked lens of his glasses, he looked every bit the fiery Islamic radical.

Shawish didn't stand to greet me but pointed to a space on his rug that he wasn't already taking up. "So you want to learn about Islam?" he asked. So far, so good; he hadn't challenged the cover story.

Shawish launched into a sermon about the sorry state of Islam. That morning he was particularly irked that Jerusalem had become the epicenter of the Middle East conflict. "There are only two holy cities in Islam," Shawish said, still speaking calmly. "Medina and Mecca."

For the next hour, he provided a detailed exegesis of exactly where Jerusalem and the Dome of the Rock stood in the canons of Islam. Every other sentence was a quote from the Qur'an or the sayings of the prophet. (I silently thanked Khalid for throwing me into the deep end of classical Arabic.) I knew we were coming to the end when Shawish launched into a tirade against Yasir Arafat. Shawish accused him of having politicized Jerusalem solely for the Palestinians' sake. "Arafat is a dog and a liar," he said in not very classical Arabic. I recognized that as straight Wahhabi propaganda: They hated anyone who contested the supremacy of the two holy cities they occupied.

Shawish would have gone on about Arafat forever if there hadn't been a burst of machine-gun fire. It sounded like it was coming from a position opposite his house, across the Green Line.

I quickly slipped in my question: "Ever heard about Ibn Taymiyah?" It was beyond naive, but I'd pegged Shawish as not caring who I was. Even if I were to break cover, he still would have agreed to tutor me in Islam.

"Ibn Taymiyah? *Anna Abb ibn Taymiyah*"—"I am Ibn Taymiyah's father." It was Shawish's way of saying he knew more about Ibn Taymiyah than even the man himself. "What do you want to know about him?"

Shawish had extended the handle I was looking for. "I have always wanted to study Ibn Taymiyah," I said. "Would you have the time to instruct me?"

It was a lie, of course. I'd never even seen the cover of one of Ibn Taymiyah's books, but I was about to.

For the next year, every time I had a chance, I ventured down to the Green Line to see Shawish. We'd sit there for hours reading Ibn Taymiyah line by line, book by book. Considering Ibn Taymiyah wrote in the thirteenth century for well-educated Muslims, his Arabic was surprisingly accessible. His conclusions were just as accessible: Islam had to be purified. All the accretions that had attached themselves to Islam since the times of the prophet were like barnacles on a boat. They had to be scraped off. Muslims should refer only to the original texts.

For us in the West, the more important part of Ibn Taymiyah's peculiar take on Islam was that Islamic militants drew on his writings to justify the murder of Christian civilians. Since Christians supported the Crusaders, the thinking went, they deserved death. It was also the obligation of a good Muslim to die for the cause. In his book *Murder on the Nile*, J. Bowyer Bell quotes from Ibn Taymiyah's writings: "Death of the martyrs for the unification of all the people in the cause of God and His word is the happiest, best, easiest, and most virtuous of deaths." Ibn Taymiyah was the source of authority that called for assassinating Anwar Sadat. Even a Muslim deserves death if he has made common cause with Islam's enemies, and Sadat's Nobel Peace Prize, shared with Israeli prime minister Menachem Begin, proved he had done so. Ibn Taymiyah's fingerprints were all over September 11, too. The people in the World Trade Center deserved to die because they paid the taxes that went to sending aid to Israel that was used to buy the weapons that killed Muslims.

Most important, Shawish taught me that Muslim Brothers weren't alone in their devotion to Ibn Taymiyah. He reviewed the history of how, when Muhammad Ibn 'Abd-al-Wahhab started preaching in Saudi Arabia in the eighteenth century, he drew heavily on the sage of Damascus. Ever since, Ibn Taymiyah has been the mainstay of Wahhabi Islam, later joined by the Brothers' radical interpretation of Islam. No wonder the two of them got along so well: It was like the Brothers were coming home.

MY LESSONS with Shawish were strictly off the books. The CIA had sent me to Beirut to look for the hostages kidnapped by Iran. The first taken was David Dodge, the acting president of the American University in Beirut. He was kidnapped in 1982, but scores more were snatched in the following years. President Reagan had taken a personal interest in their fate. More than that, the hostages' captor, Iran, had obsessed the Reagan administration.

In November 1979 Iran had unofficially declared war on the United States when partisans of Ayatollah Khomeini occupied our embassy in Tehran. On April 18, 1983, Iran blew up our embassy in Beirut. On October 23, 1983, it killed 241 Marines with a truck bomb, and Reagan was forced to pull American forces out of Lebanon. On December 12, 1983, Iran struck again, bombing the U.S. and French embassies in Kuwait. On March 16, 1984, it kidnapped Bill Buckley, Beirut's CIA chief, effectively closing down American intelligence operations in a city that used to be our main listening post for the Middle East. In other words, in four short years, Iran had run the United States out of two countries—Iran and Lebanon. That's why Beirut was preoccupied with the hostages and had no time for Shawish or Sunni fundamentalism. Obviously, I'd figured this out, but I wouldn't understand how distracted the Reagan administration was until I was given a front-row seat to one of the silliest operations the Central Intelligence Agency ever ran.

It was a typical Beirut day for me. Before the sun was up, I headed to the tennis court for an hour of hitting the ball with the club pro. Perched in a pine grove on a hill north of Beirut, the tennis club had an unimpeded view of the Mediterranean. You'd think you were on the French Riviera . . . until about seven A.M., when the first Syrian 155-mm shell of the morning would whistle over on its way to one of the Palestinian refugee camps south of Beirut. The shells were a daily reminder that Arab solidarity was a myth, albeit one that seemed almost impossible to destroy.

By eight I was back at my apartment, sitting on my balcony with my first espresso of the day. My Motorola radio, which I was supposed to keep within reach twenty-four hours a day, crackled alive. "Lone Ranger, Lone Ranger." It was Bill ▮▮▮▮▮▮ my boss.

Bill had been in Beirut a little less than a year. When he first stepped off the Blackhawk at the embassy's helo pad and fixed me with his Marine "you cross me and I'll break your neck" glare, I figured my Beirut days were numbered. As promised, things didn't go well at first. Morning one, Bill tore up one of my cables, barking that I could either tighten my prose or catch the next helicopter out of Beirut. Mornings two and three weren't much better, but then something clicked between us. Maybe it was my knowledge of Hizballah; maybe it was Bill's loyalty to anyone under him who worked hard.

"Lone Ranger," Bill growled again. "Get your ass in the office—*now*."

Bill was sitting in the dark when I arrived. The electricity was off, and for some reason, the generator hadn't kicked in. Between the one-foot steel antirocket walls, the Mylar-coated window, and the filthy curtains, which might have been new in 1947, you could barely tell it was day. The one difference between Shawish's bunker on the Green Line and this lair was Bill's Coleman lantern.

Bill was sitting at his desk, looking, as usual, Buddhalike. (He'd put on about fifty pounds since his Marine days.) Two Delta Force shooters stood at parade rest in front of his desk. I knew both of them from the practice range. They could empty their Glock 9-mm pistols on a target from fifty feet and manage to clump every round into a hole about the size of a quarter. I will call them Mack and Striker.

"Now that Baer has graced us with his presence, we can start," Bill said, moving his lantern to see us better. Every other chair in Bill's office was occupied with flack vests, rations, and ammunition, so I stood with the shooters.

"Do you know how *fucking* stupid Washington is?" Bill asked.

He started his business day the same way every day, usually after he finished reading the morning cable traffic from headquarters. I knew better than to respond. Striker and Mack didn't say anything, either. Delta shooters usually keep their politics to themselves.

Bill started off on a Washington riff but then suddenly changed his mind and started talking about an old hijacking. On June 11, 1985, Fawaz Younis and a couple of bangers from his southern-Beirut-suburbs neighborhood hijacked a Royal Jordanian airliner preparing to take off from the Beirut airport. After subduing the guards, Younis demanded that the pilot fly to Tunis, where he intended to address the Arab League. When that didn't work, he settled for off-loading the passengers and blowing up the airplane where it sat.

Although no one died during the hijacking and it didn't involve an American airplane, two Americans had been on board. Technically, that put the hijacking under American legal jurisdiction. The Department of Justice indicted Younis and issued a sealed arrest warrant.

No one would have paid any attention to Younis or the DOJ's arrest warrant—it was unclear whether he was a terrorist or just insane—if not for a confluence of events. The CIA's Counter-Terrorism Center still hadn't had a clearly identified success, especially one that it could make public. Meanwhile, the bloody, spectacular terrorist events mounted, and the White House was looking for a success, any success, to hold up in response. Coincidentally, the CIA found out that the Drug Enforcement Agency's office in Nicosia was running a narcotics source named Jamal Hamdan, who happened to be Younis's friend. It took CTC about five seconds to concoct an operation to snatch Younis.

It went like clockwork. An unarmed Younis was lured onto a pleasure boat in international waters off the coast of Cyprus, arrested, and sent back to the United States. You could almost hear the champagne corks popping from Nicosia to Langley to 1600 Pennsylvania Avenue. The FBI was delighted, too. It got one of its first international collars, and the fact that female agents took part in the arrest helped the bureau pretend it was as politically correct as the next bureaucracy in Washington. Even State was happy. By arresting Younis away from Cyprus in international waters, it avoided irritating another client. *The Washington Post* and *The New York Times* got to fill a few extra columns with a little real-life drama. It was win-win-win all the way around. Heck, the hijacked Americans are probably still dining out on the story.

The only person who wasn't happy, it seemed, was Bill ████████ "Do you know how *fucking* stupid Washington is?" he asked again.

I already knew about Fawaz Younis's arrest. I'd followed it in cable traffic as well as in the press. I assumed Striker and Mack knew something about it, too, but since they didn't say anything, there was no way of knowing for sure.

"Now they're sending this son of a bitch here for us to run. I don't like it, but I don't have a choice."

Bill told us that Washington had decided Jamal Hamdan had done so well in setting the trap for Fawaz Younis that it would turn him loose in Beirut to find the hostages. It didn't matter that Hamdan didn't have the slightest idea who was holding them or even where to start looking. This was a headquarters decision. Bill could comply or go back to the Marines.

"So why do we have to run him?" I asked. Cyprus could have put him on a plane directly to Beirut International Airport, which was in the west, where the hostages were being held.

Bill grinned like the Grinch who stole Christmas as he handed me a sheaf of Arabic documents: murder indictments from the Lebanese state prosecutor's office. When I looked closer, I noticed they all bore the name of Jamal Hamdan—the same Jamal Hamdan the Beirut ███████ was supposed to handle. The last person he was accused of killing was his sister. He'd put a twelve-gauge shotgun to her head and blown it off. She'd apparently dated a guy Jamal hadn't approved of.

"The reason we have to take the son of a bitch here in the east is because he can't go to West Beirut. He'd be immediately arrested for murder," Bill answered.

As it turned out, Jamal had conveniently killed all of his victims in West Beirut. Although the Christians in East Beirut knew he was a murderer, they would never honor the arrest warrant of a Muslim prosecutor. Legalisms aside, killing Muslims was the point in East Beirut in those days.

Bill turned to the Delta shooters. "Baer's going to run Hamdan. But you don't take orders from Baer; you take them from me. And right now all I want you to do is pick Hamdan up from the helicopter and follow Baer to a safe house. Hamdan is not to leave the safe house. If he as much as touches the doorknob like he's going to leave, or attempts to climb out of the window, shoot and kill him."

Ah, finally some emotion from the Delta boys! Until then they'd probably thought Bill had gone soft since becoming a CIA spook. Now he was starting to make sense.

That night I didn't get any sleep. Hamdan was restless and paced around the safe house like a caged animal. Every time he got within a foot of the front door, Striker would reach for the Glock under his vest, eyeing the spot in the back of Jamal's head where he planned to double-tap him. I hurriedly steered Hamdan away from the door. I could just imagine the cable exchange with Washington.

Over the next two days, I drove Hamdan from one public telephone to another so he could call his contacts in West Beirut. As Bill had predicted, Hamdan never produced a reliable piece of information on the hostages. By day three, we had all had enough. Bill called the head of European Command, to whom Beirut's Blackhawks technically belonged. I'll never forget his bellowing at whatever the four star's name was: "It's none of your goddamned business why I need the helicopters. The only thing *you* have to think about is making sure they're on the LZ at 1800." Indeed, two Blackhawks put down at the LZ exactly on time, and that was the last we saw of Jamal Hamdan.

He was resettled in the United States along with most of his extended family. As for Bill, he never let up in his battle against Washington. He went from one hardship post to another until headquarters discovered that he was a great secret weapon against the State Department and sent him as chief to anywhere the CIA was having a problem with an ambassador.

TODAY it sounds like a Monty Python skit. But it was while we were doing these things—chasing down Fawaz Younis and running scum like Jamal Hamdan—that we missed the whole phenomenon of militant Sunni Islam. The attempts against Nasser and Asad, Sadat's assassination, Hama: They were looked at as isolated events, strictly local problems. No one connected the dots. The shadow war against Iran had us facing entirely in the wrong direction.

The destruction of Hama was the best example. Washington put the blame for it squarely on Asad's shoulders—an act of pure inhumanity ordered by a brutal dictator. The reasoning on the banks of the pristine Potomac was that if only Damascus had a friendly, pro-Western, democratic government, Hama never would have happened. But no one thought it through. If elections had been held in Syria at the time, the Muslim Brotherhood would have won.

Dig a little deeper, and you'd have no trouble finding some Washington "never heard a shot fired in anger" think-tank hawk who looked at Hama as a good thing. Leveling the place was sure to inspire the Syrian Brothers to wreak revenge on Asad's Alawites. And how bad could that be? The Alawites might have called themselves Arab Ba'th socialists, but as far as the hawks were concerned, they were Arab communists. Considering the Alawites had their Soviet-built SS-21s trained on Tel Aviv, they were dangerous communists, at that. The feeling in this group was simple: The fewer Alawites, the better.

This kind of thinking turned out to be criminally shortsighted. Long before the World Trade Center towers fell, anyone who looked at the facts objectively understood that the Brotherhood was ready to blow up in our face. Yet even after the massacre at Aleppo and the takeover of Hama, no one in Washington thought to yell, "Fire in the hole!"

On October 26, 1988, a Brother named Hashim 'Abassi was rounded up in the so-called Autumn Leaves arrests in Neuss, Germany. 'Abassi was part of a cell of Islamic militants that included his brother-in-law and the group's leader, Muhammad Hafiz Dalkimoni, who were planning to blow up five civilian jetliners. Although 'Abassi and most of the other Autumn Leaves conspirators were behind bars when Pan Am 103 exploded, the investigators' initial hypothesis was that they still had something to do with it. The lead was dropped when the investigators settled on two Libyans as the sole culprits. Today we know this was a mistake. If someone had bothered to look into 'Abassi and his Syrian Muslim Brotherhood cell, we might have been led to the Hamburg cell.

September 11 was almost a class reunion for the Syrian Muslim Brothers. One of the key figures in the German apparatus, Mamoun Darkazanli, fled from Syria to Germany after Hama. Although Darkazanli denied advance knowledge of 9/11, he admitted to providing help to three of the hijackers. A former Syrian intelligence officer familiar with Darkanzali told me that he had participated in the attack on the Aleppo artillery school in 1979. Another key Muslim Brotherhood player in September 11, Muhammad Haydar Zammar, likely arranged for the hijackers' training in bin Laden's Afghani camps. A third, 'Abd-al-Matin Tatari, ran a Brotherhood front company in Hamburg. Tatari's son was close to Muhammad Atta and the the Hamburg cell members. Two Syrian Brothers in Spain probably provided support to the hijackers. The details are beyond the scope of this book, but the point is that although Washington disliked Asad almost as much as the Brothers did, Asad was definitely on to something when he decided the Syrian Brothers were bad news. Hama and Allepo weren't merely local problems, as we'd been told.

JUST AS WE'D MISSED the Muslim Brotherhood in Syria, so we missed it in Kuwait. We were looking the other way and didn't see Khalid Sheikh Muhammad, one of the strangest and most lethal insects to crawl out from under the wreckage of the World Trade Center and the Pentagon.

Born in Kuwait in 1965, KSM (as he's known in the alphabet soup of the intelligence world) was the son of two immigrants from Balachistan, a remote, uncivilized province of Pakistan. His parents had moved to Kuwait hoping to cash in on the oil boom. Instead, they ended up in a desert grease pit called Fahaheel, where they were treated the same way as all the other South Asians living in the Gulf—like coolies.

The one political outlet KSM's family was given, it took. His father became a local mosque leader; his mother, a corpse washer, which in Islam is a religious position. The sons would take Islam one step further, turning to its dark side. One of KSM's brothers joined the Brotherhood in the 1980s, when he was at the university. Apparently under his influence, KSM also joined.

The Brotherhood was a sanctioned organization in Kuwait, just as it was in Saudi Arabia. In fact, it was encouraged. When Yasir

Sleeping with the Devil

Arafat was forced to leave Egypt because of his association with the Brotherhood, the Kuwaitis happily took him and the other Palestinian Brothers. That burnished the royal family's Palestinian and Islamic credentials. When Arafat moved on, the accommodating Kuwaitis backed the Islamic Association of Palestinian Students as a recruiting vehicle for Hamas.

Naturally, the Kuwait Muslim Brotherhood wasn't even on Washington's radar screen. Like Hama and Sadat's assassination, it was another local problem, not Washington's concern. Let the Kuwaitis sort it out. Besides, this was the early 1980s, right in the middle of the Iran–Iraq war. Keeping in mind that the Kuwaiti Shi'a—almost a third of Kuwait's population—were believed to be sympathetic to Iran, who had time to worry about the Brothers? Christ, *our* oil fields were in range of the Iranian and Iraqi big guns. You could even hear them from Kuwait City.

In 1983, when Khalid Sheikh Muhammad applied for a visa to study at Chowan College in Murfreesboro, North Carolina, no one paid him the least attention. He was one more Middle Easterner hoping for a U.S. engineering degree, no doubt expecting to return and work in the oil industry. (The same thing would happen in Khartoum when the visa officer didn't recognize the blind sheikh 'Umar 'Abd-al-Rahman. It didn't matter that his name and face had been splattered across the front pages of the world's press as the man who'd handed down the fatwa to assassinate Sadat.)

Like his brothers, KSM found his way to Afghanistan, where he hooked up with Sayyaf, the Afghan Muslim Brother and ally of Saudi Arabia. It was in Peshawar that he met Osama bin Laden and all the other jihadi fanatics from whom he would learn the tools of terrorism. There was nothing like ambushing a Soviet armor column to test your mettle, see who would die for Allah and who wouldn't. Presumably, it was then that bin Laden came to trust KSM enough to commit mass murder on September 11.

Needless to say, the CIA in Pakistan saw none of this coming. The White House orders had been clear: Send the bastards all the arms and ammunition they need, but let them do the fighting and stay out of their hair. Anyhow, the Afghans didn't need training in murder. They learned that when they climbed out of the crib. Basically, the Afghan war for the CIA was purely a logistics exercise. It didn't even have much contact with the resistance groups, which meant that the CIA and Washington were as blind as the sheikh, and the Muslim Brotherhood was its Invisible Man. We didn't see it because we didn't want to.

This approach was never so evident as in Saudi Arabia. When Nasser closed down the Brotherhood in 1954, the militants fled to Saudi Arabia, where they were welcomed with open arms. The Brothers knew their Ibn Taymiyah; they could teach the Qur'an; and they would work for pennies. For the radical Wahhabis, this was a match made in heaven. Before long, Egyptian Brothers were occupying many of the important chairs in the religious faculties of Saudi Arabia's universities and *madrasahs*. By 1961 the Brotherhood had become so entrenched in the kingdom that it convinced King Sa'ud to fund an Islamic university in the holy city of Medina to replace Cairo's al-Azhar, the historical center of Islamic learning. The Brothers claimed that Nasser had destroyed al-Azhar.

Saudi Arabia even pimped for the Brothers. In the summer of 1971 King Faysal arranged for a delegation of Brothers to travel from Saudi Arabia to try to reconcile with Sadat. The head of the Brotherhood delegation, Sa'id Ramadan, was on the Saudi payroll as director of a Geneva-based organization called the Centre Islamique. Although Sadat and the Brothers never reached an agreement, Saudi Arabia had shown its hand. Egypt's most famous journalist, Mohamed Heikel, chronicled the meeting in his book *Autumn of Fury*.

By the early 1970s no one doubted that Saudi Arabia had become the Brothers' rear base. All along, Washington pretended the Brotherhood didn't exist, and it wasn't like folks there didn't know what it was. Call Hassan al-Banna and the Muslim Brothers what you want, but by today's definition, they were terrorists. Al-Banna's slogan for the Brotherhood left no doubt:

Sleeping with the Devil

God is our purpose, the Prophet our leader, the Qur'an our constitution, jihad our way and dying for God's cause our supreme objective.

Those could have been the final words of the September 11 hijackers.

TO SEE THE EXPLOSIVE EFFECT of mixing Brothers and Wahhabis, look at Osama bin Laden's trajectory into militant Islam. As a student at the King 'Abd-al-'Aziz University, bin Laden fell under the influence of two Muslim Brothers: 'Abdallah 'Azzam and Muhammad Qutb. 'Azzam, a Jordanian Palestinian, had been recruited into the Muslim Brotherhood as a student at Cairo's al-Azhar University. Soon he would become known as the "Amir of Jihad," and by then the only country that would take him was Saudi Arabia, which gave him a teaching job at the university. 'Azzam and bin Laden would spend time together in Peshawar, Pakistan, during the Afghan war.

Qutb was the brother of the Egyptian Muslim Brothers' most extremist militant, Sayyid Qutb. Sayyid did more to radicalize the Brotherhood than anyone. Like some latter-day Ibn Taymiyah, he sold the Brothers on the idea that all Christians and Jews were infidels who deserved to be killed. Egypt executed Sayyid in 1966, but his doctrine lived on. One of bin Laden's brother-in-laws was a fund-raiser for the Muslim Brotherhood.

As far as I can see, the reason Washington wore these blinders—especially to Saudi Arabia, which nurtured the viper at its breast for all these years—was twofold. One, the Brothers were on our side in the cold war, offering us a cheap, no-American-casualties way to fight the Soviet Union. Two, the Saudis were banking our oil. As with any other addiction, we were in no position to challenge the pusher. It felt great until the withdrawal on September 11.

By then, though, addiction had become the wrong metaphor. The Brotherhood was more like a cancer, well established in its host organ but treatable so long as it hadn't spread its tentacles throughout the body. The question was: Had it metastasized? I had begun searching for that answer almost a decade earlier, in as grim a corner of the planet as I ever hope to see.

9 / Trouble in Paradise

Bishkek, Kyrgyzstan—November 1992

THE FADED BLONDE built like a Siberian woodstove was fuming. Every time she tried to escape from behind the Aeroflot counter, a knot of stubborn, broad-faced Kyrgyz peasants blocked her way. With the last flight to Osh scheduled to depart in twenty minutes, they weren't about to move until she handed over their boarding passes. They didn't care that the flight would probably be hours late. They didn't care that handing out boarding passes wasn't her job. And they certainly didn't care that it was her Aeroflot-sanctioned tea break. One thing the Kyrgyz had learned from living on the remote edge of the Soviet empire: Passive resistance was the only way to get your way.

Catching sight of me on the other side of her counter, impatiently waving my own ticket to Osh, didn't improve the Aeroflot lady's mood. My Levi's, T-shirt, and North Face parka pegged me as one more pain-in-the-ass tourist setting off to discover Central Asia. My "first-class" Intourist ticket—the "upgrade" cost the rough equivalent of a New York City subway token—didn't make the slightest impression on her. Neither did my shiny black

American diplomatic passport. She pointed a fat finger at a broken banquette of chairs in the corner of the terminal, which I think was supposed to be Intourist's exclusive waiting lounge. "Wait like everyone else," she said.

I suppose she had seen her share of problems with Western tourists. Ever since Kyrgyzstan opened up, climbers, trekkers, and hunters regularly got lost in the Tien Shan Mountains. Aeroflot or the Kyrgyz air force then had to risk one of their helicopters to rescue them. Then there were the brigands—*basmachi*, as they're called in Russian—who would sometimes kidnap tourists. When that happened, the Kyrgyz army had to deploy troops to free the hostages and drive the *basmachi* back up into the high mountains.

One of the stranger cases I'd heard about involved a car full of Dutch who tried to retrace the ancient Silk Route from Osh to a dusty oasis town in western China called Kashgar. They had all the necessary Chinese visas, but the Chinese guards on the Kyrgyz border apparently had never seen a visa before. Or maybe they were suspicious of the bicycles tied to the top of the Dutchmen's car. Anyhow, the border guards wouldn't let them in. An appeal to Beijing wasn't possible; there were no telephone connections to Beijing. The Dutch had no choice but to turn back. Before they did, though, they slammed shut the giant iron gate that separated China from Kyrgyzstan and locked it with a bicycle chain. No one bothered to cut it for months, or so went the story.

If pressed, the Aeroflot lady probably would have told me I had no business going to Osh. For most of its modern existence, in Czarist and Soviet times alike, Osh was strictly verboten to foreigners. It was a "strategic site," and "diplomats" like me could mean only trouble. It would take a Soviet hand to explain the logic behind putting a hole like Osh off limits, or why the Soviet Union was so paranoid about central Asia. I suppose it was a hangover from the Great Game—the war of shadows Britain and Russia fought in the nineteenth century for control of the region. Russia was convinced that Britain intended to undermine its empire through Central Asia, and Britain thought Russia was trying to do the same thing in India.

Sleeping with the Devil

Britain didn't do anything to help Russia get over its paranoia. During the nineteenth century, the British infiltrated a few missions north of the Amu Darya, the shallow, muddy river that separates Russian Central Asia from Afghanistan. Most of those who crossed into places like Osh stayed a little while, patted themselves on the back for having played and survived the Great Game, and beat a retreat south for the more refined comforts of the subcontinent. Ultimately, the Russians would learn they had more to fear from Islam than they did from the British.

The first serious Islamic uprising against the Soviets in Central Asia occurred in 1918. Trading in a Czarist for a communist yoke was definitely a bad deal for Central Asia's Muslims. A month after their October 1917 victory far to the north, the Bolsheviks sent a detachment to seize the important regional capital of Tashkent. The new commissars began by requisitioning all the food they could lay their hands on and seizing the cotton crop in the name of the people's republic. A famine soon followed that would kill as many as a million Central Asians. In February 1918 Bolshevik troops put down a revolt in the ancient Uzbek caravan city of Kokand, sacking and slaughtering as they went, and the *basmachi* revolt was on.

While the Bolsheviks were occupied by consolidating their victory elsewhere in the Soviet Union, the uprising spread. Victory followed on victory. At its height, the rebellion counted maybe twenty thousand soldiers in its ranks, most of them peasant fighters, all of them Muslims. The end, though, seemed foreordained. The communists outnumbered the *basmachi;* they had heavy weapons; and after the White Russians were defeated, the rebels got the Reds' full attention. By 1920 the *basmachi* had been driven back into the mountains of Tajikistan. That's when Enver Pasha showed up.

Turkey's minister of war during World War I, Enver Pasha fled to Berlin after the defeat of the Central Powers, and then went to Moscow at Lenin's invitation. Lenin wanted to use the charismatic Turk to draw Central Asia's Muslims into the Soviet fold, but as it turned out, Pasha had a grander vision: a pan-Turkic state that would stretch from the Straits of Bosporus to Mongolia. He was only thirty-two.

In February 1922, Pasha captured Dushanbe, the capital of modern Tajikistan. By the end of spring, he had taken control of virtually all of the emirate of Bokhara. In July 1922 the Soviets were forced to react to Pasha's treachery and sent a division south to stop him. It worked. He was killed in battle on August 4 of that year. But the *basmachi* wouldn't be completely snuffed out until 1934. Some of the rebels, it was thought, holed up in the remote mountain valleys of Tajikistan. Most took refuge in Afghanistan. More than a few slipped as far away as Saudi Arabia. Some took up residence in Mecca and became dyed-in-the-wool Wahhabis.

Islamic fundamentalism wouldn't threaten Russian domination of Central Asia again until 1979, but that was a dandy. For millennia, Afghanistan was the main corridor of East–West trade, which meant that it was also subject to almost constant invasion and occupation. Afghanistan's current troubles started in 1973, when a military coup ushered in the nation's first republic, momentarily ending centuries of foreign and tribal rule. Five years later, Soviet-backed leftists seized control of the government in a bloody coup, and the new government immediately signed economic and military treaties with Moscow.

It didn't take long for the Islamic world to react. In March 1979 Muslim fundamentalists seized control of the 17th Division of the Afghan army, headquartered in Herat. The revolt immediately started to spread, promising to infect the rest of Afghanistan. Equally threatening for the Soviets, the new Islamic regime in Tehran seemed ready to fuel the uprising. A militant Islamic government in Kabul was the Soviets' worst nightmare.

They panicked. During an emergency late-night meeting on March 17, Foreign Minister Andrei Gromyko reported to the politburo: "The insurgents infiltrating into the territory of Herat Province from Pakistan and Iran have joined forces with a domestic counter-revolution. The latter is especially comprised of religious fanatics. The leaders of the reactionary masses are also linked in large part with the religious figures." In other words, the Soviet Union was unexpectedly face-to-face with an Islamic jihad. Memories of the *basmachi* revolt hung in the air like a putrid corpse. No one needed to be reminded that *that* revolt had nearly undone the October revolution, or that the Soviet Union's mountainous border with Afghanistan couldn't contain an Islamic tidal wave rolling in from the south.

The situation deteriorated by the day. When it appeared that the government in Kabul couldn't hold on any longer, the Red Army invaded. The first troops crossed the border on Christmas Eve 1979. For the Soviet Union, it turned out to be a mistake of biblical proportions. All its money, soldiers, T-72 tanks, and Mi-24 Hind gunships counted for nothing in stopping Afghans with faith on their side.

Ten years later, as the Soviet Union itself was starting to implode, the last Soviet soldier was driven from Afghanistan. As the politburo had feared, the chaos in Afghanistan sloshed across the border like a backed-up sewer. In 1990 ethnic riots broke out between Uzbeks and Kyrgyz in Osh. More than a thousand people died. The three Soviet republics that shared the Fergana Valley— Kyrgyzstan, Tajikistan, Uzbekistan—put their armed forces on a permanent state of alert, knowing the trouble would spread. In 1991 a twenty-four-year-old Uzbek named Tahir Yuldashev led an Islamic uprising in Namangan, about halfway between Osh and Tashkent. Islamic rebels paraded around thieves and prostitutes, back to front, on donkeys, beating them with whips in front of the mosques. When the uprising was brutally supressed, Yuldashev fled to Afghanistan and formed the Islamic Movement of Uzbekistan. Until the American attack on Afghanistan in October 2001, the IMU conducted a sporadic terrorist campaign against Tashkent, infiltrating cadres through the Fergana.

FOR WASHINGTON, an Islamic resurgence in Central Asia would have been of little interest except for one thing: the region's enormous oil and gas reserves, second only to the Gulf's. The bulk of the oil lies under Kazakstan, while the gas is under Turkmenistan.

At an estimated 260 billion barrels of oil reserves, and with greater gas reserves than all of North America, the Caspian region could keep the U.S. warm and lighted, and our factories humming, for a long time. The only problem was getting it out. Kazakstan and Turkmenistan are out in the middle of the remote, inhospitable, and landlocked Eurasian steppe.

Under the Soviet Union, Central Asia's energy was exported west to Russia and Eastern Europe via an intricate web of pipelines. That had been the rub with Central Asian gas and oil. Nearly all of the pipe it traveled through passed through Russia. The Russians could and did shut down exports at will, which gave them a stranglehold over the countries that owned the energy. Energy has value only when there's a delivery system. Otherwise, it's better left in the ground.

As soon as the Soviet Union collapsed in 1991, Washington decided it could turn Central Asia's energy into a strategic asset. Why not bypass the Russian pipeline system by finding alternative export routes? Doing so would pry Russian's dead hand off the Central Asian states and make them economically independent. In no time, democracy would bloom. Even better in some ways, with the Caspian's 260 billion barrels of oil fully and freely exportable; we wouldn't need Middle Eastern oil. Let Saddam invade Kuwait again. Who cared? For that matter, let him invade Saudi Arabia. On paper, it was a sure winner, if only new pipelines could be worked out.

The Great Game seemed to be back on, but this time with the U.S. squared off against the two largest regional powers: Russia and Iran. Naturally, American oil companies queued up to play. Chevron and Mobil, the biggest participants, bought giant concessions in Kazakstan. Amoco bought a mega-field in Azerbaijan. Unocal, the gutsiest of the American companies, drew up plans for a pair of pipelines across Afghanistan.

Everyone seemed to have conveniently ignored the endless political instability in the region—and the absence of any energy transport grid. How would Chevron, Mobil, and Amoco get their oil out of the Caspian? The safest pipeline route was through Russia to the Black Sea, and from there via tanker to the Mediterranean, but Russia and the Russian mob liked nothing better than black-mailing American oil companies. They charged, on average, three dollars for every ton of oil they put into the system. There was an alternative route to Turkey, but that would have to pass through either Georgia or Armenia, both embroiled in civil wars; Afghan-istan, too, was in the middle of a vicious civil war. It would be a long time before anyone laid five feet of pipe there.

Saudi Arabia, meanwhile, watched in disbelief. It was pure folly to think of Central Asian oil as an alternative to Middle Eastern oil, the Saudis said. Forget the political instability. Just look at the costs. The capital expenses for lifting Caspian Sea oil was roughly six dollars a barrel, while lifting a Saudi barrel cost only one to two. In the oil business, that was not an insignificant split, especially in the early and mid-1990s, when oil was dragging the bottom close to ten dollars a barrel. Throw in the price of building two main oil-export pipelines—adding up to something like $7 billion—and the Caspian Sea made no sense at all, particularly to the Saudis.

The Saudis knew why the oil companies were buying in: It boosted their paper reserves. They could "overbook" all those exotic Caspian Sea reserves, and the average shareholder wouldn't be any the wiser; he wouldn't understand how difficult it would be to get them out. But what Saudi Arabia couldn't figure out was what the United States government was up to. The cold war was over, so who cared whether Central Asia was independent from Russia? Saudi Arabia knew Washington, whether it made economic sense or not, might put its financial weight behind Caspian oil. If the U.S. invested enough money, it might make the fantasy come to life. Even worse in some ways, the Saudis felt jilted. They had spent tens of billions of dollars to finance the Gulf War. The cost was ruinous in a down market for oil, but the U.S. had insisted that the war was necessary to maintain the status quo—to keep Saddam from invading Saudi Arabia and to assure that the House of Sa'ud would remain the world's banker of oil.

Angry at Washington and wary of its motives, the Saudis kept their own finger on the pulse of the Caspian. Delta Oil, associated with Crown Prince 'Abdallah and other powerful Saudis, invested in a concession in Azerbaijan. (Anger at Washington, it should be noted, didn't prevent Delta Oil from enlisting two American partners in the cause. Business is business.) After I left the CIA, I learned that Saudi intelligence under Turki Al Faysal partnered with the Argentine company Bridas to build a gas pipeline from Turkmenistan to Pakistan, passing though Afghanistan. It was the perfect match for Bridas, because Turki had better relations with the Taliban than any Saudi. He'd dumped hundreds of millions of riyals into them.

Black gold, ethnic conflict, Islamic fundamentalism, civil war, Russian irredentism—the Great Game was back on for sure. But who was playing and who wasn't? And what were the rules this time around? That's what I intended to find out.

THE FORTY-MINUTE FLIGHT from Bishkek to Osh gave me a chance to collect my thoughts about what I expected to learn in the Fergana and how. Islamic fundamentalism was waging a war without fronts or faces. Back at headquarters, I had tried to find a picture of the IMU leader, Yuldashev. There wasn't one. How would I know if I was staring him in the face? Worrying about things like that kept me from looking out the airplane window as the Yak-40's right wing passed within spitting range of a 4,875-meter snow-covered peak.

I had a lot of time on my hands. The month before, in October 1992, I had been evacuated from neighboring Tajikistan in the midst of a civil war between ex-Soviet apparatchiks and Islamic fundamentalists. CIA headquarters ordered me back to Washington, where I was supposed to wait until I could go back and reopen the place. Since there was nothing worse than being assigned to headquarters with little to do, I used all the skills of persuasion I'd learned in the agency to convince the head of the Central Eurasian

Sleeping with the Devil

Division, John McGaffin, to let me take a grand tour of Central Asia. He didn't see the problem. He even approved my spending time on my Farsi in Samarkand, the ancient capital of Uzbekistan, home to a succession of conquerers from Alexander the Great to Tamerlane.

A couple of days after he'd signed my travel orders, McGaffin cornered me in the hall. "They speak Farsi in Samarkand?" he asked. I wasn't sure, but I'd read somewhere they did in the fourteenth century. If then, why not now? Things don't change overnight north of the Amu Darya. McGaffin let it pass.

WALKING DOWN THE GANGPLANK and stepping onto the tarmac at Osh, I wondered if my grand-tour idea had been all that smart. It was difficult to decide what was thicker: the putrid cloud of haze, dust, and smog that blocked any view of the Tian Shan, or the utter depression that wafted off the industrial wasteland and the shriveled vegetation that stretched as far as I could see. I now understood how Osh—which means "soup" in Persian—got its name. Any romantic notions I had about the Silk Route instantly evaporated.

Fortunately, my guide was waiting at the airport. A six-foot-six giant, he was standing next to an ancient Zhiguli. On the other side of the Zhiguli was a tiny old man bent at the waist like a broke-open shotgun. It took me a minute to figure out that the old man was the driver. How would he see over the steering wheel?

Ibramov, as I will call the guide, turned out to be a great traveling companion. Although he knew only about six words of English—enough to teach English literature at the local technical college—we got along fine using my Tajik, Russian, and German. More important, he was willing to take me anywhere in the Fergana.

The next morning we set out on an hour's drive to Namangan, supposedly the crucible of Islamic fundamentalism in the region. We motored from mosque to mosque, but no one suspicious was hanging around. Incendiary posters weren't pasted on the walls.

There wasn't any graffiti. Even though it wasn't Friday, the Muslim holy day, there should have been some outward sign of fundamentalism. Instead, the place looked like Osh—listless. I decided to poke around one of the mosques. Before I could get out of the car, though, Ibramov grabbed my arm and pointed at a Lada parked by the sidewalk in front of the mosque. Three men were sitting in the car, looking straight ahead. They weren't talking. The engine was off.

"Let's go," Ibramov said. I didn't object. I'd obtained permission to travel around Kyrgyzstan's part of the Fergana, but we were in Uzbekistan now. The Kyrgyz had no jurisdiction here. "I suggest we go to Kokand," Ibramov said. "There are not so many problems there."

As we drove away, I could see one of the men in the Lada copying down our plate numbers.

Two hours later, Ibramov accompanied me into the only hotel in Kokand with reliably running water. The place was empty except for an Uzbek man dressed in a grease-stained wool suit who occupied one of the two chairs in the lobby. Without standing, he asked what we wanted. When Ibramov pointed at me and said I needed a room, the Uzbek got up and walked over to me. "Passport, please." I noticed his two incisors were gold.

"You don't have permission to visit Kokand," he said, fanning the pages of my passport without bothering to look at them. Obviously, someone had informed him that I was on my way and lacked the proper papers. Technically, I'd broken the law. Although Uzbekistan won its independence in 1991, it never discarded the old Soviet system of requiring passes to visit cities and regions it deemed sensitive. Uzbekistan didn't trust foreigners any more than the Soviet Union had.

The man walked around the reception desk and made a call. Not more than two minutes later, two uniformed militiamen showed up with Kalashnikovs slung over their shoulders. The Uzbek got into an animated conversation with Ibramov. It was all in Uzbek, and I didn't understand a word. The upshot was that Ibramov smiled wanly, shook my hand, and left. I never saw him again.

Sleeping with the Devil

When I went up to my room, the two militiamen followed me and posted themselves outside my door. *This is silly,* I thought. After all, I was traveling on a diplomatic passport. I wasn't indigent, and I certainly didn't look like a *basmachi*. I headed back downstairs to find out what the story was. One of the militiamen followed me.

My Uzbek minder was still there. I asked if I was under arrest.

"No, we are here to protect you. It is very dangerous in the Fergana. The *basmachi,* you know."

"May I take a walk around Kokand this evening?" I asked.

"No. There are too many *basmachi* at night."

Dinner—a bowl of leek soup, a piece of stale bread, and one pockmarked apple—was brought to my room. Somewhere out in the night, presumably, *basmachi* were swarming thick as deer flies. Whether they were plain old brigands or the heirs of the proud Muslim revolutionaries who'd taken on the Bolsheviks, I had no idea.

THE NEXT MORNING my Uzbek minder knocked on my door. "We can visit Kokand this morning," he said.

A Russian-looking man stood behind him, dressed in a suit nearly identical to the Uzbek's. He didn't introduce himself, and I couldn't figure out who he was.

I passed on the Uzbek's offer to tour Kokand's main textile factory and instead asked to visit the main mosque. Ibramov had told me it ran a popular *madrasah*. The Uzbek and the Russian looked at each other and shrugged.

The mosque was built along traditional Central Asian lines, with a tiled cupola. I wandered through it for a while, peering into the empty classrooms, before I found a man of about sixty-five, dressed in flannel robes and the ornate half-round cap that Central Asian clerics wear. He was sitting on the floor, listening to a boy recite a sura from the Qur'an. The boy's Arabic was nearly perfect, but I doubted he understood a word. My two escorts stood in the door, while I sat on the floor and talked to the cleric, or tried to.

The cleric looked at me uncomprehendingly when I greeted him in Tajik. Either he didn't speak Tajik or didn't want to speak it in front of my minders. "I don't understand," he said in Russian.

When I tried Arabic, the cleric's face brightened. In stilted but grammatically flawless Arabic, he asked if I was an Arab. I decided to sidestep that one. If I told him the truth, he would clam up. Even in remote Kokand, they've heard of Langley, Virginia. Besides, I figured my cleric friend would be more willing to confide in me if he thought I was a believer. I told him a parallel truth: that I was from California. He smiled; maybe he thought I was in the movies.

I noticed that my minders were nervous. They were whispering to each other, no doubt because the cleric and I were speaking in a language they couldn't understand. *Pick up the pace,* I told myself.

"Who's paying for these?" I asked, pointing to a stack of new Qur'ans sitting on a table in the corner.

By way of an answer, the cleric got up and brought me one. He opened it and pointed to the stamp on the inside cover, which said it had been donated by the International Islamic Relief Organization, the richest and most active Islamic charity in the world, the same one that was raided after September 11. Now we were getting somewhere. Founded in 1978, the IIRO is a private, independent charity, at least on paper. In fact, it is a Saudi government institution, fully under the control of the royal family. King Fahd's full brother Salman personally approved all important appointments and spending. But it's more than a matter of control: The creation of the IIRO was an important milestone in Saudi Arabia's veer to militant Islam.

Like other charities sponsored by the House of Sa'ud—indeed, like so much of the history of the modern Middle East—the IIRO roots lie deep in the Arabs' humiliating defeat in the June 1967 war with Israel. Although Saudi Arabia hadn't fought in the war, the royal family was soon caught up in the backwash of recriminations. Why hadn't its oil revenues gone to building an army that might have turned the tide of victory against the Israelis? Why had the Al Sa'ud princes been gambling in Monte Carlo when they should have been on the front with other believers? Saudi Arabia was the keeper of the holy shrines of Islam, yet it had sat on the sidelines as Islam was crushed. Sensing this post-1967 resurgence of faith and eager to cover their rear ends, the royal family started flooding charities with money, the IIRO among them.

When Saudi Arabia decided to fund the Afghan *moujahidin* in the early 1980s, the IIRO proved a perfect fit, a money conduit and plausible denial rolled into one. If the IIRO was caught breaking some country's law, or one of its employees strayed and joined a terrorist group, Saudi Arabia could simply disclaim responsibility, a sleight of hand that has spared the royal family a lot of embarrassment over the years.

The IIRO was a backer of Abdul Rasool Sayyaf, the Afghan Muslim Brother it favored in 1980 when it and the United States decided to fund a holy war in Afghanistan. Sayyaf, in turn, had taken under his wing bin Laden and the other young Saudi and Muslim firebrands who came to help drive out the heathen Russians.

Knowing the IIRO was proselytizing in Central Asia was a small but important piece of the puzzle, but what message was it pushing? Was it backing a Central Asian Sayyaf? A new jihad? Or was it only handing out Qur'ans, simply trying to recall Central Asian Muslims back to the faith? My two minders decided it was time to go and motioned me to follow them. I had time to ask my cleric one last question. It had to be a good one.

"Did Saudi Arabia ever send you any of Ibn Taymiyah's works?"

If the Saudis were handing out his works, that meant they were doing more than proselytizing.

"Who?" the cleric asked.

Damn, I thought. I'd fired my best shot and missed. Before I could ask another question, my minders came to drag me away.

On the way to the airport, seated in the backseat of the Uzbek's Lada, I got around to talking with my Uzbek escort and his Russian friend. They were from "the security services," they told me. The Uzbek worked for Uzbekistan's KNB, the successor organization to the old KGB's Second Chief Directorate. The Russian was "from

Moscow," which I took to mean he was some sort of Russian intelligence adviser to the Uzbek KNB.

In a weird way, that was the last piece of the puzzle. If I was reading the signs correctly, this time the big battle would be between Russia's ex–Central Asian regimes and Wahhabi Islam. The Qur'ans donated by the IIRO were only a start, a foothold for a full-fledged jihad. The cleric may not have known about Ibn Taymiyah, but as my plane lifted off from Kokand, I was convinced that one day he would. Where the IIRO was, and Ibn Taymiyah was coming, the Saudis were sure to be lurking behind the curtain.

How about the United States? Was it prepared for what was coming? Well, I was one of a handful of CIA officers to ever visit the Fergana. That ought to tell you something.

WHEN I CHECKED INTO Tashkent the next morning, I told the chief about my visit to the mosque and asked him what he thought the Saudis were up to in the Fergana. He'd been in the country only six months, but he had good Russian and had gotten around a lot.

"I don't have a clue," he said. "Saudi Arabia is not a target. And I haven't been to the Fergana."

He had the same problem I'd had in Beirut when I was cultivating my Muslim Brother Zuhayr Shawish. Without a directive from Langley to look into Saudi fundamentalism in Central Asia, a CIA chief wasn't even supposed to think about it.

"I could ask the Uzbeks," he continued, "but I already know they wouldn't tell me a damn thing. They'd say it was an internal matter, and that would be that."

As for the Uzbeks, I got the distinct impression that they treated militant Islamic fundamentalists the same way the Soviet commissars had treated the *basmachi* revolt: dismissing them as bands of criminals.

I spent a week in Tashkent living in the embassy community. Right away I noticed that survival was on everyone's mind. The housing was lousy. The plumbing never worked. There was always a shortage of gasoline. If there was any time left at the end of the day, the embassy staff was always saddled with some Washington project, like setting up the Peace Corps or teaching the Uzbeks how to operate voting machines, never mind that there hadn't ever been a democratic election in Uzbekistan. In the meantime, no one had any idea what the IIRO and Saudi Arabia were up to in Central Asia.

I NEVER MADE IT to Samarkand to study Farsi. The CIA reopened the Dushanbe office in January 1993, and I was back in business. It wasn't long before the subject of Saudi Arabia raised its head like a maniacal jack-in-the-box.

About three A.M. I heard someone pounding on my door. I couldn't imagine who it was. To get to my office/bedroom, which was permanently lodged in the Oktoberskaya Hotel along with the Russian and Iranian embassies, you had to pass two heavily armed Tajik guards in the lobby. And once you got to the third floor, you were met by a platoon of Russian *spetznatz,* or special forces.

I opened the door to find myself nose-to-nose with the dough-faced local Russian chief intelligence chief. Boris Sergeivich, as I will call him, was stumbling drunk.

"Yop tavaya mat!" he yelled, spittle flying. In Russian, it means "Go fuck your mother."

When I got Boris quieted down, he explained to me why he was so pissy. Earlier that evening, a Tajik Islamic rebel group had crossed the Panj River from Afghanistan and managed to overrun a Russian border post and cut off all the guards' heads.

"It was your tit-sucking Saudi Arabia." Boris's anger had returned. "The goddamn war is over. Tell them to leave us alone."

I couldn't figure out what Saudi Arabia had to do with the attack. It didn't have any troops in Afghanistan, at least officially, and the part of Afghanistan the rebels had crossed from was controlled by a group we assumed took orders from Tehran.

Boris said I was wrong. The rebels were under the command of Rasool Sayyaf's Ittehad-e-Islami, bin Laden's Afghani protector.

I didn't believe that. The Russians seemed to blame everything on Saudi Arabia, from the war in Afghanistan to ethnic fighting between Armenians and Azeris in Azerbaijan. They also accused the Saudis of stoking the Chechen separatists who declared their independence in 1991. Saudi Arabia may have paid for the Afghan war, but that didn't mean it was doing the same thing in Central Asia. Saudi Arabia was our ally; it would have told us if it was conducting a covert campaign in Tajikistan. Naive me.

I played along with Boris. I told him I'd help him find out what Sayyaf was doing, or whether Riyadh had anything to do with the attack. He said something under his breath about trusting the CIA when hell froze over. I pushed him out the door with a bottle of Black Label scotch in each hand.

Two days later, Boris knocked on my door again. He handed me a neatly typed list of names. "You will know who these bastards are," he said. "They're Arabs, and they're all with Sayyaf. They were behind the attack on our border post."

I didn't bother sending the names to headquarters because I wasn't supposed to be coordinating with the Russians. Instead, I sent the names to Islamabad, where Beirut Bill ▆▆▆ was now chief. Bill, I thought, would understand what I was trying to do. And if any place would know about the fundamentalists, it was Islamabad. After all, that was where the Afghan war was run from. Another two days later, Bill sent his reply: He couldn't find anything about Boris's Arabs because we didn't have any agents in Sayyaf's camp.

It was hard to believe. Sayyaf was our creation. We'd helped him set up in Peshawar. He was one of the Peshawar Seven, the original Afghan resistance groups backed by the National Security Council's Special Coordination Committee. Good enough, but you learn in Espionage 101 never to get involved in covert action unless you know for certain what your surrogates are doing. To know that, you need a source in the group. Obviously we didn't have a source in Sayyaf's group, or one who lasted through the Afghan conflict. From a spy's perspective, it was a fatal mistake.

Boris, for one, would have found this incomprehensible. The Soviets never ran a covert campaign unless they controlled it from A to Z. If they asked the East Germans to run a campaign in Africa or South America, they made damn sure they knew what was going on. They never would have trusted the Pakistanis or Saudis to tell the truth.

I avoided Boris for the next few weeks. When I couldn't help passing him in the dim corridor we shared, he smirked as if to say: *See, I told you so.* I'm sure he was convinced we knew what Sayyaf, his master, Saudi Arabia, and the rest of the fundamentalists in Afghanistan were up to. I would have been embarrassed for myself and my country had he learned otherwise.

The attacks on Russian troops along the Tajik border continued until I was transferred out of Dushanbe in 1994, but Boris would never again ask me to trace any names.

THINGS WOULDN'T GET any better. In 1997 Bill Lofgren, the chief of the Central Eurasian Division, which covered the former Soviet Union and East Europe, had borrowed the director's Gulfstream to take a quick tour of Central Asia and the Caucasus. Six stops and God knows how many gallons of vodka later, we still didn't have the answer we had come for: Was militant Islam a threat to the Caspian Sea region or not? No one would say a word about it, even the most senior officials who were presumably authorized to talk about it. It was the same sort of thing as Washington and Saudi Arabia—a consent of silence.

The telling part of the trip came on the return. The morning we were getting ready to fly back to London from Alma-Ata, the pilot filed a flight plan to Tbilisi, Georgia. No problem with that—at first. We were told we could refuel and spend the day touring Tbilisi if we wanted. But as soon as the plane landed, we knew things were going wrong. A gun-toting soldier appeared at the Gulfstream's door and yelled at us to close it back up and stay in the plane. Thirty minutes later, a man in a dirty jumpsuit appeared. He carried a bucket in one hand and a paintbrush in the other. He proceeded to paint a circle around the Gulfstream. As soon as he connected the ends, the border guard with the assault rifle reappeared. "You can get out now, but don't step outside the circle." An hour later, we were fueled up and on our way to London, missing out on our last chance to find out about the Islamic-fundamentalist threat. Ironically, our flight path took us over Georgia's Pankisi Valley, a bin Laden stronghold.

I DIDN'T UNDERSTAND how right Boris had been until 1998, when I came across some Russian documents related to the Chechen war.

Chechnya declared its independence from Russia back in 1991, but it wasn't until 1994 that Russian president Boris Yeltsin moved to bring the wayward child back into the Russian fold. I watched clips of Russian armor and artillery flattening Grozny. I read everything I could about the conflict, but the reporting was sparse. True to form, the CIA didn't have a single source among the Chechen rebels. Other countries in the region, like Georgia and Azerbaijan, claimed to have no idea who was paying for and arming the Chechen rebels. The conflict seemed to go on forever. It had to be costing hundreds of millions of dollars.

After I left the CIA I found my answer in a batch of Russian intelligence reports that drew a convincingly direct link between the Saudi government and the Chechen rebels. It was not a question of Saudi charity money finding its way to the Chechens. One report described how on June 22, 1998, forty Chechens were quietly brought to a secret military camp located seventy-five miles southeast of Riyadh. Over the next four months, they were trained in explosives, hand-to-hand combat, and small weapons. A lot of time was set aside for indoctrination into Wahhabi Islam. Salman, the governor of Riyadh and the full brother of King Fahd, was the camp's sponsor.

If the reports were accurate, Saudi Arabia's critics had it wrong. The country wasn't just committing sins of omission where the extremists and their jihads were concerned. Boris had been right to be so angry—the Saudis were directly sponsoring terrorism. But why?

Part III
Going Down

10/Hard Landing

FOR AMERICAN ARMS MAKERS, Saudi Arabia is an industry subsector all its own, with its own peculiar rules. We buy oil from Saudi Arabia, refine it, and put it in our automobiles, and a certain small percentage of what we pay for it ends up funding terrorist acts against America and American institutions at home and abroad. With the money it earns from oil sales, the Saudi royal family purchases arms from us to protect itself from within and without, but mostly from within. We sell the Saudis those arms knowing that X amount of the purchase price will go to cover the astronomical "commissions" paid to the very few Saudis who control the arms industry, and of that X amount, a smaller Y amount will go to funding Saudi-based groups that intend to do harm to the West, because otherwise, those same groups might do harm back home in the sunny suburbs of, say, Riyadh.

It all sounds a little nuts. But buying armaments not only helps to protect the Al Sa'ud from its own subjects; it's also the easiest way for rapacious Saudi princes to siphon money out of the national treasury. The financial transactions of Saudi Aramco, the national oil company, are still run by Westerners and too transparent to cheat on. That leaves two subsidiary industries, armaments and construction, as the greatest targets of opportunity, and the Bakr bin Laden family gets the lion's share of the graft in the latter. From the U.S. point of view, selling Saudi Arabia its armaments is also the simplest way to make sure that our oil expenditures return to the United States in the form of defense-industry revenues. If that means having to hold our noses at the stink of corruption, well, that's just realpolitik.

The U.S. Arms Export Control Act requires that the executive branch inform Congress of all proposed government-negotiated foreign military sales agreements and direct commercial sales in excess of $14 million. Among the goodies approved for the kingdom in the six years beginning in 1994:

- Upgrades of 1,500 Raytheon AIM-9L missiles and 300 AIM-7M air-to-air missiles. (Ex–CIA director John Deutch sits on the board of Raytheon.)
- Upgrades of 700 GBU-10 Paveway II Laser Guided Bombs.
- A hundred and thirty 90-mm turret weapon systems for integration into light-armored vehicles, 130 M240 machine guns and M2 .50-caliber machine guns, and nearly 170,000 rounds of 90-mm ammunition.
- Maintenance and support of airborne warning and control systems (AWACS), KE-3 aerial refueling tankers, and HAWK and Patriot air-defense systems.
- Upgrades of Raytheon Hawk surface-to-air missiles.
- Five hundred and fifty-six guided-bomb units for the Rockwell GBU-15, and on and on.

But those are just the small-ticket items. In all, ever since then Secretary of State Henry Kissinger set up the arms-for-oil mechanism in the early 1970s, the Saudis have bought upward of $100 billion in U.S.-manufactured fighting machinery and related construction and support, everything from AWACs to Abrams M-1 tanks, fighting vessels, and more. For years upon years, the Saudis have been the world's number-one consumer of American armament and weapon systems.

For every deal, there's a commission; and for every commission, there's a Saudi royal waiting behind the door to take his cut. But there are other ways to get into the till than making a grab. The protocols that govern American foreign military sales to the Saudis call for funds to be taken from the Saudi treasury and placed in a trust fund administered by the U.S. Department of Defense. Specific payments to vendors are then disbursed from the trust fund. All of which might work fine if the Saudis paid their bills on time, but since they habitually don't, an end-run system called reverse collection was set so that money could be paid to the Royal Saudi Air Force and, in theory, simply held there until needed. (Reverse collection is deeply complicated. Imagine a father who decrees that his children can have their allowances only if they meet certain strict criteria, then—because he's rarely around to hand out the money—sets up an allowance account the kids can dip into whenever they declare themselves eligible.)

Because reverse collection essentially takes military purchases off the books, it proved a godsend. Using it, the Saudis have been able to purchase advanced weapons systems, including the electronic reconnaissance Rivet Joint Aircraft, without the knowledge of the U.S. Congress, a clear violation of the intent of the legislation authorizing foreign military sales.

Reverse collection has also sparked individual entrepreneurs. When a shipment of new Saudi uniform pants arrived without belt loops, the Saudis went ahead and reverse-collected $2.1 million to pay the local vendor. One Saudi lieutenant was sufficiently upset by the corrupt disbursement that he tracked the money down. A million dollars actually made it to the vendor. The other $1.1 million simply disappeared into someone's pocket, a little better than par for the course. The American who knew the story about reverse collecting, by the way, worked for the Royal Saudi Air Force under contract with BDM, back when it was a subsidiary of the protean Carlyle Group.

Prince Bandar once estimated to a PBS interviewer that of the roughly $400 billion the Saudis have spent since the early 1970s to create a modern state, maybe $50 billion has been lost to corruption. ("So what?" Bandar memorably told the interviewer. "We did not invent corruption.") Using that ratio as a guide, perhaps $12.5 billion of the $100 billion in armaments purchased from the U.S. has been kicked back to the Saudi royal family in bribes, about $800 million a year. On both sides of the equation, there has been plenty of opportunity to get filthy rich.

IN THE SUMMER of 1992, George H. W. Bush approved the sale of up to seventy-two F-15s to Saudi Arabia, at a total cost of $9 billion, including weapons and ground support. Developed by McDonnell Douglas (now part of Boeing), the multirole fighters could carry over twelve tons of air-to-air and air-to-ground weapons, including Sidewinder and Sparrow missiles and more than 160 bombs on a single run. Although they were barely operational a year earlier, the F-15s had played a role in the first Gulf War, a prime demo run for potential Arab purchasers with a front-row seat to the action.

Early in 1994, before delivery could begin, the Clinton administration approved the sale of up to twenty-five F-15s to the Israelis. (The Saudis' fighters are designated F-15S; the Israelis', F-15I, in case you're keeping score.) For Boeing McDonnell Douglas, this is the sort of drive toward regional arms parity that fuels the bottom line and keeps the factories humming, but the Israelis have more reason than most states to worry about the massive sales of sophisticated weaponry to a government that sits atop a powder keg of Wahhabi-inspired Islamic extremism. As history has proved time and again, arms sales to unstable nations have a way of circling back and biting the seller in the ass. (The same, of course, could be said of CIA help provided to the Taliban when they were Afghan freedom fighters.)

Sleeping with the Devil

Strangely, though, it was a civilian aircraft sale to the Saudis that might have done the most harm to the stability of the kingdom. The contract was inked on October 26, 1995, at the kind of White House Oval Office signing ceremony that usually marks a major piece of legislation or a military or diplomatic pact. With President Clinton looking on along with the chairman of Boeing and the president of McDonnell Douglas, Prince Sultan, the Saudis' second deputy prime minister and minister of defense and aviation (as well as Prince Bandar's father), pledged that Saudia Airlines, whose board he also chairs, would purchase sixty-one jetliners manufactured by Boeing McDonnell Douglas. Included in the purchase were twenty-three long-range 777–200s, five 747–400 passenger jets, four MD-11F cargo planes, and twenty-nine MD-90s, as well as engines from General Electric and International Aero Engines, a joint venture of Pratt & Whitney and Rolls-Royce PLC. At a total price tag that topped $7 billion, the order was the largest single purchase of commercial airliners ever by a Middle East carrier. To celebrate the deal, Defense Secretary William Perry hosted an official dinner for Prince Sultan at Blair House, the official guest residence, a short walk from 1600 Pennsylvania Avenue.

For Bill Clinton, the Saudia contract was the best sort of broadly distributed political windfall. The aircraft would be constructed at Boeing's main facility in Washington State and at McDonnell Douglas in California. The General Electric engines would come from Ohio, the Pratt & Whitney engines from Connecticut. Missouri, Kansas, Arkansas, and Utah also got pieces of the pie. In all, the states represented in the deal stood to cast 122 electoral votes in 1996, out of 538 total votes. In a press release that accompanied the signing, the White House calculated that the Saudi order would provide work for a hundred thousand Americans—this right as the U.S. economy was starting to regain steam after the economic collapse in the final years of the Bush I administration.

Always the campaigner, Clinton had lobbied hard for this one. In February 1993, barely a month in office, he sent Secretary of

State Warren Christopher to Saudi Arabia to pressure King Fahd into buying Boeing. Commerce Secretary Ron Brown followed in May, spending two hours lobbying the king. Clinton got into the act directly in July, asking Prince Bandar to stop by the White House for a tête-à-tête. A month later, Bandar returned from Riyadh with news that the king was inclined to place the entire order with Boeing, rather than splitting it, as previously contemplated, with Europe's Airbus. On October 28, 1994, Clinton met with King Fahd at King Khalid Military City, near the Saudi borders with Kuwait and Iraq, to push the Saudis toward finalizing the arrangement.

Clinton wasn't the only head of state interested in landing the Saudia contract. By the early 1990s, the world market for commercial aircraft was in decline. Jobs and votes were at stake, as were whole industry sectors. Whom the Saudis would buy from, how much they would buy, and what they would pay had become a matter of international significance and intrigue, as well as electoral survival.

Not to be outdone by Christopher, Brown, and Clinton, the French president, François Mitterrand, flew to Saudi Arabia to meet with King Fahd and the royal family and argue the case for Airbus. John Major, then the British prime minister and soon to be the Carlyle Group's man in the Middle East, jumped on the Riyadh shuttle in support of Airbus's corporate partner, British Aerospace. Behind the scenes, both the CIA and the National Security Agency were pressed into service to "sniff out French bribes and generous financing terms," according to a *Washington Post* article. Undoubtedly, the British and the French unleashed their own official snoops and sneaks on the U.S. This was a global stage, and much was at stake.

But it was beneath the surface and away from government offices where the real groundwork was being laid. Every deal with the Saudis involves rake-offs, commissions, theft, bribes, graft. Call it what you want, that's the cost of doing business with our self-styled best friend in the Arab world. Generally, though, the details stay murky, hidden in complicated transactions, protected by the Middle Eastern equivalent of the code of omerta. Not so the Boeing deal. Thanks to a prolonged lawsuit that played its way through the Washington State Superior Court, we have a pretty clear picture of what it takes to land a major contract with the Saudis, and just how far one of America's leading corporate lights was willing to raise its skirts to land a fat chunk of Saudi Arabia's trade.

The case, *Tahir Bawazir v. the Boeing Company and Sheikh Khalid bin Mahfouz,* was filed on June 16, 1998, but its roots go back to the beginning of the decade. As soon as it became evident that Saudia Airlines was looking to update its aging fleet, Boeing swung into action. Business was flat; layoffs, imminent. High inflation and recession, in the U.S. and elsewhere, were causing customers to rethink their needs and, in some cases, cancel or delay existing orders. Just as bad, the company was about to roll out its wide-body 777 line without sufficient customers to pay for the launch.

All Saudi airline purchases, military or commercial, must be approved by the royal family, and Boeing executives knew from previous experience that meant they would need a human conduit to the king and his entourage, including Prince Sultan. The search for a well-positioned consultant led the airplane manufacturer to Khalid bin Mahfouz. At the time Mahfouz was serving as deputy general manager and chief operating officer for the National Commercial Bank, one of Saudi Arabia's largest financial institutions. (The Mahfouz family was the majority shareholder in NCB.) More important, Khalid bin Mahfouz enjoyed a reputation in Saudi Arabia as "banker to the king," an invaluable entree.

Mahfouz met with Boeing executives about the Saudia deal in 1991. To allay the Americans' fear that his global financial holdings would distract him from the work at hand, Mahfouz agreed to form a partnership with someone who could oversee the day-to-day work the consulting relationship required. That someone turned out to be Tahir Bawazir, a Yemeni residing in Saudi Arabia. The Mahfouz clan had multiple business relationships with his family, going back several decades.

In March 1992 Boeing approved the team and signed the first of a series of one-year consulting agreements. Compensation would be on a purely contingent basis: a percentage commission to be calculated on the price at delivery of the aircraft—at least 5 percent of the total sales price, court documents suggest, more likely in the 10- to 12-percent range, the benchmark for such deals with the Saudis.

Not long after that agreement was inked, Khalid bin Mahfouz began to have troubles, and we're leaving aside his close links to royal charities whose money may have ended up with bin Laden, al Qaeda, and other terrorist organizations. Among Mahfouz's holdings was a major stake in the Bank of Credit and Commerce International, the soon to be infamous BCCI. In July 1991 a New York grand jury indicted the bank, four of its affiliates, and two officers for fraud. A related indictment came down a year later for Mahfouz, and a warrant was issued for his arrest. Almost simultaneously, the United States Federal Reserve Board filed a civil complaint against Mahfouz charging that he violated federal banking laws. On July 8, 1992, U.S. District Judge Kimba Wood issued an order prohibiting the sheik from "withdrawing, transferring, removing, dissipating, or disposing of assets or other property which he owns or controls . . . within the jurisdiction of the United States." Boeing, among others, was informed of the order and instructed that any proceeds from its consulting agreement with Khalid bin Mahfouz would be subject to attachment.

Undeterred by the fact that its lead consultant on the Saudia deal was under indictment, unable to visit the United States for fear of arrest or to move his assets out of or around the country, and deeply embroiled in a global financial scandal, Boeing renewed the consulting agreement in May 1993 and continued to renew it annually for four more years. Clearly, the Boeing commission, if it was ever to be paid, wouldn't be based on time spent on the job. Just as clearly, Boeing knew what it had hired bin Mahfouz for.

In December 1993 Mahfouz paid about $225 million to settle U.S. claims against him and another $245 million to settle a similar set of problems in Europe. In both instances, he was not required to admit any wrongdoing. By then he had other issues to worry about. According to Bawazir's suit, a senior member of the Saudi royal family had begun pressuring Mahfouz in the spring of 1993 to withdraw from the deal so that another member of the royal family could take his place—and the commission after the deal went through. Bawazir contends in his suit that he, not Mahfouz, crafted the strategy that held off the royal interloper; he, not Mahfouz, did virtually all the work; he, not Mahfouz, kept the whole deal alive.

All of that is easy to believe. Khalid bin Mahfouz would have been busy enough with his own vast holdings, even without the BCCI albatross around his neck; and Saudi royals are famous for swooping in on commoners' business when the pickings get rich. Whether Mahfouz stiffed Tahir Bawazir out of his fair share of the commission once the Saudia deal went through—that's the basis of Bawazir's suit—is unclear. The Superior Court of Washington refused to rule on the merits of Bawazir's case, noting simply that Washington didn't have jurisdiction to decide the matter. What the records do show is that by the time the matter made it to court, Boeing had sent Mahfouz over $15 million in commissions, his share of the earnest money the Saudis sealed the deal with. What seems almost certain is that much more was to follow. I've seen the figure $700 million bandied about, but rumor in both America and Saudi Arabia has it that royal Saudi fixers along with bin Mahfouz pocketed a cool $1 billion on the deal.

Boeing, in any event, was happy with the services rendered. When Khalid bin Mahfouz flew to Seattle on May 24, 1994—after he was able to enter the U.S. legally again—he landed at Boeing Field, where he was met by CEO Frank Shrontz and others and taken on a tour of the company's 777 factory. The politicians were happy, too. Tom Foley, then a congressman from Spokane and speaker of the House, hailed the Saudia sale as "a great day for the country." Clinton touted the domestic jobs the deal would support. Indeed, there was only one small problem with the whole rosy arrangement: The Saudis couldn't afford it.

ON NOVEMBER 13, 1995, eighteen days after the Boeing-Saudia pact was inked at the White House, a car-bomb explosion outside a U.S. training facility in Riyadh killed seven people, including five Americans, and injured forty-two. The explosion ripped the front from a building where nearly four hundred Americans had been training the Saudi National Guard to use weapons purchased from U.S. manufacturers. A group calling itself the Islamic Movement for Change took credit for the attack. Subsequently, the Saudis arrested dozens of suspects. On May 31, 1996, it executed four of them, although there remained some doubt about their guilt. Amnesty International accused Saudi Arabia of taking advantage of the bombing to get rid of political opponents. The FBI had wanted to talk to the four before they were executed, but the Saudis said no. Without a thorough, unbiased investigation, no one could be sure Osama bin Laden was not behind the attack.

The chances are close to zero that the bombing had anything to do with the Boeing pact, but the timing of the two didn't go unremarked. Bin Laden was motivated by such contracts. He accused the royal family of sacrificing Islam—the sanctity of Saudi Arabia, the home of Islam's two holy cities—for money, bribes, dirty deals. If bin Laden wasn't behind the bombing, he still applauded it.

Saudi Arabia operates the world's most advanced welfare state, a kind of anti-Marxist nonworkers' paradise. Saudis get free health care and interest-free home and business loans. College education is free within the kingdom and heavily subsidized for those who study abroad. In one of the world's driest spots, water is almost free. Electricity, domestic air travel, gasoline, and telephone service are all available at far below cost. For citizens of a basically third-world country, Saudis travel first class—so first class that many of the kingdom's brightest, the best educated, and in theory most prepared for the work world are reluctant to do any work.

About a quarter of Saudi Arabia's population, and over a third of all those aged fifteen to sixty-four, are foreign nationals, allowed into the kingdom to do the dirty work in the oil fields, to be domestics, but also to program computers and manage the refineries. Seven in ten of all jobs in Saudi Arabia—and closer to 90 percent of all private-sector jobs—are filled by foreign laborers simply because the Saudis won't do them, or are otherwise trained and inclined.

Among males, the Saudis have an admirably high literacy rate, especially for a country that was inhabited mostly by nomadic tribesmen only three generations back. About 85 percent of Saudi men age fifteen and older can read and write, as opposed to fewer than 70 percent of Saudi women of the same age. But because so much of the Saudi education system has been entrusted to Wahhabi fundamentalists, its products are generally ill-prepared to compete in a technological age or a global economy. Reportedly two out of every three doctorates earned in Saudi Arabia are in Islamic studies. Domestic doctorates in computer science, engineering, and other secular skills are rarer than hens' teeth.

That's problem one. Younger Saudis are being educated to take part in a world that will exist only if the Wahhabi jihadists and their Muslim Brother allies can succeed in turning back the clock a few centuries. In an increasingly open world, rank-and-file Saudis see events through an increasingly narrow lens. Western news is censored and often simply banned. The Saudis have pioneered the use of Internet filters and blocks. Most Saudis are limited to local newspapers and TV like al-Jazeera, through which Osama bin Laden has chosen to distribute his communiqués.

Problem two is common to developing nations: demographics. There are way too many young Saudis with nothing better to fill their hours than sitting around the mosque or watching al-Jazeera. Saudi Arabia possibly has one of the highest birth rates in the world outside Africa—approximately 37.25 births for every thousand citizens in 2002, almost exactly twice the birth rate in archenemy Israel. Almost one in ten Israelis is sixty-five or older; 97 percent of all Saudis are sixty-four or younger, and half the population is under eighteen. Leave aside the implications for regional security in those numbers (and for the Israelis, they are vast, since the Saudi birth rate and age distribution are mirrored in Palestine and elsewhere); the presence of so many people of working age, and especially so many ready to enter the workforce, places enormous pressure on an economy that is no longer capable of absorbing those who want to work while providing sustenance for those who would rather contemplate original intent in the Qur'an. Middle classes stabilize society. Saudi Arabia's is falling apart at the very moment it should be forming and solidifying. "Something unexpected happened," a former Western diplomat who had served in Riyadh told *Time* magazine. "Instead of this wonderful utopia, where young men were attracted to academia to learn about Islam, you got thousands of religious graduates who couldn't find jobs."

That gets us to problem three: The world's most advanced welfare state is predicated on the oil prices of the mid- and late 1970s and early 1980s, when the system was instituted, not on the oil prices that have prevailed since the mid-1980s and beyond. In 1981, when the entire kingdom was in effect put on the dole, oil was selling at nearly $40 a barrel, and per capita income was $26,000. A decade later, just before Iraq invaded Kuwait, refiners were able to buy oil for about $15 a barrel. The Gulf War spiked prices back up to about $33 a barrel, but by 1994, when Bill Clinton was leaning on Riyadh to do business with Boeing, oil was selling for $12.50 a barrel. As of 2001, a barrel of oil fetched in the very low twenties, and per capita income had sunk to below $10,000 just as the Saudi baby boom was beginning to achieve its majority—a classically disastrous combination for social harmony.

Because roughly 85 percent of Saudi Arabia's total revenues are oil-based, every dollar decline in the price of a barrel of oil translates to about a $3 billion loss to the Saudi treasury. From there, the math is easy. In the early 1980s the kingdom boasted a cash reserve on the order of $120 billion. By 1994 the reserve had shrunk to about $15 billion. (Cash reserves as of the start of 2003 are estimated to be about $21 billion.) A year earlier, Saudi

Arabia had secured a $4.5 billion line of credit from J. P. Morgan to help cover its share of the cost for Operation Desert Storm. As Clinton was working overtime to get the kingdom to commit to the airline deal with Boeing, the Saudis were stretching out payments to Boeing McDonnell Douglas and others for military jets and equipment.

For Bill Clinton, as for virtually every other American politician dependent on keeping the Saudi cookie jar filled to the brim, Riyadh's necessary course of action seemed obvious: PMO, pump more oil. To ease the burden, the U.S. Export-Import Bank agreed to guarantee low-interest loans of over $6 billion. (The Ex-Im Bank sometimes seems to exist solely to provide bridge loans for oil nations so that American corporations can be paid in a timely fashion.) But robbing Peter to pay Paul wasn't as easy as it looked because there was yet another demographic issue to contend with: the population explosion in the House of Sa'ud.

The royal family kept growing by leaps and bounds—a prince will have multiple wives and sire forty to seventy children during a lifetime of healthy copulation—while the resources to support that growing population were shrinking. Young royals were pushing up from below, chafing against a leadership that was slipping into its high seventies and eighties. The incapacitated King Fahd turned seventy-nine in 2002; Crown Prince 'Abdallah was seventy-eight. Many of the most active court intriguers were in their seventies. That, too, is a formula for social instability, though at a higher level of society.

Absent the survival skills their great-grandfathers had grown up with in the desert, far more familiar with camel's-hair coats than with camels, the younger generation of princes, princelets, princelings, and other royals occupied itself increasingly with dissipation and fringe criminal activities, muscling in on honest shopkeepers and hoping for a shot at the big time. Locked in an increasingly fin de siecle mentality—this game can't last forever!—the older royals grabbed for everything they could get from a steadily shrinking pie. Everything we heard in Washington portrayed a royal family obsessed with gambling, alcohol, prostitution, parties, and the "commissions" and other considerations to afford their vices.

Meanwhile, the numbers game sat out there like some huge Islamic buzzard staring hungrily into the window of the royal palace. Already, the House of Sa'ud stood at thirty thousand members. Simple math and average screwing suggested that number would double in another twenty or thirty years, maybe much more. What would the barrel price of oil have to be in the year 2025 to support even the most basic privileges Saudi royals had come to enjoy? Once there were sixty or a hundred thousand royals, would there be a free seat left on Saudia Airlines for a mere commoner who wanted to fly out of Riyadh or Jedda? Reformers among the royal family talk about cutting back the perks, but that's a hard package to sell.

SOME OTHER NATION faced with shrinking revenues, heavy obligations, and a platinum-plated resource such as the planet's largest known oil reserve might go to the World Bank for a loan, to tide things over until the price of oil rose or the books could get balanced—no one is suggesting imminent bankruptcy in the Saudis' case—but the World Bank demands at least a modicum of transparency in its dealings. Saudi Arabia would have to open its books to outside inspection, and that would risk revealing to its own populace how many billions of dollars in national revenues are being siphoned off by the House of Sa'ud.

How, for example, to explain that $7.2 billion for the Boeing commercial jets and accessories? Accounting has become more creative all around the world, but someone would be bound to notice that at least 10 percent of the purchase price the Saudis had agreed to pay Boeing disappeared in commissions. Follow the money even partway, and it would soon be obvious in which direction the money flowed: from the royal treasury to Khalid bin Mahfouz and others, then back to the royals. Bin Mahfouz also was forced to put some into Sa'ud-sponsored charities, and who knew what happened to it from there.

Officially, military expenditures consume 13 percent of Saudi Arabia's gross domestic product. Throwing in off-budget military spending, the total is much, much higher. In Israel, a nation in a constant state of warfare, armed to the teeth and surrounded by enemies on every side, military expenditures claim only 9 percent of GDP. If the books were opened up, someone would begin to wonder why the Saudis were spending so much more of their GDP on weaponry than the Israelis, especially when the U.S. protects the Saudis from outside enemies. For decades the Saudi royals and their subjects have followed their own "don't ask, don't tell" policy, though such disciplines are a lot easier when there's no end to the money.

A second approach would be to bite the bullet, heed the old guns-and-butter lessons, and tighten the belt. But this path, too, is fraught with peril. Cut back on the butter, and you violate the social contract that has allowed the Al Sa'ud to govern despite the ruling family's deviation from the theocratic principles of the Wahhabis. Thus the welfare state continues. Thus the mosque schools. Thus the kingdom is now dotted with state-of-the-art hospitals that would provide excellent free care if only the funds existed to staff and open them.

If you cut back on the guns, you risk the wrath of your American protectors; the British, who are also major suppliers of arms and armaments (John Major, please call home); and the whole complicated web of private and public Western interests that you worked so long and hard to build up and maintain. You also piss off some of the most powerful members of your own ruling clan, who depend on the commissions from arms sales and ancillary activities—base building and the like—to support their harems, castles, jets, yachts, warehouses full of suits, and so on.

That leaves only one other choice: Continue to exhaust the treasury and run up national debt by buying guns and providing butter, placate the jihadists in whatever ways you can (money;

sanctuary; a network of mosque schools for breeding the next gen-eration of terrorists, some of whom will undoubtedly want to cut your throat; training camps for Central Asian adventurers; and so on), and pray to Allah every chance you get that the moment of inevitable reckoning will not come soon. That appears to be the path the ruling family has chosen.

In 1979, 127 Saudi troops and 117 Saudi insurgents died in a pitched two-week battle after Wahhabi fanatics seized the Grand Mosque at Mecca. The insurgents carried the same message that Wahhabi clergy are preaching in the mosques today: The House of Sa'ud is defiling Islam. (As one Saudi diplomat said memorably in the wake of 9/11, "What shocks me most is why they hit America and not us.") King Khalid was on the throne when the Grand Mosque was seized. Not anxious to duplicate his experience, King Fahd gave $25 billion to expanding and modernizing the holy shrines at Mecca and Medina, and billions more to the new univer-sities that are turning out the Islamic scholars who have no jobs waiting other than agitating people against the West and their immediate benefactor.

The massive public-works projects at Mecca and Medina had an immediate financial beneficiary: the Bakr bin Laden family, which oversaw the construction and restoration and pocketed bil-lions in payments and commissions, a portion—maybe a large one—of which undoubtedly found its way to cousin Osama, al Qaeda, and other violent fundamentalist groups. That's the way things work in Saudi Arabia today: It's an end game. The only ques-tion is when does the end come.

The West and the United States especially have left the Al Sa'ud little choice. While most Saudi royals look the other way and hope the future never comes, Washington fiddles and pretends Riyadh won't burn, watching passively as wealthy Saudis channel hundreds of millions of dollars to radical groups in hopes of buying protection. Washington pretends that all the loudspeakers in all the mosques throughout all the kingdom that are blaring out their messages of hate against the West haven't been paid for with contributions from the royal family that America so readily declares to be its best friend and ally in the Middle East. America welcomes leading royals like Prince Salman to our shores even as we know that he controls distributions from the International Islamic Relief Organization with an iron hand and strongly suspect that the IIRO played a leading role in funding the terrorists who tried to blow up the World Trade Center over eight years before al Qaeda, another IIRO beneficiary, succeeded.

Leading American corporations like Boeing McDonnell Douglas hire and rehire indicted Saudis to represent their interests so they can land the deals that will pay the commissions back in Saudi Arabia that will further erode the budget and thus further divide the ruling class and the underclass. Former CIA directors serve on boards that have to hold their noses to cut deals with Saudi companies because that's business, that's the point of entry, that's the way it's done. Ex-presidents, former prime ministers, onetime senators and members of Congress and Cabinet members walk around with their hands out, rarely slowing down because most of them know that this charade can go on only so long. The trick is to get on that last plane loaded with gold before the SAM launchers are set up around Riyadh International. The status quo is too compelling, the rewards too great to do otherwise.

Was John O'Neill, the former head of counterterrorism for the FBI who died in the 9/11 attack on the World Trade Center, quashed because he refused to kowtow to the Saudis, their oil, and its American Fifth Column? I honestly don't know. I've read the stories: how the State Department barred O'Neill from entering Yemen, even though he was heading up the investigation into the terrorist attack on the U.S.S. *Cole*. O'Neill knew he was being stiffed by both State and the Saudis, and when he started to complain, it wasn't long before the knives came out. FBI management started leaking his personnel file to the press. Realizing he was outgunned, he retired and took a job as chief of security for the World Trade Center. (The irony never stops in these matters.) When I met O'Neill, I knew right away he was someone who was ready to go off message and take on official Washington. If I'd known what I know

now, I could have told him that by violating the consent of silence, he would only end up signing his own death warrant.

Back in 1997, during my waning months with the CIA, I tried to get some twenty-something staffer on the National Security Council to attend to what I'd seen in the Fergana Valley and Dushanbe and Kokand: The U.S. was closing its eyes while Muslim extremists set up shop in the very places we most needed to stop them—the oil-rich former Soviet states of Central Asia. I was ignored, of course. The only thing the NSC had its eye on was Caspian oil. Big Oil had what amounted to a permanent seat on the NSC in the Clinton administration, and having cut its deals with the Saudis and formed partnerships to exploit the energy resources of Central Asia, it didn't want my message anywhere within hearing of the White House. I can't imagine Big Oil's NSC seat has been any less secure during the tenure of Condi Rice, the former Chevron board member and intimate of the Bush family and its oil-man buddies going back two decades.

What Big Oil wants more than anything else is a stable apple cart. That's what nearly everyone who counts wants, but this isn't just about the apple cart. It's not just about whether Henry Kissinger's client base takes a beating, or the Carlyle Group partners have to put up in a Holiday Inn in Riyadh instead of a $4.6 billion palace on the outskirts, or Colin Powell can't go back to hawking Gulfstream jets once his State Department gig is done. It's not just about the Clinton people, not just about the Bush people. Saudi Arabia is more and more a breathtakingly irrational state—a place that spawns global terrorism even as it succumbs to an ancient and deeply seated isolationism, a kingdom led by a royal family that can't get out of the way of its own greed. Is this the fulcrum we want the global economy to balance on?

11/Kiss It Good-bye

I F I HAD TO PICK a single day when the wheels started flying off
Saudi Arabia, it would be November 29, 1995, when King Fahd
suffered his near-fatal stroke. It was clear to those close to him that
he would never again rule Saudi Arabia. But since he was clinically
alive, Crown Prince 'Abdallah couldn't take over.

Without a king, Saudi Arabia drifted into chaos. The proof was
everywhere. Royal corruption turned to theft on a scale never seen
in Saudi history. Government finances went into a free fall. Wahhabi militants, all adherents of Osama bin Laden's violent interpretation of Islam, were off the reservation. The government in Riyadh
stopped any meaningful cooperation with Washington on terrorism.
And Washington did what it always did when it came to Saudi Arabia—pretended nothing was wrong. It even used the opportunity of
Fahd's stroke to extort more money from the kingdom.

AS SOON AS the royal family heard about Fahd's stroke, it went to
battle quarters. From all over Riyadh came the *thump-thump* of
helicopters and the sirens of convoys descending on the hospital

where Fahd had been taken. Among the first to arrive was his clos-est family—his fourth and favorite wife, Jawhara, and Azouzi. Fahd had come to depend on Jawhara, and Azouzi was the apple of his father's eye. Fahd doted on him and indulged him in everything. Everyone had heard the stories about Azouzi riding a Harley-Davidson around his father's palace, chasing servants and smash-ing furniture. Most of the Al Sa'ud found the king's indulgence strange. Azouzi was pimply, craven, and a bit slow. But Fahd's favorite soothsayer had reportedly told him that as long as Azouzi was by his side, the king would have a very long, fulfilling life. Azouzi was his father's good-luck charm.

Next to arrive were Fahd's full brothers—Defense Minister Sul-tan, Interior Minister Na'if and Governor of Riyadh Salman. To outsiders, they were a tight bunch. Their mother, who was from the Sudayri clan, had taught them from an early age that they would have to stick together or risk being elbowed out by the other forty or so sons of Ibn Sa'ud. They took the lesson to heart, and although they did not particularly like each other, they always closed ranks when the going got tough. The pillars of Fahd's rule since he became king in 1982, the brothers all arrived at the hospital about the same time.

Other princes hurried to the hospital, too, from all over the kingdom and the rest of the world. You could see private executive jets lined up at Riyadh's airport, wingtip to wingtip. They couldn't get anywhere near Fahd, but by being close, they could pick up more reliable news and, just as important, demonstrate their fealty. Fahd's health wasn't a minor question for them. Most of them lived off his largesse—royal stipends, which ran as high as $270,000 a month, to as many as twelve thousand people. The recipients knew they were breaking the treasury. Would Crown Prince 'Abdallah cut back their funds or even eliminate them? They had to stick around to find out.

As soon as it was clear that Fahd would live, his full brothers were on the phone with doctors in the United States and Europe. Their questions seemed bizarre: What would it take to keep Fahd's heart beating and his body warm? They didn't seem to care whether he would recover his mental capacities or what kind of life he would have; they merely wanted to keep him clinically alive, and money wasn't a problem. If necessary, they told the doctors, they would lease as many Boeing 747 cargo jets as needed to bring in mobile hospitals and medical teams.

The doctors couldn't understand the desperation to keep Fahd alive, but then again, they didn't understand the politics of the kingdom. What the family knew and the doctors didn't was that Crown Prince 'Abdallah was out there somewhere in the desert, a wolf ready to rip through the flock as soon the shepherd was dead. The only way to keep him at bay was to keep Fahd's heart beating and his brain waves measurable, however faintly, for as long as possible—even, God willing, until after 'Abdallah died.

'Abdallah had always been the odd prince out. For a start, his mother was from the Shammar tribe, traditional rivals of the Al Sa'ud. Ibn Sa'ud married her to cement a truce with the Shammar, but though the Shammar inside Saudi Arabia were now all loyal subjects, 'Abdallah was still mistrusted by Fahd's full brothers. Almost alone in the top tier of the royal family, 'Abdallah had consciously chosen the way of the desert, turning his back on the palatial luxuries of Riyadh, Jeddah, and Ta'if. He never went to Europe on vacation. He preferred, when he could, to spend his time in a tent, drinking camel's milk and eating dates. He interspersed his conversation with peculiar Bedouin turns of phrase and aphorisms. All of his children were raised according to the customs of the desert, a rough egalitarianism and a vow of poverty. Maybe 'Abdallah's worst heresy was to forbid his sons from the fat commissions that so many of the royal offspring were scrambling after.

The Al Sa'ud hated being reminded that they had abandoned their Bedouin roots, but what they hated still more was that 'Abdallah wanted to cut back royal corruption and perks. 'Abdallah had made no secret that when he became king, he would put an end to their thieving. It had become completely out of hand. Aping the senior members of the family, the lesser princes had fantastic expectations of the way they should live, and their stipends didn't cut it. The third-generation princes were getting something like $19,000 a month, a fraction of their needs. It cost $1 million a year to keep even a modest yacht on the French Riviera. What were they supposed to do?

In order to make ends meet, they were getting into nastier and nastier business, from stealing property to stealing state assets, from selling immigrant visas to selling heroin. One trick they'd discovered was borrowing money from a private bank and simply refusing to pay it back. It wasn't like the Sa'ud had any built-in discipline or sense of shame. There were so many princes that they didn't even know one another.

For a while it looked as if 'Abdallah might get his way even before becoming king. In the mid-1990s, when Saudi Arabia was facing catastrophic financial difficulties, he persuaded Fahd to appoint a handful of reformist ministers. 'Abdallah had them zero in on property seizures. The practice had become so widespread that it was completely alienating Saudi Arabia's traditional merchant and fledgling middle classes. A prince would walk into a restaurant, see that it was doing well, and then write out a check to buy the place, usually well below market price. There was nothing the owner could do. If he resisted, he'd end up in jail.

The senior princes used their government positions to do the same thing on a much grander scale. One would pick out a valuable piece of property—maybe a particularly good location for a shopping mall, or a piece of land he knew was needed for a new road—then order a court to condemn it in the name of the state and have the king award it to him. The money involved was staggering, and the practice was becoming more flagrant. Senior princes had started to rely on it to keep up with their bloated personal budgets. So the senior princes united and started to pick off 'Abdallah's reformist ministers one by one.

The first to fall was 'Ali Sha'ir, in 1994. Taking his ministerial duties and 'Abdallah's reform campaign seriously, Sha'ir tried to block a deal engineered by Prince Talal, who had arranged for a court to seize a particularly valuable piece of property owned by a prominent businessman. Talal naturally screamed bloody murder and denounced Sha'ir for having deprived him of his "God-given" rights. He immediately enlisted the governor of Riyadh, Salman, and Interior Minister Na'if. Unable to withstand the pressure, Fahd let Talal have his property and sacked Sha'ir.

In 1995 the same thing happened to the minister of municipal and rural affairs, Muhammad ibn 'Abd-al-'Aziz Al Shaykh, when he tried to prevent a similar seizure by one of Sultan's sons. Al Shaykh confided in a friend that "the only land the royal family had not reached to grab was the moon." Sultan went crazy. He didn't care so much about his son being out of some money, but he could see how far 'Abdallah intended to take his reforms. One day it was his son; the next day it would be him. 'Abdallah lost, and Al Shaykh was fired.

Sultan was absolutely right about being in 'Abdallah's sights. For the crown prince, the crooked property deals were a small piece of the tapestry of corruption. The off-budget deals were the bigger pieces, bankrupting the country, and no one was more up to his ears in them than Prince Sultan.

With off-budget spending, revenue from oil sales went directly to special accounts, bypassing the Saudi treasury. The money was then used to pay for pet causes, from defense procurement to construction projects. With no government audits or any sort of accountability, commissions and bribes were enormous.

The most notorious off-budget deal became known as the Yamama project, after the Riyadh palace it was signed in. The deal, which dates back to 1985, called for British Aerospace to trade Saudi Arabia forty-eight Tornado fighter airplanes for six hundred thousand barrels a day of oil, but it was not a onetime deal. Yamama allowed for upgrades of hardware, spare parts, and so on. According to BAE's publicity flacks, the trade was a good deal all around— British Aerospace had an assured market for its hardware, and Saudi Arabia for its oil. But Yamama was a huge commission-generating machine. British Aerospace overcharged for its hardware and spare parts, with the difference going to commissions. Most of the commissions went to Sultan, his family, and a legion of middlemen. Some estimated the commissions from Yamama went as high as 45 percent.

Needless to say, Fahd received his consideration. Since he didn't want his hands dirtied by the money, he let Jawhara's brothers and half brothers handle it for him. The Ibrahims, as they were called, were good at it. They had been raking off commissions unseen for much of the kingdom's history. Through the 1980s and early 1990s, if you wanted an arms deal, you had to see the Ibrahims. If your construction company was ailing and you needed to be cut in to some government public-works project, you went to see the Ibrahims.

Normally, facts about the Ibrahim deals are hard to come by. But on December 12, 1997, 'Abd-al-'Aziz Al Ibrahim brought legal action against Rolls-Royce in London, claiming that the company, which had supplied the engines for the Tornados, had reneged on a commissions agreement with his own firm, Aerospace Engineering Design. Like the Boeing suit, this one makes for fascinating reading if you're interested in how corruption works in the Middle East.

For 'Abdallah, the issue wasn't so much who got what out of Yamama. He just wanted the money—the revenue from the six hundred thousand barrels a day—put back under treasury control so it would be harder for the jackals to get at it. In September 1996 'Abdallah thought he had a chance to do that. With all the rake-offs, Yamama had become an intolerable burden on Saudi finances. By early 1996 Saudi Arabia was no longer able to top off the fund from oil revenues, and British Aerospace was forced to borrow $400 million to keep Yamama solvent. Still, Yamama was a bad deal for the Saudis: They were effectively getting a lot less for their oil; and worse, one day they would have to pay back British Aerospace. But they didn't dare pull out. Doing that would screw up the Challenger 2 tank deal—another British Aerospace package they wanted to slip into the Yamama folder. It was an infernal cycle. No Yamama. No new tank deal. No new commissions. If Yamama was going down, 'Abdallah would have to muscle it through every step of the way.

Sleeping with the Devil

Initially, 'Abdallah signed an order to Saudi Aramco to halve the money going to Yamama. That failed. Then, during a cabinet meeting on September 5, 1996, 'Abdallah tried to get the ministers to vote Yamama out. Sultan put up a staunch defense. Since he couldn't argue that hundreds of millions in commissions would be lost—exactly what 'Abdallah wanted stopped—Sultan defended Yamama by arguing that Saudi forces were too dependent on British hardware to change. Sultan also said that if Yamama was canceled, Saudi Arabia would have to rely even further on the United States for weapons, which was politically unacceptable.

At the end of the day, Sultan got to keep Yamama, and Yamama continued to sap Saudi Arabia's finances. By June 1997 Sultan was putting pressure on the Saudi International Bank to come up with $473.1 million to top off Yamama once again. His loan application probably didn't mention that the fund needed help because Sultan was bleeding it dry.

Another off-budget project that 'Abdallah wanted back under treasury control was the expansion of the Two Holy Mosques project. This sweetheart deal involved tearing down and rebuilding the old Medina and Mecca mosques. As with Yamama, the $25 billion allocated came from the direct sale of oil. The bin Laden family was responsible for construction and took care of bribes paid to royal family members who ensured the funding never stopped; it also took care of the kingdom's American friends, particularly American construction companies with clout in Washington. York supplied the largest air conditioner in the world for the project.

By the mid- to late 1990s, the total amount of oil going to off-budget programs was about a million barrels a day, a sixth of Saudi Arabia's exports. At current prices, that meant Saudi Arabia was hemorrhaging something like $30 million a day. With the money out from under Saudi Aramco control, anyone with enough clout could pillage as much as he wanted. That's what happened with Old Mecca. Key government ministers and their Wahhabi allies would decide that one more part of the historic site needed to be torn down and rebuilt. The government then would order Aramco to put aside, say, $100 million, and the royal family would send a check to the Bakr bin Laden group, commissioning the work. But rather than have the full $100 million go to construction, somewhere on the order of 90 percent went back to the senior princes, charities, and Wahhabi clerics. Everybody walked away a winner. Well, almost everybody. The average schmuck on the street didn't get a penny, but he could always go to Mecca or the other thousands of Bakr bin Laden–built mosques and pray (for free) for better days. 'Abdallah wanted to end that. At the very least, he wanted to put some of the Mecca mosque reconstruction money into creating jobs for young, unemployed Saudis so they wouldn't be spending all their days in the mosques.

Add it all up, and 'Abdallah was Al Sa'ud's worst nightmare. Even Fahd had his worries about him. In October 1995 Fahd got it in his head that 'Abdallah might want to seize control of the country, maybe conspiring with Foreign Minister Sa'ud Al Faysal. Fahd had noticed that every time Sa'ud got into trouble, he went to 'Abdallah for help. Later, Sultan and Fahd agreed that they could never be out of the country at the same time. Someone had to watch 'Abdallah.

'Abdallah was kept out of the tight circle that formed around Fahd after his stroke. They couldn't take him out of the line of succession, but they could lie to him about Fahd's health. Nine months later, when Fahd needed knee surgery, 'Abdallah wasn't included in the debate over whether it was better for Fahd to remain bedridden or risk dying under the knife. 'Abdallah wasn't even told the names of Fahd's doctors.

Within the family, bitterness against 'Abdallah was so deep that he was blamed for Fahd's stroke. One version had it that Fahd and 'Abdallah were on the telephone arguing about who would attend a meeting of the Gulf Cooperation Council in Oman; although it was an unimportant decision, relations between the two had become so acidic that a vein popped in Fahd's head. Another version held that Fahd and 'Abdallah had been arguing about what they always argued about: the looming financial collapse. There were whispers that 'Abdallah had intentionally provoked Fahd, knowing his health couldn't withstand a shouting match. We'll never know because neither is talking.

A year and a half after Fahd's stroke, Sultan had come to so despise 'Abdallah that he stopped attending cabinet meetings chaired by him. The feeling was mutual. In July 1997 'Abdallah bypassed the Council of Ministers, which was heavily stacked in favor of the Sudayri, and tried to get Fahd to sign off on decrees and laws that he thought should be passed. Jawhara and Azouzi teamed up to thwart him once more.

IT WASN'T as if the rest of the Fahd clan was united. Sultan, Salman, and Na'if might have arrived at the hospital in a great show of solidarity—or to make sure none of the others got there first—but they were in for a rude shock once they pushed through the front doors. Jawhara and Azouzi had set up camp outside of Fahd's hospital room, deciding who would get in and who wouldn't. That included ministers, senior princes, doctors, petitions, decrees, and everything else. In other words, there had been a de facto coup d'état.

Fahd's brothers were furious, but there was nothing they could do. It wasn't as if they could arrest Jawhara and her son. The other choice, making 'Abdallah regent, was unthinkable. Their only consolation was that Jawhara and Azouzi were more or less on their side. Jawhara would always be a handful, but they reassured themselves that they could handle Azouzi. Let him ride his Harleys around the palace and steal a piece of property here and there. They needed to make sure Fahd outlived 'Abdallah so Sultan could assume the throne and the Sudayri would be back in power. As it turned out, they'd misjudged Azouzi.

For a start, they hadn't plumbed the depths of his bottomless greed. He was the biggest leech in Saudi Arabia's history. He had learned about money at the feet of the masters—the Ibrahims, his mother's clan. In one deal, the $4.1 billion AT&T contract, Azouzi not only landed a staggering $900 million commission, he outmatched his own brother Muhammad "the Bulldozer" bin Fahd, who represented Ericsson. Muhammad bin Fahd, who won his nickname through his predatory business tactics, wasn't one to gracefully give up a commission. But things got even worse when one of the Bulldozer's retainers embezzled $22 million from him and then stole his yacht. He couldn't do anything because Jawhara and Azouzi didn't care enough to get it back.

Azouzi did have his expenses to look after, including that legendary palace outside Riyadh. From the moment the first slab of marble was laid, it was clear he intended to outdo anything ever built by the Al Sa'ud. You enter the palace by going through four separate arched gates, and that's for starters. And he did have the family spirit. In September 1997, when Jawhara had to make her husband sign a petition to put more of the Ibrahim on the state payroll, Azouzi stood foursquare behind her.

For Sultan and the other full brothers, Jawhara didn't make things any easier. Sultan found himself cut out of military procurement, at one time his exclusive *chasse gardee*. On August 20, 1996, he desperately tried to get Fahd to process some defense contracts he knew had already been approved. No one in the king's palace would return his calls. He finally cornered Jawhara's brother Walid Al Ibrahim, who promised to do something about them. Jawhara pushed the contracts through, but at her own pace. Meanwhile, it drove Sultan and almost everyone else crazy that a queen ruled the most male-chauvinist country in the world.

By March 1997 the situation had become intolerable, even for Fahd's family. Sultan teamed up with Salman in an attempt to block one of Azouzi's property deals. I'm not sure what the outcome was, but if they succeeded, it was a Pyrrhic victory. Azouzi's theft would only spread, soon to be accompanied by a brazen power grab.

Sleeping with the Devil

SAUDI SUCCESSION doesn't proceed according to primogeniture. By tradition, senior princes come to a consensus on succession, usually based on experience and wisdom. The system had served the royal family well. The incapable were taken out of the line of succession, and everybody got his turn. (Following King Khalid's death in 1982 and Fahd's ascension to the throne, the princes had made 'Abdallah the new crown prince, perhaps because he commanded the powerful National Guard.) Now Fahd's brothers were afraid that Azouzi was trying to upend custom.

Azouzi started involving himself more and more in national security, from foreign affairs to intelligence. Even the Americans noticed. When the commander of U.S. forces in the Middle East, General J. H. Binford Peay, came to Riyadh to meet Fahd on July 13, 1997, he was surprised to find Azouzi at Fahd's side, whispering in his father's ear. Where was 'Abdallah? What had become of Sultan? Peay had to meet 'Abdallah separately, and even then the crown prince studiously avoided the issues that should have been at hand.

But what really worried the family was Azouzi's funding of radical Wahhabi causes. Azouzi seemed to have rediscovered his faith. He was obviously courting favor with the Wahhabis, knowing he would one day need their support to become king. Also, by giving generously to the radicals, he was buying insurance they would shut up about his $4.6 billion amusement park.

In December 1993 Azouzi authorized $100,000 for a Kansas City mosque. On September 15, 1995, he opened the King Fahd Academy in Bonn, and on September 17, 1995, he dedicated a new mosque there. Nine days later, he invited the head of the Islamic Society of Spain, Mansur 'Abd-al-Salam, to Riyadh. In May 1996 Azouzi and Jawhara arranged for King Fahd to release Muhammad al-Fasi from prison. Fasi had been imprisoned for opposing the Gulf War and the presence of American troops in Saudi Arabia: In other words, he shared one of bin Laden's platforms for kicking the United States out of the Gulf. 'Abdallah strongly opposed Fasi's release, knowing that outside a prison cell, he would mean nothing but trouble for the Al Sa'ud.

Even the interior minister, Na'if, had to admit that Saudi Arabia had a problem with Islamic militants. In November 2002 he said, "All our problems come from the Muslim Brotherhood. We have given too much support to this group. The Muslim Brotherhood has destroyed the Arab world." Na'if went on to accept, at least minimally, Saudi Arabia's responsibility for militant Islam. "Whenever they got into difficulty or found their freedom restricted in their own countries, Brotherhood activists found refuge in the kingdom, which protected their lives"—even though, as Na'if was quick to add, "they later turned against the kingdom." He failed to mention the unbreakable bond between Saudi Arabia's homegrown Wahhabis and the Brothers.

'Abdallah had a more immediate concern with the radicals. In September 1996 the newly appointed air force chief commissioned five followers of bin Laden. There was already open discontent in the Ministry of Defense and Aviation about the U.S. presence in the region. Officers of all ranks felt that the U.S. exaggerated the threat of Saddam Hussein as an excuse to keep troops in Saudi Arabia and other countries in the region. The officers opposed even the prepositioning of equipment in their country. The appointment of those five Islamic radicals was sure to aggravate the situation, but no one was willing to reverse the commander's decision, including 'Abdallah and Sultan. Over the next five years, Wahhabi militants continued to worm their way into military and intelligence jobs. By October 2002 the Saudi police were informing contacts in the American expat community that they could no longer count on the loyalty of junior military and intelligence officers. The arrest of several Bahraini military officers with ties to al Qaeda in February 2003 seemed to justify the Saudis' fears.

The spread of Islamic radicals inside the military only encouraged Azouzi to give more to radical causes. In September 1997 he coordinated a $100 million aid package to the Taliban. It didn't make the slightest bit of difference that the Taliban were protecting bin Laden, a man who had vowed to overthrow the Al Sa'ud. All

Azouzi cared about was the support of the Wahhabis, come hell or high explosives.

In December 1999 the press caught wind of Azouzi's arrangement with the Islamic militants. It turned out that he had been funding a fellow bin Laden traveler, Sa'd al-Burayk, who in turn was giving the money to Islamic groups in Chechnya to slaughter Russians, military and civilian alike. Any leftover money, Burayk shipped on to militant Islamic causes. With all the bad press, Na'if had no choice but to declare a moratorium on Azouzi's spending and bring his charity back under control; he also promised to put Burayk under house arrest. But Na'if did nothing at all, and Azouzi continued to dump his millions wherever he wanted. Recall, this was the same Na'if who humiliated Louis Freeh and got away with it; the same Na'if who made it crystal-clear in all other ways that he had absolutely no intention of cooperating in the al Khobar investigation. If the U.S. didn't call him on that, what were the chances of coming down on him like a load of bricks because he failed to rein in Azouzi?

Not only did Na'if let Burayk out of the country, Burayk accompanied Crown Prince 'Abdallah on a state visit to Crawford, Texas, in April 2002 to meet with George W. Bush. Bush, ever the genial host, didn't ask about Chechnya, bin Laden, or Burayk's latest public exhortations for Muslim men to enslave Jewish women. I suppose this is what State means by "deference."

AS WITH NA'IF, it was impossible for any of Fahd's full brothers to get a rise out of Washington. Through the 1990s, Defense Minister Sultan continued to fund 'Abdallah al-Ahmar, the head of Islah, the Muslim Brothers in Yemen. Washington ignored evidence that Islah may have had a hand in bombing the U.S.S. *Cole*. When the governor of Riyadh, Prince Salman, suffered a deep conversion to fundamentalist Islam in the mid-1990s, Washington disregarded that, too, even though Salman was in charge of the charities whose money found its way into the pockets of bin Laden and the Muslim Brothers. Fahd, Na'if, Sultan, and Salman were board members of corporate Washington. They were above the law.

Then again, Washington really had no choice. It wasn't like the administration could show up in Riyadh, tin cup in hand, ask for Boeing's money and, in the same breath, censure the royal family about funding and covering for people who were killing Americans. And it certainly was in no position to chastise the Saudis for being spendthrifts. The United States had enticed them to climb on this infernal merry-go-round. American defense companies lived off Saudi contracts. The United States took the lion's share of the country's defense spending, which accounted for half of Saudi government outlays. It talked the Saudis into spending multibillions on the Gulf War. This was dollar diplomacy with a vengeance, or at least with reckless abandon.

You didn't have to be a CPA to see that the Saudis couldn't afford the $7.2 billion Boeing–Saudia deal. The contract called for an initial $500 million signing payment, but the Saudis could come up with only $60 million. By 1997 they owed $2.8 billion on the airplanes, but not a penny could be earmarked out of the budget. In better days, Sultan might have stolen the money from Yamama, but that caper was already $1 billion in arrears. He also might have gone to his own well, but he had already kicked in $67 million to the cause. In July 1997 Sultan's mad scramble led him to his own Ministry of Defense. The Boeing payment, he decreed, would have to come from that budget. To cover the tab, the ministry had to postpone the purchase of spare parts and the delivery of new aircraft, which ended up costing Saudi Arabia millions in penalties while undermining its ability to defend itself. The U.S. had to pick up that slack with its fleet in the Persian Gulf.

By late September 1996 'Abdallah was so alarmed about the kingdom's financial solvency that he tried to send a message to the Clinton administration. 'Abdallah couldn't get the American embassy in Riyadh to listen; its sole mission seemed to be getting the Saudis to pay their bills on time. Nor did 'Abdallah trust Prince Bandar as a conduit to the White House because at the end of the day, the ambassador was loyal to his father, Sultan. The best 'Abdallah could do was raise Saudi Arabia's problems with former ambassador Richard Murphy, then serving as a senior fellow with the Council of Foreign Relations. Murphy was known in the Arab world as the U.S.'s most able, balanced expert on the Middle East. 'Abdallah trusted and liked him. Moreover, he had no connections to Israel, at least that 'Abdallah was aware of. The problem was that Murphy had been out of the government for almost seven years and had little clout in official Washington. Still, 'Abdallah decided Murphy was his only chance.

At their meeting on September 23, 1996, 'Abdallah explained to Murphy that the United States needed to consult with Saudi Arabia before taking any new initiatives in the region. 'Abdallah brought up the Gulf War. The Bush administration, he said, had misled Saudi Arabia about the costs. Helping to pay for the U.S. bases in Saudi Arabia was costing additional billions. (In other words, Saudi Arabia couldn't afford the Boeings or any other expensive toys.) Moving on to regional problems, 'Abdallah said that the Clinton administration had to get rid of Saddam right away—or never. At the same time, the Arabs could not be allowed to believe the U.S. was waging a war against the Iraqi people. Finally, the United States must come to a modus vivendi with Tehran. It was simply costing the Arabs too much to be in a constant state of conflict with Iran.

Needless to say, 'Abdallah's plea fell on deaf ears back in Washington. Clinton was running for a second term. All the White House cared about was that Saudi checks kept arriving in Seattle and that no one was laid off from Boeing's assembly lines.

Meanwhile, Prince Sultan continued to buy guns that no one could afford. In December 1996 Saudi Arabia went ahead with another costly, useless arms deal, picking up forty-four model-412 Augusta helicopters that could be financed by Yamama oil, which meant even more grotesque commissions could be hidden from the Saudi street. A month later, Sultan was back in the marketplace, pricing 102 F-16 multirole combat aircraft. Later that year, the Saudis committed to a $3 billion frigate deal with France. Never mind that on the Yamama front alone, the kingdom was now $4.5 billion in arrears.

The real kicker came on December 18, 1996, when Secretary of Defense William Perry, Secretary of State Warren Christopher, and Vice President Al Gore summoned Bandar to the White House. It wasn't to inquire about the progress of the Khobar investigation. They weren't going to let Bandar go home to his Potomac estate until he agreed to give Bosnia $2 million a month in aid.

THE MORE the Clinton White House saw of 'Abdallah, the less they liked him. He was not only threatening to cut back defense and civilian aviation contracts but also demonstrating a definite independent streak on foreign policy.

He kept harping on the message he had delivered to Richard Murphy: Either overthrow Saddam Hussein, or leave him alone and lift the sanctions. Clinton's do-nothing policy on Iraq—keeping Saddam in his box, or "containment," as the White House euphemistically referred to it—was costing the United States and Saudi Arabia a lot of money, as well as what little goodwill was left in the Middle East. The average Saudi was starting to side more with Saddam than with the royal family; Islamic militants were becoming commonplace in the Saudi military. So desperate was 'Abdallah to take Iraq off the griddle that in June 1997 he sent his own emissaries to meet with Saddam, opening up a back channel the U.S. wasn't supposed to know about. The effort didn't go anywhere, but it did add to Washington's mistrust of 'Abdallah.

The crown prince also irritated Washington when he cut a deal with Iran and Mexico to raise oil prices. By 1996 oil was averaging just under $21 a barrel. At that rate, all three countries were heading toward a financial abyss. 'Abdallah arranged to make a pilgrimage to Mecca with the son of former Iranian president Akbar

Sleeping with the Devil

Hashami Rafsanjani. The details of the pricing were worked out then. The following year, the price of a barrel of oil rose to $23, a jump of almost 10 percent. Almost no one noticed in the U.S.—the NASDAQ was going ape—but the White House didn't at all like the precedent 'Abdallah had set.

Most unforgivably for the White House, 'Abdallah called the 1993 Oslo accords what they were: a lie. The accords had been sold to the Arabs on the grounds that the Palestinians would get some sort of workable state in the West Bank and Gaza—United Nations Resolution 242, more or less. But not a single settlement was dismantled under Oslo. The Jewish settler population in the West Bank went from 250,000 to 380,000, and 5,000 Jewish settlers in the Jordan Valley continued to consume 75 percent of the water, leaving the remainder for two million Palestinians to live on.

'Abdallah knew that numbers like those would only inflame the militants inside his country, but the Clinton administration—as would the second Bush administration—blissfully ignored it all. The United States had made a pact with the devil and was going to stick with it until the catastrophic end. As long as Sultan kept buying American weapons and Aramco kept banking our oil, no one in Washington cared what was happening in the kingdom.

12 / In the War on Terrorism, You Lie, You Die

A COUPLE OF MONTHS before I resigned from the CIA, I found myself wondering if there was anything not for sale in Washington. Although I was always an outsider, I couldn't help but notice that the Bandars and the Boeings, the Carlyle Groups and the Exxons ran Washington. I'd seen the campaign-finance scandal from a front-row seat, noting how a couple hundred thousand dollars bought you instant access to the president. I'd seen, too, how some midlevel oil exec could pick up the telephone and get a meeting with the National Security Council as fast as Bandar could get one with the president. But Washington had to have its limits, didn't it? Ironically, I would have to go back to the Middle East to get my answer.

When I checked out of the CIA on December 4, 1997, I had a lot of regrets. I was walking away from the place I had spent my adult life. As I headed across the parking lot one last time, my sole consolation—if you want to call it that—was that the agency I was leaving wasn't the one I had joined ▮▮▮▮▮ It had lost touch with much of the world, especially the place I felt passionate about: the Middle East. Two separate incidents had convinced me of this.

In early October 1994, when I was deputy chief of Iraqi operations, I picked up a rumor from an agent in Amman that Saddam Hussein was moving armor back toward the Kuwaiti border. Saddam was reportedly sick of the embargo and intended to reinvade Kuwait. I didn't believe it. How stupid could he be?

Sure enough, as soon as I got back to Washington, our satellites picked up the movement of Iraqi armor south toward the Kuwaiti border. The satellites were fine up to a point. But what they couldn't tell us—and what the White House wanted to know—was whether Saddam intended to actually cross the border. For that we would need a human source. The only problem was that we didn't have one. Not only did we not have someone next to Saddam, we didn't have a source in his military to tell us, for instance, whether the army was putting in logistics lines, a sign that Saddam was serious about going all the way.

My first phone call from the White House situation room came at 0834. A navy ensign informed me that the president was considering dispatching a carrier to the Gulf but wanted to hear what the CIA's directorate of operations had to say before giving the order. Now the heat was on.

I knew we didn't have a source, so it was time to think out of the box. I took a flier and called up the Saudi desk to see if they'd noticed any usual activity in Iraq. Bedouin crossed the Iraqi–Saudi border all the time. Maybe one of them had picked up a rumor. The desk officer said without missing a beat, "There's nothing at all. Nothing."

I knew she was telling me the truth, but it was still hard to believe. Saudi Arabia was supposed to be our ally. We had troops based in the kingdom. We kept a fleet in the Gulf and F-15s patrolling it because of the Saudis. Before I could ask if we could send a message to our good friends in the desert, the desk officer said, "And there's no point in asking. ████████████████ ████████████████

With Saudi Arabia out, Kuwait was my last chance. I called the chief there on a secure phone. He and I had known each other since serving together in India in the late 1970s. He'd arrived in New Delhi wet behind the ears but now was in management, on his way up.

"The Kuwaitis don't have the slightest idea what Saddam's up to," he said. "I can have them call up to the border to see what's going on." It was grabbing at straws, but there was no choice.

He called me back fifteen minutes later. He said a Kuwaiti border guard with a pair of binoculars could see an Iraqi tank and its crew. "They're only digging in, eating lunch," the chief said.

Coincidentally, two minutes later, George Tenet was on the line from the White House. At the time he was head of intelligence programs at the National Security Council, responsible for relaying updates on the crisis to the situation room. "What the fuck is going on in Iraq?" he shouted.

I passed on the chief's remarks. Tenet, clearly not satisfied, grunted and hung up.

It went on like that all day and the next. I would call Kuwait and stay on the phone until someone could get ahold of the Kuwaiti border guard with the binoculars. As I waited, I wondered: Is this what all that money for intelligence is buying us? A pair of binoculars?

It was at this point that I started to wonder what else we didn't know about the northern Gulf. Fine, Saddam and Iraq were closed off to the world. It was hard to collect intelligence there. But what about our friends like Kuwait or, better, Saudi Arabia, the heart that pumped our economic life blood?

I started reading the reports coming out of Riyadh. There was essentially nothing. They all had to do with the travel of some congressional delegation, cultural events, book fairs, all spin, no substance. There was not a word about divisions in the royal family or their relations with the Wahhabis. If you went by the embassy reporting, the officers weren't even meeting the Wahhabi clerics, who seemed to be getting more powerful than the Al Sa'ud.

I looked through the databases back to 1986. There wasn't much you couldn't find in the newspapers and academic journals.

It was like the Kuwaiti and the binoculars: When it came to the Gulf, we were blind. If the place were to go up in flames, we wouldn't know until it was too late.

As I headed across the parking lot that day in December 1997, I figured I could do better on my own, particularly if I was living in the Middle East. In fact, I was headed to Beirut that afternoon.

IT DIDN'T TAKE LONG to see that the Beirut I landed in wasn't the Beirut I'd left in 1988. Then it was a city divided by civil war; now it was one huge, sprawling construction site. Prime Minister Rafiq Hariri was in the middle of restoring the old downtown, calling on the services of the world's best architects. He had even excavated a part of the old Roman Beirut. An ultramodern tunnel was being dug under the city to clear up its notorious traffic. There was a new freeway to the airport. Give the place a few years, and it would rival Paris and London.

Still, it was the Middle East, and a lot of open wounds needed to be sewn up before it could be whole again. On Christmas Eve that year, the taxi driver who took me from the Muslim west to the Christian east said that it was the first time he'd crossed the Green Line—that no-man's-land of the civil war. I'd soon be reminded that things weren't what they seemed in the Middle East.

It started when a friend back in Washington asked me to look into the Qatar opposition that had taken refuge in Beirut and Damascus. He was interested in a rogue prince, a very close relation of the current Amir. His name was Hamad bin Jasim bin Hamad Al Thani. I give you the full name because it seems that almost every prince in Qatar has a Hamad or a Jasim in his name. The foreign minister's name is Hamad bin Jasim bin Jabir Al Thani. The Amir's name is Hamad bin Khalifah. For simplicity, I'll call the exiled Hamad bin Jasim the black prince.

The black prince was the former minister of economy and the chief of police. He had tried to overthrow the Amir in February

Sleeping with the Devil

1996, with the backing of the Amir's father, Khalifah, who himself had been overthrown by his son in 1995. If it sounds confusing, it is. But the point is that Qatar is the center of intrigue in the Gulf. Saudi Arabia, Egypt, and Syria all backed the February 1996 coup attempt and were continuing to undermine the Qatari government. Qatar was not only wobbly and a source of fascination to anyone who cared about Gulf politics; it was also a big prize for the world's oil companies. In addition to its oil reserves, Qatar owned one of the biggest gas fields in the world. It was also flirting with the Israelis, and that meant the black prince was a figure of importance to a lot of people in Washington.

To even find out where the black prince lived wouldn't be easy. I started by looking up my old friends in Beirut. After something like fifty meetings in Hamra's smoky coffeehouses, I found someone who knew the prince was living in Damascus, in a compound reserved for senior military and intelligence officers. That put him out of reach. It wasn't like I could go and knock on his door. I wouldn't have made it past the gate guards. I pulled out my Rolodex and got back on the phone.

Eventually, I got to one of the black prince's "business" associates, who agreed to set up a meeting in Lebanon. The one condition was that it take place in the Park Hotel, in the Biqa' Valley. The Park Hotel, outside Shtawrah, was run by Syrian intelligence. The black prince must have figured that I would never dare grab him there, if that was my intention. After all, Qatar and the United States were close friends, and in the black prince's view of the world, it would be logical for his cousin the Amir to send an American to do his dirty work.

A mystery writer could not have picked a better night. Sheets of freezing rain swept across the Biqa', knocking branches off trees. Shtawrah was deserted, black as a grave. Even the Syrian checkpoints along the main Damascus–Beirut highway were abandoned.

The lights were out at the Park Hotel. I wouldn't have been able to find it if not for the driver. When we pulled up, half a dozen gaunt, bearded men stood under the hotel's portico, cradling

AK-47s. They didn't say a word when I got out. Not even a nod of welcome. They followed me into the hotel.

Inside, the lone concierge was waiting for me. He motioned me to follow him up to the second story. We walked down a long, pitch-black corridor, the gunmen still behind. The concierge knocked on a door that looked like the rest. The black prince opened it. A bit heavy, dressed in fatigues and combat boots, with a black-and-white kaffiyeh around his neck, he looked like a Palestinian fighter, not a Gulf prince. The room was dark except for a gas-burning stove in the corner. As the black prince made tea, he said, "You know, I was with Arafat in the early days, at the beginning of the civil war. I trained in his camps. I fought alongside him."

I already knew that, but it was important to hear it from him. He was trying to tell me that I shouldn't take him for one of his soft Al Thani cousins or Saudi royalty. He was a fighter. A revolutionary. Someone I shouldn't mess with.

It didn't take long for him to come to the reason he'd agreed to see me. He wanted to know about the relationship between Washington and his country's foreign minister, Hamad bin Jasim bin Jabir Al Thani, or "good Hamad," as he was known to Qatar's Washington lobbyist. The foreign minister was a Washington darling, having hosted several Arab economic summits to which Israel was invited. He'd also allowed Israel to open an economic mission in Doha, one step toward diplomatic recognition. He had promised democratic elections, women were now allowed to drive, and Enron had recently been let into a multibillion-dollar natural-gas deal. On top of it, the foreign minister was almost as socially acceptable as Bandar—he owned a tasteful estate on Foxhall Road, maybe D.C.'s most expensive neighborhood. With those kinds of credentials, he could wander in and out of the White House anytime he wanted, just like Bandar had. The black prince, though, wanted to know if the foreign minister had the White House in his pocket.

"So has my cousin bought a seat on your National Security Council?" the black prince asked.

Sleeping with the Devil

"No one buys and sells Washington," I shot back. "He's the goddamn foreign minister, and he's rich. Sure he can pretend he owns the place, but he can't buy it."

"Hmm . . . you have a lot to learn, my friend. We need to talk."

THE BLACK PRINCE and I kept in touch. As things warmed up in the spring and he trusted me more, we met in restaurants in the mountains above Beirut. We usually sat outside and smoked water pipes until late in the night.

We talked about Qatar, mostly. It was clear right away that the black prince wanted to make another stab at overthrowing his cousin and his nemesis, the Amir and the foreign minister. At one point he asked me if I could help him find landing craft. Going along with the ploy, I called an arms dealer in Paris who sent me some data on military landing craft for sale in the Ukraine. It worked like a charm. The black prince invited me to his home in Damascus. He had built himself a two-story house in a military compound northwest of Damascus. It had a pool and a football-field-size lawn. It wasn't exactly a palace, but then again, we were in socialist Syria.

The first part of the afternoon, we sat around the pool drinking lemonade. His new Egyptian wife joined us for a while. I noticed a man barbecuing next door. He was wearing an apron and a baseball cap. He could have been one of my uncles.

"Who's that?" I asked.

"General Khuli," the black prince said, waving across the fence to him.

Muhammad Khuli had been the chief of Syrian air force intelligence. He was removed in the mid-1980s when he was implicated in trying to blow up an El Al flight departing London at Heathrow. A bomb had been planted in the suitcase of an unwitting pregnant Irish girl. I wouldn't say it was an intelligence coup to watch Khuli cook a hamburger, but I couldn't help remarking on the irony that I'd had to leave the CIA before I could get this sort of access to the bad guys.

Before I could think about it too much, the black prince said, "Let's take a drive."

We piled into his new American SUV and headed for the Israeli border, to the Syrian side of the Golan Heights. We pulled off the main road and headed up the side of a hill. It was now dark, and every once in a while the bodyguard got out to remove boulders that had tumbled into the road. Finally, we pulled off onto a piece of ground that had been leveled by bulldozers. "This beautiful plot is mine," the black prince said. "I just bought it. One day I will build a house here that will look onto liberated Palestine." He was referring to Israel.

While we walked around, the driver and the bodyguard made a fire from wood we'd brought along. They set up two camp chairs and put a pot of water on the fire for tea. Although it was late spring, it was cold, and the wind had started to pick up. Sparks from the fire blew across the mountain in a long arc. When we were comfortably seated in the camp chairs and under thick blankets, the black prince launched into what he'd brought me here to tell me.

"Do you know anything about my cousin Hamad bin Jasim bin Jabir?" He was talking about the foreign minister with the estate on Foxhall.

By now I felt I could level with the black prince and he would understand what I was saying. I told him about running into the foreign minister in the office of Leon Feurth, Al Gore's national security adviser. I mentioned how I'd been asked to leave so Gore could have a one-on-one with the foreign minister.

The black prince turned his head to get a better look at me. I think he wanted to see if I was telling him the truth. Was that all I knew about the foreign minister?

"Look, my friend, I don't know whether you will be honest with me or not. But your government is playing a very dangerous game."

I asked him what he meant.

"Let's start with bin Laden. The foreign minister is one of his main backers and hates the Saudis. He would make a bargain with the devil to fuck the Al Sa'ud."

I knew that much. When I was still in the CIA, I'd heard Sultan and the other senior princes refer to the foreign minister as "the dog." I also ran across some information that Sultan had indeed backed the black prince and the former Amir in the February 1996 coup attempt. But since the Saudis had refused to talk to us about it, we could not be absolutely sure.

"What do you mean, back bin Laden?"

I knew that the interior minister, 'Abdallah bin Khalid, had met Osama bin Laden on August 10, 1996, but that didn't mean a damn thing. A lot of Arabs were making the pilgrimage to Khartoum to see bin Laden. Iraqi intelligence had met with bin Laden on several occasions. Although we couldn't be positive, we assumed the emissaries were only taking bin Laden's measure, making sure he wasn't about to turn on them.

"I mean back him. Do you know who Khalid Sheikh Hamad is?" In Qatari Arabic, the "mu" is dropped on the word "Muhammad." The black prince was referring to Khalid Sheikh Muhammad.

"No," I said. I wanted him to tell me the story from beginning to end.

"He is bin Laden's chief of terrorist operations. His target of choice is airplanes. In 1995 I was chief of police when he landed in Qatar. He'd come from the Philippines after a couple of his henchmen were arrested. He was immediately taken under the wing of the interior minister, 'Abdallah bin Khalid, who is a fanatic Wahhabi. The Amir then ordered me to help 'Abdallah. The first things he asked for were twenty blank Qatari passports. I know he gave them to Khalid Sheikh, who filled in the names."

"Do you have proof of this?"

"Yes. I still have the numbers in my safe back in Damascus, and a lot of other stuff."

It was becoming clear to me that the black prince wanted me to do something with this information. By now he had checked me out and found that I was a former CIA officer. I'm certain he thought—most Arabs do—that I was still working for the place. I wasn't about to disabuse him of his belief. I wanted to hear the rest of the story.

"Where is Khalid Sheikh now?" I asked. (KSM was still at large then, with a starting price tag on his head of $2 million.)

"Flew the coop. Gone. Sayonara. You know as well as I, so don't play stupid."

"I want to hear what you heard." When Khalid Sheikh Muhammad left Qatar in 1996, I wasn't sure of the circumstances.

"As soon as the FBI showed up in Doha, the Amir and the foreign minister ordered 'Abdallah bin Khalid to move KSM out of his apartment to 'Abdallah's beach estate. In the meantime, agents of the Ministry of Interior cleared out Khalid Sheikh's offices—the former police academy, a farm, and a place called the north depot."

The black prince could see I was incredulous. He called the bodyguard over to bring me a pen and paper. "You write all this down and check with Washington."

"Where did they go?" I asked.

"Maybe Prague. I know at least Muhammad Shawqi Islambuli went there." Islambuli was the brother of Khalid Shawqi Islambuli, the Muslim Brother who'd emptied an AK-47 magazine into Anwar Sadat's chest in 1981. Muhammad himself was wanted in Egypt for murder.

I didn't say anything while I made a few notes. When I finished, I asked, "And you have proof of all this?"

"And a lot more. Remember, I was the minister of economy. Whenever it came time to put money into U.S. elections, I did it."

I DIDN'T CARE about foreign governments putting money into U.S. elections. But I did care about Khalid Sheikh Muhammad, and I already knew about the so-called Bojinka plot—KSM's plan to blow up U.S. passenger airlines. I had to take the black prince seriously. But how could I get the information to the CIA? In spite of what the black prince thought, once you're out of the CIA, you're out.

I did the only thing I could. I e-mailed a friend still in the CIA and asked him to pass on my information to the Counter-Terrorist Center. As insecure as that connection was, I included all the data, including the black prince's name. If nothing else, I figured, that should ring a bell. I hoped Washington would send out someone to talk to him and collect whatever he had locked up in his safe. It couldn't hurt to hear the guy out.

My friend wrote back the next week: no interest.

I was never one to give up, so I called a *New York Times* reporter named Jim Risen. If the black prince's story checked out—especially the documents—the *Times* would probably run a story and force someone to pay attention to one of our allies in the Gulf supporting bin Laden, by this time one of the world's most lethal terrorists.

By the time Risen had enough to pursue the story, I'd moved to New York. The black prince was still prepared to spill his guts. Unfortunately, just as Risen was about to get on a plane to go see him, the black prince was kidnapped in Beirut and flown back to Doha. At this writing, he is locked up in a windowless jail, and his family says he's being injected with debilitating drugs. As soon as he disappeared into the black hole that is the Gulf, hard facts became nearly impossible to get.

EVEN AFTER THE BLACK PRINCE was gone, I wasn't done with the story. In New York I looked up one of his associates. Born in Sri Lanka, the man was now a naturalized American citizen. He once worked for the Qatari mission in the U.N. but now owned a ski lodge in Vermont.

He was worried about talking to me. "It's been very bad for me and my family with the government. I don't want any more trouble."

After I convinced him I was a friend of the black prince, he told me his story. In 1995, when the current Amir overthrew his father, he made the tactical error of siding with the father and the black prince, which made him the enemy of the foreign minister and the Amir. One day the foreign minister showed up in New York and told him that he could either change sides and inform on the black prince, or risk being turned in to American authorities. "What for?" he asked. "I haven't broken the law." The foreign minister answered, "It doesn't matter; you'll soon see."

Soon after, the FBI showed up at his Bronx apartment building. Agents went door-to-door asking the Sri Lankan's neighbors whether they were aware he was a terrorist. Separately, agents went to New York University and questioned his children, who were students there. The grilling took place in a squad car parked in front of a university building so other students could get a good look. The Sri Lankan's children were let go, but not before being humiliated. He and his wife were held at the FBI Manhattan field office for twelve hours before being released. Surveillance on the Sri Lankan and his wife continued for over a month. Even their lodge in Vermont was watched.

There was no way I could put all the pieces together. But it was obvious to me that the foreign minister had a lot of clout in Washington. The money he put into lobbying and public-relations firms from 1997 to 1999—$24,628,799.36, to be exact—bought him a piece of the U.S. justice system. The money allowed Qatar to stiff the FBI team sent to Doha in February 1996 to arrest Khalid Sheikh Muhammad. It also harnessed the FBI to intimidate Qatar's opposition, maybe even a source of information that could have prevented September 11. Not bad for a country that lived off of American oil companies.

Unfortunately, that wasn't the end of the story. In 1998, when I was living in France, I got a call from a young *Wall Street Journal* reporter named Danny Pearl. We met in Geneva. With a wiry frame and intense eyes, he was one of the most thorough, dogged, and honest reporters I'd ever come across. You knew right away he would never give up on a story. I told him about KSM and Qatar. He listened, took notes, and promised to follow up on it one day. We saw each other from time to time in Washington. He would bring up the Khalid Sheikh Muhammad story, but neither of us had anything new to add.

Two days after September 11, I received this e-mail from Pearl:

> *Hi, how are things? Did your book come out? I hope you weren't near the Pentagon Tuesday.*
>
> *Like half the paper, I'm being roped into reporting on bin Laden's network . . . some of the suspects supposedly had UAE passports, and I remember you talking once about how Fujairah was a hot spot for fundies.*

Pearl called me the next day. I reminded him about our talks on KSM and Qatar. "Worth thinking about," he replied.

I have no way of knowing whether Pearl went to Karachi and asked about Khalid Sheikh Muhammad. *The Wall Street Journal* says no, that he was working on the shoe-bomber case. But I can't help but be struck by the fact that one of the witnesses in the Pearl murder trial fingered Khalid Sheikh Muhammad as his murderer.

THE FINAL CHAPTER came to me indirectly, from a friend in London who told me that a few days after September 11, Pearl called the foreign ministry in Qatar to ask whether Khalid Sheikh Muhammad was behind the attacks. I didn't need to be told that the Qataris adamantly denied knowing anything about September 11 or KSM. Still, I wonder whether the Qataris called KSM and told him that Pearl was on his trail. Maybe by the time this book appears in print, we'll have that answer from his own mouth. It's certain that no one in Washington is going to demand an answer from Qatar, our new best ally in the Gulf.

But we're not going to find the answers to a lot of life-and-death questions until our government gets serious about terrorism and starts demanding the truth from places like Qatar and Saudi Arabia. And believe me, there are more questions than answers after September 11. Another Qatari told me that in the late 1990s, Ayman Zawahari, bin Laden's Egyptian Muslim Brother deputy, and a dozen other bin Laden associates were all given refuge in Qatar—with the knowledge of the government. As for Saudi Arabia, we still don't have an answer why Omar Bayyumi showed up in San Diego with hundreds of thousands of dollars and helped to settle two Saudi hijackers. He is out of the FBI's reach, living quietly somewhere in Saudi Arabia.

I often wonder if the money for Colin Powell's speech at Tufts University came from the same Saudi defense ministry account used to pay Omar Bayyumi. Unlikely but not impossible, considering the nature of Washington's fifty-year marriage with the kingdom. But it's not history that should worry us; it's truth. Until we start demanding the truth from Saudi Arabia—and telling ourselves the truth, too—there will be more September 11s and more tragedies like Danny Pearl's murder. That much you can take to the bank.

Epilogue

> *A desperate disease requires a dangerous remedy.*
> —GUY FAWKES, 1570–1606

WASHINGTON'S ANSWER for Saudi Arabia—apart from the mantra that nothing's wrong—is the same as its answer for the rest of the Middle East: Democracy will cure everything. Talk the royal family into ceding at least part of its authority; aid and abet the reform-minded princes; set up a nice little model parliament; compromise the firebrands with a Cabinet position or two, a couple of political parties, and some money to grease the skids; send Jimmy Carter in to monitor the initial election; and in a few generations, Riyadh will be Ankara, or maybe even Stockholm. The governmental mechanism might not work all that well, but the people who run the government day to day are, for the most part, committed body, mind, and spirit to rooting out corruption, rounding up terrorists, and recognizing the right of the people to self-govern.

An article in the October 6, 2001, *National Journal*—a reliable organ of Washington Think—sums up the approach and the problem. Ned Walker, the former U.S. ambassador to Israel and Egypt and the number two man in the Riyadh embassy in the 1980s, told the *Journal:* "You don't get real economic development without democratization. For the long-term stability of the governments in the region, we should encourage democratization, which means we have to help them build civil societies in the context of their cultures."

Chas W. Freeman, a former ambassador to Saudi Arabia, was bullishly reassuring: "Al Qaeda is directed first and foremost at the overthrow of the Saudi monarchy. You can be damn sure that any al Qaeda operative is on the Saudi wanted list and that any senior operative is high on that list."

"Saudi Arabia has fought its own counter-terrorism battles," added Anthony Cordesman, late of the Defense Department and now a Middle East expert at the Center for Strategic and International Studies. "Saudi Arabia is in the process of massive social and economic change. It's change that's led a small minority to turn to violence."

You can hear this tune all over Washington, from Foggy Bottom to the think tanks to the local op-ed pages, even out at the CIA, an organization never much for social engineering. Democracy will triumph in the desert as it triumphed in America and Europe. People are people, and we all want the same thing.

It's utter nonsense. As far as I can tell, democracy's proponents are talking about free and fair elections in Saudi Arabia—one person, one vote; the whole nine yards. Let's start by taking a look at the last time there were true democratic elections held in an Arab country: Algeria in late 1991 and early 1992. When it became clear the fundamentalists were about to win an overwhelming majority and impose an Islamic constitution, the army stepped in. The country was immediately plunged into a civil war that killed hundreds of thousands of people. It's still going on today.

Why would we expect Saudi Arabia to be different? According to one poll conducted in October 2001, 95 percent of educated Saudis between the ages of twenty-five and forty-one support bin

Laden. There's no reason why we should accept the results as hard facts, but in the absence of any other information, we pretty much have to. In October 2002 I asked a leader of the Saudi opposition, Muhammad al-Masari, what he thought. There was no doubt in his mind that an Islamic government would succeed the Al Sa'ud if the Saudis were allowed to decide their own political destiny. I couldn't resist asking al-Masari if either the British or American governments had asked him what he thought about democracy in Saudi Arabia. "No one from either government has ever asked me anything," Masari said.

THE OCTOBER 2001 POLL didn't answer why the Saudis support bin Laden, though I suppose it doesn't really matter. Maybe it's that bin Laden dares to do what the United States of America refuses to do: stand up to the thieves who rule his country. Or maybe, as Washington's neoconservatives say, it's that they just hate the West and its values. Whatever the reason, the practical effect is that a democratic election in Saudi Arabia would bring to power a militant Islamic government more hostile than Khomeini's Iran. Goodbye, cheap, subsidized oil. Hello, $144 a barrel, just as Osama promised.

The only reason this fairy tale about the triumph of desert democracy lives on, as far as I can tell, is that it allows those who matter in Washington to sleep soundly in their Georgetown town houses and suburban mini-mansions and faux châteaus. If Riyadh is only an election removed from a European-style parliament, then it's okay to keep grabbing for the petrodollars; okay to turn a blind eye to the billion-dollar commissions; okay to conveniently forget that the ambassador prince who showers gifts and sinecures all over Washington is as deep in the muck as the princes back home; okay to ignore the fact that even when the Al Sa'ud were offered Osama bin Laden's head on a platter by the Sudanese, they said no, thank you;

okay to build up that client list and make the calls to sell those private jets so you can pull down your seven-figure stock-option profits.

Ned Walker, who is all for democratization in Saudi Arabia, is president of the Middle East Institute, supported in part by Saudi princes who would rather crawl on their knees to Mecca than sit still for a popular vote. Chas Freeman, who is so certain that the Saudi monarchy is leaving no stone unturned in its search for al Qaeda, is president of the Middle East Policy Council, whose board members, last I looked, included Frank Carlucci and Fuad Rihani, research and development director of the Saudi bin Laden Group.

And those are just the small fry, for God's sake, the innocents—the ones who are feeding off the crumbs left from all those consulting firms run by former CIA directors and onetime secretaries of state. At the same time the Defense Policy Board was shocking official Washington by suggesting that Saudi Arabia might be the real evil axis of global terrorism, the board's chairman, Richard Perle, was serving as a managing partner of Trireme Partners, a venture-capital firm that invests in companies specializing in technology, goods, and services related to homeland security and defense. While Perle was excoriating the Saudis and urging war against Iraq, his partners were meeting with leading Saudi businessmen in an effort to raise $100 million in new investments, according to an article by Seymour Hersh in the March 17, 2003, *New Yorker*. The chief middleman in arranging the meetings, Hersh writes, was Adnan Khashoggi, the same Khashoggi who seems to have conveniently left behind that briefcase stuffed with $1 million during a visit to Richard Nixon at San Clemente. Hersh writes that Perle himself took part in one of the meetings—in France, at a Marseilles restaurant in early January 2003—but he assured Hersh that he would never confuse his public and private roles. Perle resigned subsequently as chairman of the Defense Policy Board. This pattern of behavior that Sy Hersh paints is one repeated time and again in the nation's capital. Ask the Saudis for money, and if they don't pony up, squeeze them for it. Foment crisis, then figure out how to capitalize on it.

EPILOGUE

This fantasy of a democracy is corrupting foolishness. We all know what version of "democracy" the State Department has in mind for Saudi Arabia. (Think Kuwait.) It's insulting to try to make us believe it's the real thing, just as it's degrading for all those executive-branch officials and spokespersons who get trotted out to pay lip service to the myth. Say that the truth is something else for long enough, and you'll forget what the truth really is.

There are something like seventeen million Saudis. (It's the five million plus "guest workers" who bring the total population up over twenty-two million.) The average Saudi is too poor, oppressed, and afraid to express any sort of genuine political opinion. They make do with what they're given by the Al Sa'ud: mosques, the Qur'an, subsidized food, one-way tickets to Afghanistan. But they're not the people I'm talking about. I'm talking about the people who run the country, the people who control the oil money, the people who take the bribes and pay the protection money and fly over to Morocco whenever they want to get laid by someone other than their eleven wives. These are the people who would rather keep Saudi Arabia stuck in the ninth century and spend the oil money on themselves than build a stable country.

Washington abetted the whole thing, even encouraged the Al Sa'ud to run a kleptocracy. The result is a kingdom built on thievery, one that nurtures terrorism, destroys any possibility of a middle class based on property rights, and promotes slavery and prostitution. We can't get around the fact that the House of Sa'ud underwrites the mosque schools that turn out the jihadists, just as it administers the charities that fund the jihadists. It channels the anger of the jihadists against the West to distract it from the rot in the House of Sa'ud. And by the way—in case I didn't make myself perfectly clear earlier—the royals wouldn't allow a real popular vote unless you wrapped them in Semtex and attached a burning ten-second length of detcord to help them make up their minds.

Saudi Arabia is, in a phrase, a goddamn mess, and it's our goddamn mess. The United States made Saudi Arabia the private storage shed for our oil reserves. We reaped the benefits of a steady petroleum supply at a discounted price and grabbed every Saudi petrodollar we could lay our hands on. We taught the Saudis by example what was expected of them and neglected the fruits of our own creation. The Saudi Arabia of today flows in a direct, unbroken line from the $1 million that Adnan Khashoggi allegedly forgot to carry away from San Clemente in 1968, through Boeing's reupping Khalid bin Mahfouz as its consultant on the Saudia airline deal, to all the hands still dipping furiously into the Saudi till even as the place gets ready to implode.

We can walk away from the moral consequences of our actions, but we can't walk away from economic consequences. We crow about democracy and talk about someday weaning ourselves from a dependency on foreign oil, but in the entire history of America's dependence on foreign oil, there has never been a single honest, sustained effort to reduce long-term U.S. petroleum consumption. The oilmen who now occupy the White House would rather host a Marilyn Manson concert on the South Lawn than get serious about alternative fuels. Not that I want to let the Clinton people off the hook, or the first Bush team, or the Reaganites, Carterites, Fordites, or Nixonites: Screwing up Saudi Arabia might be the most successful bipartisan undertaking of the last half century.

Not all the wishing and hoping in the world will change the basic reality of the situation, which is as follows:

- The industrial world is dependent on the oil reserves of the Islamic world and will be for decades to come, whether it's the already developed reserves of the largely Arab states or the soon to be developed reserves of Central Asia.
- Of the Islamic oil states, none is more critical than Saudi Arabia, because (a) it sits on top of the largest proven reserves; (b) it serves as the market regulator for the entire global petroleum industry; and (c) it has the money, the political will, and the religious zeal to pursue control of the Arab Peninsula and Central Asia.

- Of all the oil-consuming states, none consumes more than the United States, none enjoys anything like the most-favored-nation status that the U.S. enjoys with the Saudis, and thus none is more dependent on Saudi oil to fulfill its appetite and to keep doing so at a compliments-of-the-house rate.
- If Saudi Arabia tanks, and takes along the other four dysfunctional families in the region who collectively own 60 percent of the world's proven oil reserves, the industrial economies are going down with it, including the economy of the United States of America.

Like it or not, the U.S. and Saudi Arabia are joined at the hip. Its future is our future. So what can America do?

Counterintuitive as it might seem, Syria offers one way out of the mess. Twenty years ago, Syria was Saudi Arabia: not in the vast sums of money (it's not a major oil producer), not in the ruling kleptocracy, but as the epicenter of Islamic terrorism. When I first set foot in Damascus in 1980, I estimated that Hafiz al-Asad would have maybe three or four years before he went under. The Muslim Brothers owned the street. The mosque schools were teaching jihad, just as the Saudi *madrasahs* do today. The mosque public-address systems blared out a message of hate and revenge, just as they do in Saudi Arabia today. Lebanon next door was an arms bazaar: You name it, someone had it. Asad had seized power in a military coup in 1970. What goes around comes around, I figured; the guy's going to get strung up on a light pole in downtown Damascus like a lot of other Syrians. Instead, he died in his sleep at age seventy, wasted by disease but ruler to the end.

We've already been over why: the ruthless assault on the Sunni stronghold at Hama, the way Asad took control of the mosque schools and silenced and killed dissent when it wouldn't shut up, his total control of the armed forces, and so on. Pretty it wasn't. "Democracy" it certainly isn't. But Hafiz al-Asad forced a rule of law on the Syrian people, the same rule of law the Al Sa'ud have refused to force on the Saudis, most notably themselves. When Asad handed the country over to his son, it was as stable a dictatorship as any in the Middle East.

Whether there's anyone in the Al Sa'ud willing to impose the rule of law in the kingdom, I don't know. Whether anyone has the guts or determination to even try, I'm not sure. From what I know, Crown Prince 'Abdallah might. He's related to Asad through marriage; maybe something of Syria's determination has rubbed off on him. But 'Abdallah will be eighty years old soon, and he has enough enemies in the family to block anything he might dream up. In case he or someone else wants to try, Syria is a model, much as the bloodless policy wonks in Washington might blanch at the suggestion.

At the end of the day, what we need in Saudi Arabia and the Middle East is rule of law. I'm not talking about a Bill of Rights, the Magna Carta, a free press, freedom to worship, or the right to bear arms. I'm talking about something more basic—outlawing righteous murder, jihad, the Muslim Brotherhood. That would be a start; then you could move on to outlawing grotesque commissions, theft, and bribery. Only when you address those problems can you think about other rights or true democracy.

It would also help if we imposed a rule of law on ourselves, like enforcing the Foreign Corrupt Practices Act, stopping bribery, and putting an end to officials retiring from the U.S. government on Friday and going to work for a foreign government on Monday. A little decency in Washington—and in Europe and the rest of the world that has lived off the oil bonanza—would go a long way toward cleaning up the mess in Saudi Arabia and beginning the process of telling the truth about what's going on in that country.

Failing that, there's always the 82nd Airborne.

IT'S NOT LIKE the United States has never thought about seizing Arab oil fields. On August 21, 1975, the Congressional Research Service presented to the Special Subcommittee on Investigations of the House Committee on International Relations a document entitled "Oil Fields as Military Objectives: A Feasibility Study." By the time the document was entered into the record, the OPEC oil embargo had been over for almost a year and a half, but the memory lingered on.

Gerald Ford, who ascended to the presidency on Nixon's resignation, and the holdover secretary of state, Henry Kissinger, had talked publicly about the possibility of seizing Persian Gulf facilities should the embargo escalate into a strangulation of American industrial capacity. Doing so, the Research Service estimated, would be no cakewalk, even in the best of circumstances:

> *If nonmilitary facets were entirely favorable, successful operations would be assured* only *if this country could satisfy all aspects of a five-part mission:*
>
> - *Seize required oil installations intact.*
> - *Secure them for weeks, months, or years.*
> - *Restore wrecked assets rapidly.*
> - *Operate all installations without the owner's assistance.*
> - *Guarantee safe overseas passage for supplies and petroleum products.*

Achieving American objectives, the Research Service summarized, would require two to four military divisions, maybe sixty thousand troops, "tied down for a protracted period of time." To keep the oil fields running, "drafting U.S. civilian workers to supplant foreign counterparts might be mandatory." Because "U.S. parachute assault forces are too few to cover all objectives quickly [and] amphibious forces are too slow," skilled localized sabotage teams could be expected to "wreak havoc" before invasion forces were in place. "In short, success would largely depend on two prerequisites: slight damage to key installations [and] Soviet abstinence from armed intervention."

Even if we confine a takeover to Saudi Arabia, we couldn't count on it going smoothly. Whether the House of Sa'ud were still in power or had been supplanted by some sort of Wahhabi putsch, we would still have to contend with all those weapons Washington sold the Saudis, and all those fighter pilots and infantry officers trained by American military personnel and private contractors to use the planes and other weapons. Happily, the U.S. has an adequate base of operations in Qatar. Additionally, U.S.-trained Saudi forces would realize the futility of resisting, in part because they know that however many planes and missile launchers they have, the U.S. has the next generation in far greater numbers. Also, corruption in the kingdom is so thorough that spare parts for its planes and tanks would quickly be truly spare and sparse.

Sure, terrorism would likely increase, locally and globally. Al Qaeda, the Muslim Brotherhood, Hamas, you name it—none is going down without a fight. Even if the Saudis aren't widely loved in the Middle East, the enemy of my enemy is still my friend. Vilified for the invasion of Iraq, the U.S. would take an even worse beating in international public-opinion polls. We would have to run rough-shod over international organizations and our own long-standing principles, although the newly promulgated "doctrine of preemptive warfare" would certainly provide cover. But would all that be worse than standing idly by as the House of Sa'ud collapsed and the world's largest known oil reserves fell into the hands of Muslim Brotherhood–inspired fundamentalists dedicated to jihad against Israel and the West? I don't think so. Some things are more calamitous than others, and if the Bush-Cheney administration knows anything well, it ought to be how to rebuild and run an oil field.

THE CONGRESSIONAL RESEARCH SERVICE feasibility study on seizing Arab oil fields has mostly disappeared from history, in part because it's embarrassing for Congress to be identified with such schemes and in part because the study is almost embarrassingly naive at times. ("The resultant survey covers the immediate future only, through the 1970s," the authors write. "Thereafter, new

United States and allied sources of energy could make armed intervention against petroleum producers an irrelevant act." Right.) But the magazine article on which the CRS study builds—Robert W. Tucker's "Oil: The Issue of American Intervention," from the January 1975 issue of *Commentary*—has been nibbling at the dreams of out-of-the-box Washington thinkers for more than a quarter century. Unlike the CRS bureaucrats, Tucker doesn't beat around the bush. He wants to seize the Saudi oil fields, straight and simple:

> *Since it is impossible to intervene everywhere, the feasibility of intervention depends upon whether there is a relatively restricted area which, if effectively controlled, contains a sufficient portion of present world oil production and proven reserves to provide reasonable assurance that its control may be used to break the present price structure by breaking the core of the cartel politically and economically. [Remember: This was 1975.]*
>
> *The one area that would appear to satisfy these requirements extends from Kuwait down along the coastal region of Saudi Arabia to Qatar. It is this mostly shallow coastal strip less than 400 miles in length that provides 40 per cent of present OPEC production and that has by far the world's largest proven reserves (over 50 per cent of total OPEC reserves and 40 per cent of world reserves). Since it has no substantial centers of population and is without trees, its effective control does not bear even remote comparison with the experience of Vietnam.*

There is a second factor to consider: the Shi'a–Sunni split in Islam. The Saudi Shi'a in the Eastern Province, the majority of workers in Aramco, are ripe for a revolution. They are a poor, oppressed minority, not allowed to express their faith, forbidden from holding any important government position or serving in the military. From time to time, they're subject to Wahhabi pogroms. If they're lucky enough to own any property, it's liable to be seized by the Al Sa'ud. Until U.S. and British forces started rolling into Iraq in March 2003, I would have bet that if we had offered the Shi'a a deal to rule the Eastern Province—the heart of Saudi Arabia's oil industry—they would have instantly agreed. Now, I've got plenty of doubts. Iraq's Shi'a didn't exactly welcome their "liberators" with open arms as the script called for. But the war still goes on as I write. Maybe by the time it ends, America won't seem so arrogant to the Arab world, so intolerant of any world view but its own. That's a steep learning curve, but winning over the Shi'a would be worth the effort.

The idea is not as far-fetched as it seems. Already the Pentagon has made an alliance with Ahmad Chalabi, head of the Iraqi National Congress and a Shi'a, to set up a government in a post-Saddam Baghdad. Even if he were to take power, Chalabi isn't likely to last long. He left Iraq in 1958, still a child, and has spent his adulthood in the West. He has no political base in Iraq. Few Iraqis know his name. Also, in 1989 he was convicted in Jordan of defrauding his own bank. If we're ready to consider a Shi'a with all that baggage, couldn't we consider a Saudi Shi'a for the same role?

If you carry the logic forward, it would be possible to extend an arc of moderate Shi'a governments from Tehran to Kuwait to Bahrain to the Eastern Provinces, all countries with a substantial Shi'a population. Before September 11, any talk about nation building on this scale would get you ejected from any serious policy discussion in Washington. Now we're faced with the House of Sa'ud's dissolution, and we may have no other choice. An invasion and a revolution might be the only things that can save the industrial West from a prolonged, wrenching depression.

Was it all inevitable? No, which brings me to the final thing I want to say in this book. Washington made us lie down with the devil. It made the bed, pulled back the covers, and invited the devil in. We whispered in his ear and told him we loved him. When things went a little wrong, Washington held his hand and said it was all right. And all that time we had our eye on his bulging wallet, lit by the moonlight on the dresser.

Afterword

On March 2, 2003, I was in Newport Beach, California, finishing the last edit of *Sleeping with the Devil*, when I got a call from ABC News. "Do you want to go to Iraq to help us cover the last days of Saddam?" It didn't take me a second to decide. "You bet. When do I leave?"

I wasn't about to let the opportunity pass me by. However long it took to topple Saddam and run him into the ground, one thing was certain in my mind: The moment American troops crossed the border into Iraq, the Middle East would never be the same again. The Arab world is like a spider web, intricately interconnected. Disrupt it anywhere, and you disrupt it everywhere, especially those places where it is already most combustible: places, that is, like Saudi Arabia. I wasn't sure what was coming—I'm still not—but here was my chance to be present at the inception.

No sooner had I returned from Iraq than it looked as if the war there might have claimed its first out-of-theater victim. On May 12, 2003, Islamic militants carbombed a foreign residential compound in Riyadh, killing thirty-five, including nine Americans, and sending the royal family into panic. Within hours, a Saudi spokesman was popping up all over the American cable news networks, telling us that the bombing was the kingdom's "wake-up call." Saudi Arabia is a victim of terrorism as much as the United States, or so went the party line. (Subtext: Please, please give us a pass on the inconvenient fact that fifteen of the 9/11 hijackers were Saudis.) Even Crown Prince Abdallah lost his cool when he confessed that Saudi Arabia is in the middle of "a decisive battle against the power of evil."

With running gun battles between police and militants breaking out all over the realm and a second residential compound in Riyadh hit on November 9, Washington panicked, too. Travel advisories, canceled flights, a U.S. embassy draw-down—everywhere one looked, the wheels seemed to be coming off the old guns-and-oil alliance. Soon, American companies were reassessing their Saudi investments. Exxon-Mobil, for one, pulled out of a mega gas deal.

President Bush's Ambassador to Riyadh, Robert Jordan, added his own fuel to the fire by telling a reporter that he could imagine a scenario in which the "whole thing [Saudi Arabia] comes crashing down." The unrest, he went on, was "certainly the greatest threat, I think, to the regime since 1932." Not to be outdone, CENTCOM Commander Army General John Abizaid in late January 2004 described Saudi Arabia, along with Pakistan, as a long-term strategic challenge to American interests. In Pentagon speak, "strategic challenge" translates into a whole mess of trouble.

But maybe not. Sure, the shoot-outs with militants go on, and the Saudis continue to unearth scary arms caches, but the car bombings seem to have stopped. More important, radical Wahhabi clerics are taking back their calls for jihad, and doing so on the front pages of Saudi newspapers and on TV. Finally, the royal family might be getting the upper hand on the clergy. If so, stabilization could be in the air. But with Saudi Arabia, there's really no way for us in the West to know for sure.

Wake-up call or not, Saudi Arabia remains a country closed to foreigners and objective, first-hand analysis. Now more than ever, the expatriate community is confined to its gilded ghettos. Internally, freedom of the press is a joke. Journalists and academics who manage to get visas spend their time in five-star hotels and wandering around sterile malls. Saudi officials are closemouthed as ever. So is the royal family. And, as usual, the internal Saudi opposition is invisible, or nearly so.

Saudi Arabia, in short, is a country you have to get at in crab-like fashion. Just as Saudi watchers used to pick up their best information in Beirut, much of my understanding of the place comes from putting my ear to the ground in neighboring countries. In this case—thanks to ABC and the Bush administration's determination to topple Saddam—I got a look at Saudi Arabia through the prism of the Iraq war. I'll reconstruct as best I can the conversations I had with key players in the region. You'll find no Saudi royals in the pages that follow, nor any Bush administration members or Washington think-tank thumbsuckers. They all have their places in the ecology of the Middle East, but to get the real story, I contend, you can't sit in marble palaces in Riyadh, Jeddah, or along the Potomac.

ON APRIL 9, 2003, the day Baghdad fell, I was in Amman, Jordan, but not by my own choice. The Iraqis wouldn't give me a visa, and the Syrians weren't about to let me cross the border into Iraq without one. The Iraqis have long memories, and my name was inextricably tied to a 1995 coup attempt against Saddam.

Waiting for Saddam's border guards to defect, I made what I took to calling a jihad tour of Jordan, Lebanon, and Syria. I wanted to hear what Islamic militants had to say about the war and its reverberations. Even though they weren't fighting in it, I suspected they would go a long way to determining the shape of the peace, or absence of it, throughout the region.

My first call was on Muhammad Husayn Fadlallah, a radical Lebanese Shi'a cleric who became famous in the '80s, thanks to his flaming anti-American sermons. Back in 1985, he had been the target of a car bomb that ended up killing eighty-five bystanders. The Lebanese generally held the CIA responsible although it had nothing to do with it.

Most Saturdays Fadlallah spends the day in his office outside Damascus, a few blocks from the Shi'a holy shrine of Sitt Zaynab. I'd been told that Fadlallah considers it important to keep an office there to broaden his constituency beyond Lebanon, particularly among Iraqi Shi'a who often make the pilgrimage to Sitt Zaynab.

As I shook Fadlallah's hand, I had a hard time squaring the fact that the U.S. government officially considers him a terrorist. He was calm, poised, and thoughtful. His beard looked more grandfatherly than Komeiniesque. Fadlallah smiled benevolently through the meeting. Still, I wondered what he thought about sitting down with an ex-CIA officer, probably a first.

Time was short, so I came right to the point: "Are you going to call for a jihad against American troops in Iraq?"

If Fadlallah was surprised by the bluntness of the question, he didn't show it. "No," he said. "It's not necessary. The United States has violated international law. It has invaded another country. And now it is the recognized right of Iraqis to defend themselves. We, the Iraqis and all Arabs, will expel the Americans . . . sooner or later."

Fadlallah went on to say that he would advise against a jihad, because a jihad would implicate the Middle East's Christians, who in fact opposed the Iraq war. In this regard, he noted, it was crucial that the Pope had come out against the war along with Lebanon's Christian Maronites.

Fadlallah paused for a minute to collect his thoughts. "Actually, Arab determination to oppose an American occupation will have the full force of jihad. The culture of resistance is a potent force. To be certain, no one can stop you from removing Saddam. But that doesn't mean we accept foreign occupation. You Americans can count on a long, bloody war. "

"But Saddam killed hundreds of thousands of Shi'a," I said, ignoring his comment about occupation. "Surely Iraq will be better off without him."

"Saddam's a murderer, no doubt. He needs to be brought down. But that doesn't mean Americans should do it. Would we invade your country if your president oppressed you? No. That's your business."

That's all I was going to get out of Fadlallah. He wasn't interested in talking about Saudi Arabia or what effect the war in Iraq might have on it, but in his own way he had rattled the spider web with his talk about de facto jihads, and I felt certain the Saudis were feeling the effects back in Riyadh and Jeddah.

Sitt Zaynab functions as a sort of minor Vatican for the Shi'a. Other influential leaders are represented there, including Ayatollah Ali Sistani, the Najaf cleric who upended Washington's plan for an intermediate Iraqi government by demanding early representative democracy. Ali Sistani's envoy was just as polite as Fadlallah, but he declined to make any political comments, suggesting instead that I raise the issue with Ayatollah Sistani himself if I got to Najaf.

NAJAF, THOUGH, was still not possible. From Sitt Zaynab I made my way to Sidon, Lebanon, to see a militant Sunni cleric, Mahir Hammud. Several Lebanese contacts had warned me that Hammud was a stalking horse for Usama bin Ladin, but I didn't hear any hard evidence to back it up. In any case, Hammud was as close as I was going to get to Al Qaeda.

Again, I got right to the point: "If a young Muslim comes to you and asks whether he should go to Iraq to fight the Americans, what do you tell him?"

Hammud thought about the question for a few seconds, twisting his long, salt-and-pepper beard in one hand. "I'd advise him to wait in Lebanon because soon he will be fighting the Americans here, at home. George Bush obviously does not intend to stop at the Iraqi border. He eventually will attack Hizballah. It doesn't matter, though, because Hizballah will fight. And we will fight with them. This, we all know, is the final battle against Zionism, which we will win, or we will die as martyrs."

Suddenly, the energy waves from the war in Iraq were broadening and strengthening. Hammud was predicting a long bloody war and a broad resistance, and, as with Fadlallah, my inclination was to take Hammud seriously. Both men had played an important role in the Islamic Resistance that expelled Israel from southern Lebanon—the first time Israel was defeated on the field of battle. Still, these two weren't soldiers, the ones who would be throwing the grenades and rigging themselves with explosives. I'd have to keep looking.

'AYN AL-HILWAH, a Palestinian refugee camp just outside Sidon, is one of the most dangerous places in the world. A group affiliated with Usama bin Ladin controls half the camp; the other half is under the thumb of a radical faction of Yasir Arafat's Fatah. Although the Lebanese army has a checkpoint outside the main entrance, no Lebanese soldier now dared set foot in the place. The last one that tried was shot down within a few feet of the entrance, and the army was too outgunned to go in and look for the assassins.

The man I went there to see was Munir Al-Maqdah, a senior Fatah commander. Like Fadlallah and Hammud, Maqdah was an important player in the Islamic Resistance, but Maqdah had always operated in the field, leading several successful attacks on Israeli units. Maqdah was also rumored to be involved in international terrorism. He was accused of trying to assassinate Israeli Prime Minister Sharon and of having a part in the 2000 Millennium plot, which among other objectives targeted the Los Angeles International airport and American tourists in Amman. The Israelis, Jordanians, and Lebanese all have a price on his head—high praise, indeed, in the circles Maqdah moves in.

The meeting arrangements were all the proof I need that Maqdah was a hunted man. For about twenty minutes we sat in our car in a junkyard in the middle of 'Ayn Al-Hilwah, just waiting, while a gunman, AK-47 slung over his shoulder, watched us from a distance. At last, on his signal, we got out of the car and followed him through a rabbit's warren of makeshift cinder-block houses, their windows and doors covered in plastic sheeting. Sewage ditches crisscrossed the terrain.

I started to get the feeling we were being led around in circles when someone appeared out of a doorway, pulled us into an unremarkable cinder-block house, and silently led us upstairs to a tidy room, probably Maqdah's office. Although the electricity was off, a computer sat on the only desk, along with a fax machine. An AK-47 was propped in the corner.

I'd never met Maqdah, but I knew him the instant he walked through the door. Tall and slim, with a nine-millimeter Glock on his hip, he had the clear respect of the bodyguards that followed him in.

"Jihad?" he laughed at my question. "Call it anything you like, but American blood will flow in rivers in Iraq. You can count on it."

Maqdah went through the same litany as Fadlallah: Saddam was a loathed tyrant, but it wasn't the place of Americans to remove him.

"Look at it this way," Maqdah said. "Muslims do not see any difference between Israeli tanks rumbling into Janin, knocking down houses and running over women and children, and your tanks rumbling across the border from Kuwait into Iraq. You're the enemy. No, I take that back. You're the main enemy now."

To illustrate his point, Maqdah showed me a fax from the Al-Aqsa brigades, recruiting volunteers to fight the United States in Iraq.

"You know, it sounds strange coming from a Palestinian," I said. "America, the Palestinians' main enemy."

"As an American, you have no idea what effect an American invasion of Iraq will have. You don't understand what Baghdad means to Muslims."

Maqdah then recited in classical Arabic a saying of the Prophet: A martyr in Baghdad equals seventy anywhere else.

Maqdah and I talked for maybe a full hour. As he warmed to me, it became clear that he looked at the war in Iraq as an historical opportunity to galvanize Muslims across the world to fight the United States, colonialism, and Israel. More than once he made reference to the corrupt Arab regimes, Saudi Arabia most prominent among them, who he promised would pay a heavy price for their support to the United States.

NOT UNTIL I got into Iraq, two days after Baghdad fell, did I really begin to get a glimmer of the impact the war would have on Saudi Arabia. Sure, I'd heard what the Islamic fringe—I *hope* they're still the fringe—had to say, but the promised fire and brimstone was absent so far. What I saw on the ground was much more immediate.

The first thing I noticed driving along the Amman-Baghdad road was the burnt out Iraqi armor, mostly T-72 main battle tanks with big black holes caused by American rockets. Some had their turrets blown off. By the time we got to Baghdad's outskirts, the ruins of what was once the world's fourth largest army were everywhere—whole fields of burned-out armor and artillery. The accuracy of the American anti-armor assault was devastating. Some of the tanks were destroyed in narrow alleys, others under bridges, the surrounding structures untouched.

Looking at the destruction, I couldn't help but remember how Arabs, especially the Saudis, described the Iraqi army as "the shield of the Arabs." These same destroyed T-72 tanks I was seeing had stopped waves of Iranians at Faw during the Iran-Iraq war. Now the shield was gone. What was going to stop the next Iranian attack? Without the American military to stop them, the Iranian army could be across Faw and into Saudi Arabia's oil fields literally in hours.

But it wasn't just the ruined armored divisions that alarmed me. The Iraqi army was what had held Iraq together for centuries; it was the glue that stopped the country from spinning apart into its three main ethnic divisions—the Shi'a Arabs, the Sunni Arabs, and the Sunni Kurds. In the CIA, we had always assumed the Iraqi army would always be there to hold the country together. No one thought a representative democracy or a loose federalism would ever substitute it. Who or what was going to replace that glue now?

That answer—or one version of it—arrived a few days later in Karbala, the Shi'a holy city in southern Iraq.

I was standing outside the tomb of Imam Hussein, the grandson of the prophet martyred near Karbala, when an older man in plastic sandals, faded cotton pants, and a soiled white shirt approached me. "Would you like to meet the Imam?" The surprise still hadn't worn off that Iraqis had become so open so soon after Saddam's ouster.

The Imam's office was across the street from the Hussein mosque in a four-story apartment building. I was shown into a room furnished only with threadbare, synthetic carpets and Styrofoam bolsters.

The Imam, maybe forty-five years old and dressed in a black turban and robes, showed up thirty minutes later. Although clearly a busy man, he looked pleased to receive another Western reporter, but his presentation sounded canned.

"Things are running very well in Karbala," he assured me. "During the fighting, the electricity, the post, and the schools were only interrupted for a few days. There has been no crime. The people are safe at home and in the street."

"But I thought the police all ran when the Americans came. They fled with the military and the Ba'th Party."

The Imam smiled at my naïve question. "Of course, they did. But now in Karbala we have our own police."

I already sensed where this was going but asked the question anyhow. "But there's no mayor, no government. How can that be?"

"I'm the mayor."

That's when it struck me: Yes, U.S. Marines were patrolling the main roads; and, yes, the Iraqi army no longer existed. But that didn't mean Iraq was without a military and police force. The Shi'a clerics were Iraq's new glue; they would keep the peace if anyone would. In effect, our invasion of Iraq has established a Shi'a Islamic republic. And there is probably no way we will ever be able to change that.

OF COURSE, THIS might not sound like much of a revelation. Ayatollah Sistani has called publicly for a representational democracy. If achieved, it would almost certainly legitimize a Shi'a takeover of Iraq since the Shi'a claim as much as 65 percent of Iraq's population. But what people aren't talking about is what effect this will have on the rest of the Gulf and, to get back where this began, on Saudi Arabia.

Iraq and Saudi Arabia have much in common: a wide-open, 840-kilometer border; large, resentful Shi'a populations; and an abiding xenophobia. Saudi Arabia's Shi'a minority, somewhere between a seventh and an eighth of the population, have always been second-class citizens. In the early '80s, on the heels of the upheaval in Iran, the Saudi Shi'a came to the edge of revolt. What will happen when Iraq's Shi'a are empowered? Keep in mind that the Saudi Shi'a look to Najaf and Karbala, the two Iraqi Shi'a holy cities, for spiritual guidance more than they do Qum, Iran's spiritual center. For the moment, the kingdom's Shi'a are quiet, at least on the surface, but for how long?

And let's say Fadlallah and Maqdah are right about a culture of resistance growing in Iraq after the American invasion. How long will it be before this culture and its suicide bombs migrate south into the Arab Gulf sheikhdoms, the same sheikhdoms that possess 60 percent of the world's proven oil reserves?

I cannot speak for Ambassador Jordan, but my hunch is that if the war in Iraq goes badly, we may be a lot closer to the day when Saudi Arabia, our most reliable ally in the Middle East for half a century, comes crashing down.

Index

Note: Arabic names with the prefix al- or bin are alphabetized by their main element.

INDEX

INDEX

Burma, 22, 29, 77
Bush, Barbara, 64
Bush, George H. W., 48, 50, 55, 57,
    154, 183, 206
  Bandar friendship, 64–65, 66
  Carlyle Group and, 51, 54
Bush, George W., 51, 54–55, 56,
    64–65, 66, 67, 206
  'Abdallah and, 181, 185
  oil interests and, 206, 210

Cambridge Energy Research, 34
Capitol Trust Bank, 58
Carlucci, Frank, 48, 50–51, 52,
    204
Carlyle Group, 48–52, 54, 66, 153,
    156
Carlyle Partners II fund, 52
Carter, Jimmy, 64, 66, 100, 206
Casey, William, 64
Caspian Sea oil, xxiv, 53, 134–36,
    168
Caterair, 51
Central Asia, 129–47
  militant Islamics, 131–33,
    143–47, 168
  oil resources, 53, 56, 57–58,
    133–36, 168, 206
  See also specific countries
Centre Islamique (Geneva), 126
Chalabi, Ahmad, 212
Chechnya, xxviii, 32, 144, 146–47,
    181
Cheney, Dick, 53, 55, 66, 210
Cheney, Lynne, 53
Chevron, 53, 57, 134–35, 168
Chowan College (Murfreesboro,
    N.C.), 125
Christopher, Warren, 155–56,
    184

Churchill, Winston, 81, 83
CIA, xxix, 28, 61
  Afghanistan and, xvi, 125–26,
    144–45, 154
  arms dealers and, 8–10
  Central Eurasian Division,
    136–37, 145, 146
  cold war focus, 98, 99
  Counter-Terrorism Center,
    112–13, 129, 197
  lack of Middle East sources, 97,
    187–88, 197
  Lebanon and, 114, 117–22
  militant Islam and, 112, 122, 142,
    145, 197
  Muslim Brotherhood and, 94–99,
    112, 124–26
  Saudi policy, 35, 36, 44, 50, 55,
    58, 64, 156, 167, 188, 189,
    202, 204
  Syria and, 91, 93, 124
Citicorp, 48
Clinton, Bill, xi, 53, 54, 59, 154,
    168, 206
  Bandar and, 35, 36, 65–66
  Boeing-Saudia deal and, 155–56,
    159, 162, 163, 182–83
  Bosnia policy, 184
  Iraq policy, 183, 184, 188–89
  Qatar and, 20, 192, 194
cold war, 70, 83, 123, 135
  Muslim Brothers and, 98–99,
    100, 127
  Saudia Araia and, 89
  Syria and, 94, 95–96, 123
Cole, U.S.S., bombing, xxii, 13, 21,
    32, 167, 181
Congressional Research Service,
    208–10
Cordesman, Anthony, 202
Cutler, Walter, 59

INDEX

INDEX

INDEX

INDEX

Na'if (Saudi prince; interior minister), xi, 17–18, 20, 22, 23, 25, 33, 173, 177, 180, 181, 182

Naqshabandi, 'Abd-al-Karim, 23–24

Nasir, Sayyid Abu, 69

Nasser, Gamal Abdel, 95, 98, 99, 105, 122, 126

National Commercial Bank, 57, 157

National Commission on Terrorist Attacks, 56, 67

National Security Agency, 156

National Security Council, 34, 145, 168, 188

Nimeri (Sudanese general), 110

Nixon, Richard, 41, 43, 50, 86, 204, 206, 209

Nobel Peace Prize, 117

North, Oliver, 64

North Korea, 13, 22

Northrop, 41, 42

nuclear weapons, 38, 98

Nunn, Sam, 57

Oakley, Bob, 34

Ohliger, Floyd, 78–79

oil embargo (1973), xvii, xix, xxiv, xxv, 87, 209

oil industry, 206–11
  basic reality of, 206–7
  Central Asia, 53, 56, 57–58, 133–36, 168, 206
  history of, 74–75
  Iran, 74, 83, 184
  Iraq, xxi, 5–10, 74
  Qatar, 191, 198
  See also OPEC; Saudi oil

O'Neill, John, 167

OPEC, xvii, xix, xxiv, xxv, 86, 87, 209, 211

Osh, 129, 130, 133, 136, 137, 138

Oslo accords (1993), 185

Pakistan, xxviii, 19, 33, 136
  Afghan militant Islamics and, 132–33
  CIA policy in, 125–26
  Muslim Brothers and, 100, 124
  Saudi free oil shipments to, 34–35

Palestine, xxix, 74, 82–83

Palestinian Islamic Jihad, 69

Palestinians, 48, 66, 104, 115
  demographics, 162
  Lebanese refugee camps, 118
  Muslim Brothers and, 125
  Oslo accords and, 185

Pan Am Flight 103 bombing, 65, 96, 123

Pasha, Enver, 131–32

Pearl, Danny, 198–99, 200

Peay, H. Binford, 179

Pennzoil-Quaker State, 55

Perle, Richard, 66–67, 204

Perry, William, 155, 184

Persian Gulf
  oil and, xvii, xix, xxi, xxii, xxiv, 5, 73, 74, 78, 209–11
  U.S. defense of, 11, 182, 188

petroleum. See oil industry; Saudi oil

Philippines, 69, 195
  airliner bombing, 18

Phillips Academy, Andover, 64–65

Powell, Colin, 50, 51, 54, 66, 67–68, 200

Prague, 196

INDEX

INDEX

INDEX

NOW AVAILABLE

FICTION THIS REAL CAN COME ONLY FROM SOMEONE WHO KNOWS THE TRUTH.

Rich with the real-world tradecraft of today's counterintelligence, *Blow the House Down* is a relentlessly riveting and unnervingly plausible alternative history of 9/11. Deftly balancing fact and possibility, this is the first great thriller to spring from the global war on terrorism and the electrifying debut of a major new fiction talent.

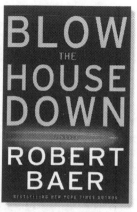

$14.95 paper
(Canada: $19.95)
1-4000-9836-X

"Engrossing and challenging—how do you act when you know what *really* happened on September 11? Baer is so persuasive, one wonders whether he in fact did know. He certainly writes as if he did."

—WILLIAM F. BUCKLEY, Jr., author of *Last Call for Blackford Oakes*

"Chilling....One of the finest espionage novels I've read since the end of the Cold War."

—NELSON DeMILLE, author of *Night Fall* and *The Lion's Game*

"Gripping...discloses a reality most Americans don't know about....There are some books that are less than they seem to be. This one's a lot more."

—SEYMOUR M. HERSH, Pulitzer Prize–winning author of *Chain of Command*

"A crackling spy thriller that moves at jet speed."

—DAVID WISE, author of *Spy*

The New York Times Bestseller

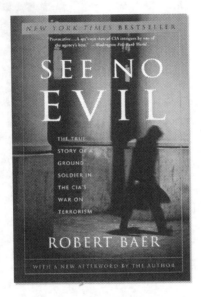

SEE NO EVIL
1-4000-4684-X • $14.95 paperback (Canada: $22.95)

Former top CIA operative Robert Baer paints a chilling portrait of how terrorism works on the inside and provides startling evidence of how Washington politics sabotaged the CIA's efforts to root out the world's deadliest terrorists.

> "A compelling account of America's failed efforts to 'listen in' on the rest of the world, especially the parts of it that intend to do us harm." —*Wall Street Journal*

THREE RIVERS PRESS • NEW YORK

Available from Three Rivers Press wherever books are sold.